KINGDOM
LIVING
IN YOUR CLASSROOM

KINGDOM LIVING
IN YOUR CLASSROOM

JOY D. McCULLOUGH

purposeful design®
p u b l i c a t i o n s

Colorado Springs, Colorado

Purposeful Design Publications is the publishing division of the Association of Christian Schools International (ACSI) and is committed to the ministry of Christian school education, to enable Christian educators and schools worldwide to effectively prepare students for life. As the publisher of textbooks, trade books, and other educational resources within ACSI, Purposeful Design Publications strives to produce biblically sound materials that reflect Christian scholarship and stewardship and that address the identified needs of Christian schools around the world.

The views expressed in this publication are those of the author, and they may not necessarily represent the position of the Association of Christian Schools International.

Unless otherwise identified, all Scripture quotations are taken from the New American Standard Bible®, Copyright © 1960, 1962, 1963, 1968, 1971, 1972, 1973, 1975, 1977, 1995 by The Lockman Foundation. Used by permission.

Scripture quotations marked NIV are taken from the Holy Bible, NEW INTERNATIONAL VERSION® (NIV®), © 1973, 1978, 1984 by International Bible Society. All rights reserved worldwide.

Scripture quotations marked Amplified Bible are taken from the Amplified® Bible, Copyright © 1954, 1958, 1962, 1964, 1965, 1987 by The Lockman Foundation. Used by permission.

Printed in the United States of America
17 16 15 14 13 12 11 10 09 08   1 2 3 4 5 6 7

Library of Congress Cataloging-in-Publication Data

McCullough, Joy D.
  Kingdom living in your classroom / by Joy D. McCullough.
    p. cm.
  ISBN 978-1-58331-096-0
  1. Teaching--Religious aspects--Christianity. 2. Teachers--Religious life. 3. Classroom management.
I. Title.
  BV4596.T43M38 2008
  242'.68--dc22
                        2008008880

Catalog #6602

Designer: Chris Tschamler
Editorial team: Mary Endres, Cheryl R. Chiapperino

Purposeful Design Publications
A Division of ACSI
PO Box 65130 • Colorado Springs, CO 80962-5130
Customer Service: 800-367-0798 • www.acsi.org

To my mom—Meryl G. McCullough—
who has taught me, and continues to teach me,
so much about that which will last for eternity.

CONTENTS

ACKNOWLEDGMENTS

The foremost word of thanks for this book must go to my heavenly Father, who has truly blessed me by giving me the desires of my heart. He gave me a year of jubilee in which I could spend uninterrupted time alone with Him and write. What a sacred privilege. He continues to show Himself strong, gracious, and gentle as I walk the journey He has set before me. Many of the truths written in this book have flowed out of my time with Him. Thank you, Papa. I love you.

I have been able to walk out many of the personal examples shared within this book because of the input and the wisdom of my prayer partner and friend, Anne Rauser, and my sister, Lorraine Koehn. Thank you both so much for your wise and prayerful counsel. God used you in powerful ways to help me walk through some difficult but beautifully life-transforming times.

To my former colleagues at Trinity Western University's School of Education, thank you sincerely for what you have contributed to my life. The road wasn't always easy, but God has used it to help me grow. As you continue to build into the lives of your students, and one other, may the peace of God rest on and abide with each one of you, and may God increasingly use you to change lives for His glory.

Thank you to my former students at Trinity Western University who gave me feedback on the preliminary drafts of this book, which we used in EDUC 400: Classroom Leadership, Management, and Discipline. May the work that God began in you during that class continue now that you are leaders in your own classrooms. I loved our times together.

Thank you to those who read through and gave input regarding the draft manuscript of this book before I sent it to an editor. You know who you are. Thank you, Carolyn McClure, for your detailed and professional input from a teacher's perspective. Thank you, Lorraine, for your personal and grammatical input from the perspective of a parent and grandparent.

To my first-ever professional editor, Jim Coggins, what can I say? Thank you so much for taking my manuscript and making it into something a publisher would want to publish. Every author should be so fortunate to have such an incredible editor. God definitely led me to you. Thank you.

I am so thankful for the team at Purposeful Design Publications that is led by Steve Babbitt. From the very beginning, I have thoroughly enjoyed the process because of the entire publishing team. A special thanks to Mary Endres and Cheryl Chiapperino, who edited my manuscript, paid close attention to detail, and answered my questions. Thank you also to the designer, Chris Tschamler, who along with the rest of the team, brought this book to completion. It's so beautiful to see how God puts all of us, who have special and unique abilities, together to create a final product that is so much better than any one of us could have completed by ourselves.

And finally, thank you to all of those who have attended my ACSI workshops over the past years and encouraged me to put these things in writing. I hope you are blessed and changed by the result.

To God be the glory!

INTRODUCTION

You have picked up this book for a reason. You may have picked it up because you want to continue to grow personally and professionally and the title caught your eye. You may have picked it up because a friend recommended it to you. You may have picked it up because it is required reading for a course. Whatever your reason, my sincere prayer for you as you read and consider the message in this book is that God will enable you to read it with an open heart, an open mind, and a teachable spirit. I pray that you will be inspired to apply its message personally and professionally and that God will use this book to change your life in ways that will bring Him glory and increase your influence in His kingdom.

The things I talk about in these pages have come together over a teaching career spanning more than thirty-two years in elementary, middle, and high school classrooms and in university classrooms preparing teachers. These years were spent in both the public and private sectors and in three countries. During these years, I was actively pursuing a knowledge of God and striving to become all He wanted me to be. I still am. More than ever, I am realizing how gracious God is to use us when we haven't yet "arrived." The ideas presented here are based on God's Word and have been proved over and over during the years in a variety of settings with different students, parents, and colleagues.

These ideas are relevant for Christian teachers, no matter at what level or in what context, private or public, they teach. They are written for all who want to maximize their influence for God wherever He has called them to serve. If God is calling you to teach in the public sector, I hope that, as you read this book, you will catch a vision for what you *can* do in your public school class-room. We often focus on the restrictions in the public setting and the things we can't do, but there are many things we *can* do! We can start by becoming a person worthy of the calling of God on our life and ministry.

Kingdom Living in Your Classroom is an invitation to you who have a personal relationship with Jesus Christ to walk forward on a journey of spiritual, personal, and professional growth. For those who are not believers, my prayer is that, as you read this book, you will accept the invitation of God to enter into a personal relationship with Him through Jesus Christ. A decision to accept this invitation has the potential to influence for good every area of your life.

This book is set up in four parts. Part One, chapters 1 through 6, is "Leadership in Community: Leading While Still Learning." I am more convinced than ever that God calls us to lead when we still have much to learn. Come to this section with a teachable and humble spirit, realizing that God may be calling you to lead before you feel ready to lead or even want to do so. This section identifies four essentials of leadership: your character, your foundation, your vision, and your relationships. The focus is on *who you are.*

Part Two, chapters 7 through 11, focuses on "Management in Community: Using Management Strategies to Motivate and Give Hope." In the past, much teaching has focused on controlling students, and so we have tended to emphasize the negative things that students do. This section has been developed to help you shift your focus from simply controlling students to motivating them to learn and grow. It will help you to ask, "What do I need to be and do in order for my students to get excited about growing into the people they were created to be?" This shift in focus can bring joy and delight to your teaching. Specific strategies will be presented to help you motivate students by managing well, getting off to a great start, arranging your classroom purposefully, managing student work with integrity, and instructing effectively.

Part Three, chapters 12 through 15, focuses on "Discipline in Community: Discipline as Opportunity for Discipleship." No matter who you are or what you do, there will be times when challenging students and situations will demand your wise attention. This section focuses on how you might deal with these opportunities within the rich and meaningful context of discipleship. As you will see, this approach to discipline goes way beyond just stopping unproductive or unacceptable behavior. Again, specific strategies will be given. The chapter titles are "Viewing Student Misbehavior," "Using Rules and Procedures in Discipline," "Applying Biblical Discipline," and "Responding to Violations and Conflict."

Part Four, chapters 16 and 17, focuses on "Personal Growth in Community: Growing Through Challenges." God invites you, as a leader in the classroom, to grow into Christlikeness. Teaching is about your growth as much as it is about your students' growth. The two chapters are titled "Growing and Leading Through Adversity" and "Moving Forward from Here." As you read this section and apply it in your life, you will begin to see adversity as an opportunity for personal growth.

My desire for you is that, in your life and in your teaching, you will be solidly planted in the Word of God and anchored in Jesus Christ. Only then will you be able to "walk in a manner worthy of the calling with which you have been called" (Ephesians 4:1). As you apply the lessons in this book, may your influence expand for God's glory!

Dr. Joy D. McCullough

PART ONE

LEADERSHIP IN COMMUNITY:
LEADING WHILE STILL LEARNING

It is becoming increasingly obvious that there is a leadership crisis in our world, our nation, our churches, our schools, and our homes. We hear almost daily of leaders who have left the road of integrity and have broken both personal and professional commitments. Leaders of major corporations are stealing money from their organizations; government officials are behaving unethically and participating in cover-ups; those who have been assigned to protect children are abusing them; spiritual leaders are walking away from their marriages; star athletes are using drugs to enhance their performance. The devastating consequences of failed leadership touch every part of our lives.

For this reason, the first section of this book will focus on who God wants you to be. You can know all the tricks of the trade and yet be ineffective as a teacher and as a leader. If you don't have a strong character built on a firm foundation, you will eventually crumble or burn out, and you will cause much hurt to those around you. God wants you to have a fruitful ministry that lasts over time, to fulfill His purpose for your life, and to become all He created you to be. It is good and necessary to learn new skills and appropriate strategies, but only godly character will allow you to be influential in ways that will make an eternal impact.

CHAPTER ONE

REFLECTING CHRISTLIKE CHARACTER

But we all, with unveiled face, beholding as in a mirror the glory of the Lord,
are being transformed into the same image from glory to glory.
—2 Corinthians 3:18

Where should we begin a book on the topic of kingdom living in the classroom? Should we start with our foundational beliefs, our relationships, or our character? Perhaps we should start by identifying what we mean by *kingdom living*.

What Does *Kingdom Living* Mean?

Kingdom living means that we live in a manner worthy of the call of God on our lives. We live according to His expectations. We take the Bible as our guide. We grow and become the people and leaders that God wants us to be. We let God transform us into people who reflect Christ within the community He has called us to serve. Kingdom living means that we choose to live in obedience to the King.

Is kingdom living about our beliefs, our character, or our relationships? It is about all three. Kingdom living is founded on solid biblical *beliefs*; it flows through us as people whose *character* is being transformed into Christlikeness; and it influences powerfully our various *relationships*.

So where do we begin talking about kingdom living? with our foundational beliefs? That is the usual place to begin. However, I have chosen to begin by discussing character, or how we apply biblical beliefs to our lives. Why? Too many Christians get so preoccupied with having the right foundation that they never build on it. Foundational beliefs rooted in God's Word are essential for life, but we can't live as God wants us to live *just* by having a right set of beliefs. Our beliefs must be balanced with godly character so that we will avoid the trap of being dogmatic and having to prove we are right at all costs. Firm beliefs without godly character can be deadly when they take the form of legalism and lifeless religion. If our beliefs have not affected our hearts, thoughts, words, and actions, and if our beliefs have not made us more loving, then we are, as the apostle Paul said, simply sounding brass or tinkling cymbals (1 Corinthians 13).

What Is Godly Character?

Godly character is the essential ingredient that allows our beliefs, relationships, abilities, skills, and ministries to flow together with integrity and bring honor to God continually. We need to allow, and even invite, God to work in our lives—hammering, chiseling, filing, shaping, and refining us to conform us to the image of Christ. In Scripture, this process is compared to a refiner's fire (Malachi 3:2–3), the blast furnace used to refine precious metals such as gold and silver. This refining of our character is not an easy process. The refiner's fire is hot and painful as it burns away those things that hinder our effectiveness. Yet God has promised to be present with us through the fire.

Character is built or torn down as a result of choices we make, either to act in accordance with biblical truth or to ignore or reject it. Character is the sum of our choices either to obey God or not to obey Him. Character is often developed at critical times in our lives, but it is developed in the everyday times, too. What is going on right now in your life that gives God an opportunity to develop character within you? Are you cooperating with Him?

In the past few years, it has become increasingly clear that the current crisis in leadership is a crisis in character. Several years ago, we witnessed an American president being unfaithful to his marriage vows and then saying that what he did in private didn't affect how he did his job as president. We've seen media coverage of a schoolteacher who became sexually active with a thirteen-year-old student and later had two children with him. Pastors have been dismissed in disgrace after various kinds of moral failure. Chief executive officers of financial institutions have lined their own pockets after picking the pockets of their investors. Employees have stolen money from their employers. Leaders of various organizations have been called to account because of inappropriate conduct. Many of these illicit practices, unfortunately, also exist within the Body of Christ. Each lapse in character causes deep hurt and destruction among many people, both the few who were closest to these leaders and the many who served and looked up to them.

How Important Is Godly Character?

Godly character is what ensures good fruit that will last. God's Word has the power to form godly character in our lives. Yet godly character will develop only as we give the Holy Spirit opportunity to work within us, as we remain open to instruction, correction, and refinement. Character is shaped not by the sum of our *information,* but by an ongoing process of *transformation* (Hayford, 1997, 71).

The refining of our character has its roots in eternity. God is preparing us to become Christ's bride. This refining is more than outward conformity to God's standards. Rather, it is a profound metamorphosis, a supernatural transformation that happens to us on the inside, beginning with a true change of heart. This transformation is not about *what we do* (although our actions can't be overlooked) as much as it is about *who we are.* Society tends to focus on image (who people *think* we are) rather than on who we *really* are. The way we handle life's situations reflects our character, and character determines the impact we make—in our homes, in our classrooms, and in the larger community.

Godly character affects leadership. Without it, we will ultimately be ineffective in the leadership positions we hold, and we may even be unable to maintain them. Without godly character, we may attempt to manipulate or control others. Our influence in Christian ministry will be determined, ultimately, by the combination of our leadership gifts and our godly character.

If we are to be influential for God's glory in our classrooms and in our lives, God must be involved in our lives. We need not fear our own inadequacies when God is in control. We can acknowledge our inadequacies, our sin, and our need to become more Christlike. God calls us and enables us to be people of integrity—people of character who have a firm grasp of moral principle, people who are upright, whole, honest, sincere, and complete. Integrity means behaving consistently in every circumstance, including our unguarded moments. We develop integrity intentionally, one step at a time, by being faithful to God's ways, even in the little things.

How Do We Pursue Godly Character?

Our pursuit of godly character should be a daily, continuous, lifelong quest. It won't just happen. God asks us to present our bodies as living sacrifices to Him (Romans 12:1–2). We must choose with all we are to let God do His transforming work within us. When we come to the point at which we can say to God, "Do whatever it takes, whenever You desire, however You choose, through whomever You will, to make me into the person You created me to be," then He will move into our lives in such a powerful and transformational way that we will never be the same again! Praise the Lord!

Circumstances in our lives do not *determine* our character; rather, situations *reveal* our character. This is a sobering truth. Think back over the past year, or even the past week. What has your response to life's circumstances revealed about your character? Did the situations you recently went through reveal your anger, frustration, intolerance, impatience, hurt, jealousy, bitterness, resentment, self-pity, fear, unforgiveness, pride, or need for others' approval? Did they reveal that your *default mode* is to blame others, to try to hide, and to shift responsibility away from yourself? I've been there. Thankfully, I can tell you that when we are open, honest, and repentant about our sin, God brings freedom and joy! We need to allow God to expose our sin to us, and to whomever else He wants to use in our lives to enable us to confront our sin. We can pray, with heartfelt resolve, as King David did: "Search me, O God, and know my heart; try me and know my anxious thoughts; and see if there be any hurtful way in me, and lead me in the everlasting way" (Psalm 139:23–24). True freedom comes only when we admit we are wrong and allow God to work in our lives to bring about true repentance and changed character.

Genuine confession, repentance, and forgiveness all have the fingerprint of eternity on them. Let me give you a personal example. I had sinned against another person in numerous interactions. Many other people knew that I had lashed out at this person, but it took me about four agonizing months to realize that I, indeed, was wrong. During those long months, I blamed everyone else and made excuses for my behavior. I thought that this person and the others didn't understand. Finally, God got through to me and showed me that *I* was the problem and that it didn't matter what the other people did or didn't do. God, in His gracious way, convicted me so deeply of my sin that

I confessed and genuinely asked for forgiveness from the very people I had been blaming for the problem. It was then that I became absolutely awed by what God did. When I admitted my sin with absolutely no excuses or explanations, when I took full responsibility for it and its consequences and asked for forgiveness from those I had sinned against, God totally and instantaneously changed my heart toward those people. In a split second, my issues with them were gone—totally gone. My heart was full of love for them. All the negative thoughts I'd had for four longs months vanished! I was in awe. How did God do that? I don't really know except to say that confession, repentance, and forgiveness somehow tap into the eternal God's value system. It's beyond human understanding. How does my asking for forgiveness for my sin change my heart toward the people of whom I was asking forgiveness? I don't know, but I'm glad it does. What a God! In a moment, He changed my heart so much that I was able to see and appreciate those people as instruments chosen by God to develop His character in me. That goes beyond anything I could have manufactured on my own, believe me! What an awesome God!

Essentials to Becoming a Person of Godly Character

There are four essentials to becoming a person of godly character. First, we must take responsibility for our own actions, words, thoughts, and attitudes rather than focus on others and what they are doing. Second, we must examine our own values and beliefs and identify what they are based on. Third, we must arrange our lives so that sin no longer looks good or acceptable to us. We need to see sin as God sees it—not as we may have become accustomed to seeing it. If our view of sin doesn't line up with the divine view of sin, we need to bring our view into line with God's. Fourth, we must develop a well-ordered heart. In *The City of God*, Augustine discusses different kinds of love and different ways of loving (1952). John Ortberg has Augustine in mind when he says that having a well-ordered heart means "to love the right thing, to the right degree, in the right way, with the right kind of love.... When the heart is well-ordered, we are not only increasingly free from sin, but also increasingly free from the *desire* to sin" (2002, 198–99; italics in the original). Relying on Christ to change us and cooperating with Him in the process are necessary for us to be transformed from within and for our lives to reflect Christlike character.

The following four areas must be addressed if we are going to develop godly character: moving beyond our past, taking our thoughts captive, breaking free from approval addiction, and guarding our hearts.

Moving Beyond Our Past

Our past can hinder us from developing godly character. Our past is like a magnet. Anytime we begin to move forward, the enemy will try to suck us back into our past by telling us lies: "Who do you think you are? Considering where you've come from and what you've done, you're not worthy to lead! If people knew what you did, you wouldn't have the position you now have. You're a victim. Your past will always define you in negative ways." These are all lies of the enemy. And he has a lot more lies that he will use to keep us chained to our past if we give him the opportunity. We need to press into a new beginning and not let our past control or define us or our future. The other day I heard a statement that really hit home: "God does not consult our past to determine our future." Praise the Lord! Let's not believe the enemy's lie that says we must live in bondage to our past. Let's rise above our past and move forward!

To rise above our past, we must reject the lies of the enemy and replace them with the truth about God's view of us and God's purpose for our lives. To rise above our past, we must confess sin, repent (turn from sin), and move into the glorious future that God has for us. His plan for us always brings hope. God is calling us to let go of the past and move into the future that He has prepared for us, so we need to stop remembering what He has forgotten! Let's not let our God-given dreams die just because we made some mistakes (and even committed some sins) in the past, or because others have done things to us in the past.

Press past the mistakes! Press past the hurt! Press past the sin! Don't give up. Christ died to set us free. Let us remind ourselves that Christ's loving and perfect payment for sin has power to heal. Let us believe fully in the worthiness of the sacrifice that Christ paid to set us free to live differently for His glory. Let us not be bound again in the slavery of sin (Galatians 5:1). As Christians, "we have this treasure [the light of the gospel] in earthen vessels, so that the surpassing greatness of the power will be of God and not from ourselves" (2 Corinthians 4:7). We are cracked earthen pots, so we need to let God's light shine through the cracks and expose what needs to be exposed. Anything we keep hidden has power over us because we will fear that it may be found out. Satan wants us to hide our sin, not to deal with it, because he knows it will keep us in bondage. But God's promise is this: "If we confess our sins, He is faithful and righteous to forgive us our sins and to cleanse us from all unrighteousness" (1 John 1:9).

Taking Our Thoughts Captive

One way to move beyond our past and handle present challenges is to take our thoughts captive. It is in our thoughts that the battle is fought. What we sow in our minds we reap in our actions (Proverbs 23:7). Our minds need to be fed just as much as our bodies do. The kind of food our minds devour will determine the kind of people we become. We must satisfy our minds with health-giving food. Wrong thoughts can be deadly. When we begin to *think* differently, we will begin to *live* differently. In other words, our lives, situations, attitudes, relationships, actions, and speech will not change until we change our thinking.

Too often we spend time thinking negative thoughts, replaying them over and over again like a broken record. These thoughts lead to discouragement and bondage. We don't need to keep replaying the facts of a situation. We don't need to rehash in our minds what someone did to us. We don't need to believe the enemy's lies. Let us throw out those broken records, or they will destroy us. Each lie of the enemy that we believe and each fact of a situation that we rehearse is a link in a chain that the enemy desires to use to enslave us. Let us cast off every wrong thought while it is still only a single link and replace it with God's truth. Let's cast off these thoughts before they start joining together to make a chain. Each time we replay a lie in our own minds, each time we rehearse to someone a grievance we have against someone else, each time we allow a thought to linger rather than take it captive in obedience to Christ, we are allowing the enemy to keep us in bondage. We must confront issues immediately and not let things fester. The enemy wants to have control of our thoughts. If he can keep us focusing on his lies rather than on God's truth, the enemy can discourage us and keep us from becoming the people God wants us to be. Because we are held in bondage by what we refuse to face and deal with, the enemy tries to keep us fearful of having our sin exposed. We must believe the truth of 1 John 1:9. It is crucial that we identify the lies we have believed—

those that make us hesitant to move into the future God has prepared for us. Then we must replace those lies with God's truth.

Breaking Free from Approval Addiction

"An addiction is something that controls people—something they feel they cannot do without, or something they do to alleviate pain or pressure. It is what people run to when they are hurting or feel lonely. It comes in many varieties, such as drugs, alcohol, gambling, sex, shopping, eating, work—and yes, even approval. Like any addict, insecure people look for a 'fix' when they get shaky. They need someone to reaffirm them and assure them everything is all right and they are acceptable. When people have an addiction the things they are addicted to are on their minds most of the time" (Meyer 2005, vii–viii).

We must break free of the addiction to people's approval. We will never become who God wants us to be if we are more concerned about what others think of us than what God thinks of us. Instead, we will do, say, and think what others want us to do, say, and think so that we can win their approval. What bondage! Approval addiction keeps us looking at other people and at our own weaknesses, flaws, and inabilities. Our flaws will certainly distract us if we pay too much attention to them. God calls us to confess our faults to Him and trust Him to change us in His own way and His own time. We must begin to see ourselves as God sees us. He is our audience of One. He loves us and created us in His image. We all need to enter God's rest concerning what people think of us and whether they approve of us. We can become so secure in Christ, so confident that our hearts are right with Him, that we will realize that whatever people think of us is between them and God and is not our concern. Let's stop speculating about what others are thinking about us. Such speculation is the enemy's tactic. (Mostly, people probably aren't thinking about us at all.) Let's not give other people that kind of power over us. Others can't control us unless we let them.

Once we recognize who we are and who Christ created us to be, we'll be set free to be that person! Let's let Christ define us. As we keep our eyes on Jesus (Hebrews 12:1–2), as we know the truth that He wove each of us together in our mother's womb (Psalm 139:13), and as we understand that He placed us on earth when and where He did so that we might learn of Him (Acts 17:

26–27), we will be set free to live the life He intended us to live (Galatians 2:20). To develop Christlike character, we must be free from the need to please others and to gain their approval. The call of God to us is to present ourselves to Him as living and holy sacrifices, free from conformity to the world and its thinking. We gain this freedom by the renewing of our minds (Romans 12:1–2) as we seek God's approval alone.

Guarding Our Hearts

Scripture admonishes us to guard the heart with all diligence because from it flow the springs of life (Proverbs 4:23). We must therefore be careful what we put into our hearts. God's Word is "living and active and sharper than any two-edged sword," and it can make an impact on whatever it touches in our lives (Hebrews 4:12). It can restore our souls, make us wise, bring joy to our hearts, enlighten our eyes, and warn us (Psalm 19:7–11). We guard our hearts by letting God's Word teach, reprove, correct, and train us (2 Timothy 3:16).

Another way of guarding our hearts is to develop a well-ordered heart. Too often people focus on having balanced lives—trying to control all their responsibilities and situations. Personally, I tried that strategy for much too long, and it didn't work. I tried to take time for family, friends, teaching, church, God, leisure, and so forth, but I found out that many times it was impossible to balance the outward situations and relationships of my life. John Ortberg, through his book *The Life You've Always Wanted* (2002), helped me to understand that I was focusing on the wrong thing. He says that having balance in our lives isn't the right focus. There are times in life when the unexpected happens and we have to "drop everything" and deal with it. When we focus on trying to keep our lives balanced, often frustration, anger, and stress emerge if people upset the balance we are trying to maintain. I can certainly attest to this. Remember the personal example I gave earlier in this chapter? What I am learning is that I still need to follow God's direction in prioritizing my day but that He wants to develop within me a well-ordered heart that can live joyfully and peacefully even when the balance gets knocked off kilter. God develops a well-ordered heart in us as we spend time in His Word and understand that He is in control. This understanding can truly be life changing.

Just recently, I was given deeper insight into this issue. A well-ordered heart is like a fulcrum that is able to balance things in life. In the diagram below, the line represents our lives. The fulcrum represents our well-ordered, Spirit-sensitive hearts. This first diagram indicates that when our hearts are well ordered and everything in our lives is going smoothly, everything in our lives is balanced.

Holy Spirit

^

However, often things in our lives don't go exactly as we expect or desire. The second diagram invites us to realize a life-changing truth. When the Holy Spirit asks us to deal with some specific thing in our lives, our well-ordered hearts move toward that area. When the fulcrum moves toward the place in our lives where the Holy Spirit wants to work, it may seem that our lives are out of balance; however, we will still have balance because we will be exactly where He wants us to be.

Holy Spirit

^

Let's determine to live lives that flow from well-ordered hearts, fully surrendered to the Holy Spirit's working.

Fighting the Spiritual Battle

Before the end of this chapter, one more thing needs to be said. Character is reflected in the armor of God that we are called to put on if we are going to stand firm against the schemes of the devil. We aren't fighting two-legged enemies of flesh and blood. Ephesians 6:12 tells us that we fight against rulers and powers, spiritual forces of darkness and wickedness. To resist this enemy and stand firm in our faith, we must prayerfully put on the full armor of God daily: truth (right thinking), righteousness (character), faith (believing what God says even though we can't see it), salvation (the basis of our relationship with God), the Word of God (His specific revelation to us), and the preparation of the gospel of peace (readiness to live as God wants us to live).

Closing Thoughts on Reflecting Christlike Character

Character really does matter! Character encompasses our personality, our goals, our values, our choices, and our relationships—and our character will be godly only to the extent that we allow God to mold us. Someone has said that the measure of our character is what we would do if we would never be found out. In spite of what the world might tell us, what we do in private has a profound effect on our life and ministry and on the lives and ministries of those around us.

QUESTIONS: REFLECTING CHRISTLIKE CHARACTER

Take the time to answer the following questions prayerfully, considering what God wants to say to you:

1. Think back to the last conflict that you were involved in. What was your part in it? What did your words or actions reveal about your character? Is there one specific area that you believe the Holy Spirit has been speaking to you about? What is it, and how will you give Him the time and opportunity to work in you?

2. What do you believe about your past? Take time to list as many beliefs as possible. Now take time to identify the lies of the enemy by checking the beliefs on your list that keep you from moving into the future without hesitation or fear. Seek the Lord's forgiveness, healing, and freedom in any areas in which you are still in bondage to those lies. Give those areas to the Lord and then take your hands off. Now check off the beliefs on your list that truly set you free to become all God intends you to become. Remember that His truth about your past will set you free.

3. You know the thoughts that play over and over again in your mind and keep you on an emotional roller coaster. What truths do you need to start believing and living? Search Scripture and ask the Lord to direct you to some verses that you can commit to memory. (A good concordance and a Bible dictionary are very helpful for serious Bible study.)

4. Are you addicted to people's approval? If so, how does that addiction manifest itself? How might you begin to wean yourself from the addiction? Joyce Meyer's book *Approval Addiction: Overcoming the Need to Please Everyone* (2005) is an excellent resource to help you.

5. When you are out of balance in your life, what character is revealed in you? In the past few weeks, what has been revealed to you about your own character? In what areas does a lack of balance result from misplaced priorities or sin? How might having a well-ordered heart enable you to develop a more godly character? In what area of your life is God, through His Spirit, desiring to work? Have you moved your well-ordered heart to that area? If not, what is holding you back?

CHAPTER TWO

BUILDING ON A FIRM FOUNDATION

Our worldview... helps us interpret the world around us. It sorts out what is important from what is not, what is of highest value from what is least.
—Brian J. Walsh and J. Richard Middleton, *The Transforming Vision*

As we continue to grow in the teaching profession, we would be wise to take time periodically and systematically to identify and evaluate the worldview foundation on which we are building. As foundations erode all around us, it would serve us well to determine whether we are building on a foundation of solid rock or of sinking sand (Luke 6:46–49, Matthew 7:24–27).

In this chapter, you will have an opportunity to answer a series of questions that will help you identify your foundation (worldview or paradigm). It is crucial that you do so because your foundation provides you with the standard by which you measure all incoming information. After you have *identified* your foundation, you will have an opportunity to *evaluate* how firm it is, and you will learn how to *respond* to challenges to your foundation.

Identifying Your Foundation

Many Christian teachers do not realize that much of what they do is based on an unstable foundation composed of personal experiences and intuitive feelings rather than on the solid foundation of God's Word. Personal experiences and intuitive feelings will shift over time and in different situations. Using these things to determine our foundation is like building our house on sand. However, a worldview based on Scripture will survive over time and across all the situations we will encounter. We identify our worldview not just by listing those beliefs we think are orthodox; rather, we must make an honest evaluation of what we actually believe in our hearts. For example, we can know of Christ's death and resurrection, and we can think therefore that this *knowledge* is our foundation. But if in reality we haven't fully given our lives to Christ, then such knowledge is not our foundation at all. True saving faith is "an anchor of the soul, a *hope* both sure and steadfast" (Hebrews 6:19; italics in the original). We must identify not only the beliefs that are in our minds but, most importantly, the beliefs that we have moved into our lives in such a way that we are deeply, personally, and sincerely committed to them.

What Beliefs Influence Teaching?

All teachers teach on the basis of their beliefs. "All knowledge exists within a framework of beliefs" (Van Brummelen 1994, 89). Knowledge is not neutral. We must recognize this truth and see its implications for us as teachers.

In the 1960s and early 1970s, much of what was taught in schools was "supposed" to be neutral, value-free—and it was certainly not supposed to be based on a teacher's personal beliefs. At that time, such neutral education was highly desired; it was even thought possible. By the early 1980s, most educators realized the absolute absurdity and impossibility of educating students in a *values-free* environment. They acknowledged that all teachers teach within their own framework of beliefs. What they value affects what they include in their lessons. They emphasize what they believe is important, and they refrain from teaching what they consider unimportant or even incorrect.

Unfortunately, some teachers still believe that their teaching is value-free. Because some teachers do not teach from a Judeo-Christian (or any recognized *religious*) foundation, they believe that they do not teach from a values-based foundation, equating religion alone with values. It takes only a minute or two to show them that they do indeed teach from their own values-based foundation. They may then say that values based on nonreligious underpinnings are more credible, more acceptable, and more relevant to what teachers do in class than are religious values. Many would say that only certain values belong in the classroom. But who decides? Are all values and all value foundations equally acceptable in the classroom? How can foundations be examined to determine whether certain ones are more truthful, more real, and more appropriate for teaching children? If all teaching is based on some values, why have so many Christian teachers bought into the lie that they must keep their faith at home and keep it private?

If everything done in education is done because of the foundations upon which people stand, it is imperative to look at those foundations critically, to discuss them openly and honestly, to evaluate them according to some standard outside ourselves, and to modify them where necessary. We must be able to identify and defend the foundations on which our practice is based.

You will have the opportunity to identify and evaluate your foundations at the end of this chapter. Take the time to do so. Former teacher education students who took the time to answer the questions posed there said that this activity was one of the most important and meaningful they have ever done.

Some Examples

Emily West (name changed) is in her second year of teaching in a Christian school first-grade classroom. She loves the emphasis the school has placed on building Christian community, and she already feels that she is a valued community member. She is excited that God has called her to teach in a Christian school, because she and her husband wholeheartedly support Christian school education. They have already decided to send their children to Christian schools. Emily sees this school as an extension of the church and the home, and she loves the strength and wisdom that come from working in relationship with the school. She enjoys using curriculum that is scripturally based, but at times she wonders if it goes far enough in addressing some of the personal and family issues her students are facing. Death, disability, and family upheaval have touched the children in her classroom this year. How does she help them to walk through these realities?

Mrs. West is encouraged by the equally high emphasis on academics, discipline, and faith at her school. She doesn't have to compromise one set of values for another. Emily wants her teaching to impact her students' lives in ways that will bring them into a personal relationship with Jesus Christ. She also takes seriously the call to teach by striving for excellence in all she does. Mrs. West believes strongly that young children need a firm foundation in language, reading, and math; therefore, she teaches these subjects daily. She uses mostly materials that have been developed specifically for Christian schools, but she supplements these materials with others when she thinks they will help her students. Her room is filled with children's books and math manipulatives. Posters brighten the classroom. Student work is displayed all around the room. Students are encouraged to look at and affirm one another's work. Can you identify what Emily believes about teaching and learning and about her relationship to Christ?

Janelle Skidmore (name changed), in her fifth year of teaching, is young and enthusiastic. She feels called by God to teach in the public school system. In her school, parents are fully involved in the education of their children. Although not a Christian school, her school upholds many of the values that she and other Christian parents want for their children. It's a good fit for her. Teaching is her passion, and she spends much of her time teaching and preparing to teach—staying up late, preparing on weekends—at times ignoring friends and family. She loves the high educational expectations encouraged by the parents and the school administration. She wants to build a highly active, participatory community of learners within a safe, inviting, and warm environment. She believes in teacher-directed learning. She has a strong work ethic and hopes to motivate her students in that direction. She created and posted a bright, cheerful, and colorful poster of the classroom rules. She has very structured systems in place to monitor student work. In her unit on families, she taught (with conviction) the traditional view of marriage and family. She struggles with suggestions being made to teach "tolerance" and even to "celebrate alternative family structures." What should she do? How does she stay true to her own convictions and yet teach in the public system? Will her foundational beliefs hinder her from educating her students within a caring community? Should she sacrifice her convictions for the sake of building a tolerant community? Everything Janelle does is based on her foundational beliefs. Take time to identify what some of them are.

Ron Champion (name changed) has been teaching for eighteen years. He loves teaching. His classroom is cheerful and bright. He invites students to take active responsibility for their own learning. He has a family, and he is strongly committed to his church. His main focus is on family and church. He knows that he has been called by God to teach, but he does not believe his teaching job should consume him. He also believes he has been called to be a husband and father. He values meaningful and productive dialogue among students and between student and teacher. He and his students together determine the rules that will guide their behavior, attitudes, work, and words in the classroom. Students decide how they will learn and how they will show their learning to the teacher.

Ron celebrates cultural differences in his classroom. He understands that many of his students have bought into the belief that they are products of their environment and thus are not responsible for their actions, and the beliefs of those students concern him greatly. They present some real challenges, but Ron is excited because he spent part of the summer break looking for and finding strategies to control his class. His unit in social studies opens the dialogue on identifying different family structures. He is careful to make no value judgments on what students say in class discussions. He believes that he can reach his students more effectively by seeking common ground and not standing strongly against what his personal convictions may say is wrong. He doesn't want his relationship with God to stand in the way of having great relationships with his colleagues, his students, and their families. All that Ron does in the classroom is based on his foundational beliefs. Can you identify them? Which ones are effective? Which ones might cause him trouble? In what ways might he be willing to compromise his foundational beliefs, and what effect might that willingness have on him and his students in the long run?

The stories could go on. Teachers differ in so many ways. What makes the difference? Personality? Beliefs? Age? Gender? There is no simple answer. Most of these things have some influence on who we are and how we teach. However, Scripture reminds us that what we *think* is the foundation of what we become. "For as he thinks within himself, so he is" (Proverbs 23:7). We become what we think. Therefore, we need to look at our thoughts and beliefs about key areas of life to determine the foundation on which we are building. God's Word says that transformation comes about by the renewing of our minds (Romans 12:2). If we hope to grow, to be transformed, we need to make sure our minds are being renewed. One way of evaluating whether our minds are being renewed is by identifying our foundational beliefs to see if they line up with Scripture.

How Do We Build a Comprehensive Worldview?

According to Brian Walsh and Richard Middleton (1984, 17), worldviews "are not systems of thought, like theologies or philosophies," but rather perceptual frameworks—ways of seeing. Kenneth Badley (1996, 17) suggests some metaphors to help us understand what a worldview is like: "a filing cabinet for organizing life," "a map that helps us find safe routes through the ups and downs of life," "a compass that provides direction or guidance," and "eyeglasses that help us see more clearly." To Walsh and Middleton (31–32), a worldview is not merely a vision *of* life, but it is a vision *for* life, a model of the world that guides its adherents' lives.

For example, the worldview of much of the society around us is that objective beliefs and convictions should be set aside and that we should talk about life only in terms of personal preferences, personal opinions, personal perspectives, and current understandings. To speak this way is supposed to reflect more tolerance of others. In contrast, God calls us as His children to build our lives firmly on truth expressed in love.

During our teacher preparation programs and our teaching careers, we were asked, and continue to be asked, to process new information. Yet, as Christians, we are not just to fill our minds with facts. Our goal is to find, embrace, and live truth. Some time ago, I was talking to a young lady who had been attending church all her life and who had completed Bible school a year prior. She would definitely have said that she is a Christian. We watched together a DVD called *Veritology: What Is Truth?* that is part of a series titled The Truth Project (Focus on the Family 2006). Through tears, she told me that she had never sought truth, had never even known how important it is to pursue truth. She acknowledged that her life was "a mess" and that she needed truth.

There are people who say that there is no truth to be pursued, that truth is to be *created*, not *found*. They say these things because they do not believe in absolute truth. What is your response going to be? How will you walk alongside people who do not value truth or who do not even know that truth exists? A good resource on this subject is the work done by Harro Van Brummelen (1994, 92–100).

In the teaching profession, we are asked to believe many different things about children, authority, right and wrong, discipline, punishment, teacher roles, parent responsibilities, motivation, rewards, and so much more. How do we know that what people are telling us is true? What criteria do we use to evaluate and organize new information?

What problems arise if we process new information solely on the basis of *prior knowledge?* What if what we already know is not true and accurate? What if it is biased? What if it is incomplete? Will we find truth if we measure new information by incomplete, inaccurate, or untrue prior knowledge?

What concerns might surface if we evaluate new information in the light of personal experience? What about people who have had experiences that are different from ours? Will truth be different for them? Maybe our personal experience is specific to our situation, culture, or gender. Is truth different for people whose situation, culture, or gender is different from ours?

What problems arise if we assess new information in light of our *intuitive feelings*? Maybe what we feel about an issue on Tuesday will be different from what we feel about it on Thursday. Maybe we will feel differently about new information in the morning than in the evening. How, then, do we decide which of our feelings will lead to truth?

What is at stake if we measure new information by *majority opinion*? When the majority believes something, does that consensus make it true? Consider the following. Years ago, almost everyone in the world believed that the sun went around the earth, yet their belief did not make it so. The earth revolves around the sun—always has, always will—no matter how many people believe otherwise. Some say people believed otherwise because of limited knowledge. True—but even when new knowledge was presented to these people, the majority did not listen. They chose to believe a lie. Isn't that still the case today? Many people choose to believe lies even when the truth is known. Many people choose not to believe the truth even when it is presented with transparent clarity. So how do we know whether we have truth if we base our conclusions on majority opinion?

What concerns arise if we measure new information by a *specific standard*? How do we know if the standard itself is true? Should all information be measured by that same standard? Is there one absolute standard for all people? Who sets the standard? What *is* the standard?

Which ways of processing information would be analogous to building on rock, and which to building on sand?

What Does Scripture Say About Foundational Beliefs?

Two portions of Scripture speak specifically about building on a firm foundation. Matthew 7:24–27 points out that the wise person (one who hears God's Word and puts it into practice) builds on the rock and stands firm when the storms of life come. The foolish person (one who hears God's Word but does not put it into practice) builds on sand and crumbles under the storms of life. Luke 6:46–49 adds the dimension of digging deeply in order to build on the rock. This metaphor implies that building on the rock is hard work.

How do we know whether we are building on rock or on sand? Is our foundation—our worldview—firm, and does it line up with God's Word? Is it able to withstand the onslaught of Satan? Is it soundly rooted in Scripture, and is it able to stand up to the bombardment of unbiblical philosophies? Do our beliefs motivate us to nurture and disciple children, and are they strong enough to stand against the misunderstanding and ridicule that may come as a result? Is our foundation stable enough to build eternity on? Are we willing to stand up for our foundation even if doing so brings hurtful consequences?

What Is Your Worldview?

I hope and pray that you will take the time now to examine and identify your foundation—your worldview. Examine it now, and never tire of examining it. It is the basis for your life and your ministry. Take every opportunity in the future to examine it again. Do not be content with pat answers. Provide detailed support for your beliefs. By taking time to think about and answer these questions seriously, you will be able to come to grips with what you believe and why you believe it. Then you will be ready either to restructure your foundation or to build upon it. Those who have answered these questions in the past have reported the exercise to be a life-changing experience, a wake-up call, a starting point from which to move forward.

Why is such an exercise worth the time it takes to do it? Every teacher is in the process of building. You need to know what you can build on your foundation and what you can't build on it. If your foundation is suitable for a one-room cabin, you will not be able to build a thirty-room castle on it. Further, you need to know not only why certain buildings won't fit on your foundation, but also why the building you want to build doesn't fit on someone else's foundation. Until you know the shape, size, firmness, and depth of your foundation, you will not be able to determine what you can build, and you will not recognize whether what others offer you will fit on your foundation. Unless you know your foundation, people will be constantly offering you "materials" to use in your building that are flawed—*and you won't know it*. If you use their flawed materials, your building will eventually collapse.

Scripture has warned us that many will be deceived and will build on things that are not supported in Scripture: "See to it that no one takes you captive through philosophy and empty deception, according to the tradition of men, according to the elementary principles of the world, rather than according to Christ" (Colossians 2:8). "Be on your guard so that you are not carried away by the error of unprincipled men and fall from your own steadfastness, but grow in the grace and knowledge of our Lord and Savior Jesus Christ" (2 Peter 3:17–18). "Be diligent to present yourself approved to God as a workman who does not need to be ashamed, accurately handling the word of truth" (2 Timothy 2:15).

Answer These Questions

To help you identify the foundation that you are building on, take the time to answer the following questions in as detailed a manner as possible, but don't take more than about fifteen pages, double-spaced, to answer all eleven questions. Answer the questions systematically and with much thought. Don't use books. If you know some Scripture that supports your answer, write it down, but don't look in a concordance. Don't use theological textbooks. Don't ask anyone else for help. Don't write what you think other people would want you to write. Be brutally honest. Sit down at your computer and type what comes to your mind and heart. The more detail you include, the more beneficial the exercise will be to you. One of the things you may realize as you answer these questions is that you don't know Scripture as well as you would like to. Maybe you have accepted what you have been told, but you don't know where to find scriptural support for your beliefs. This discovery, in itself, could be an incentive for further learning!

1. What do you believe about God? Does God exist? What place should God have in a person's life? What characteristics does God have? On what specific evidence do you base your beliefs about God?

2. Who is Jesus Christ? Who did Christ claim to be? On what evidence do you base your beliefs about Jesus Christ?

3. Who or what is the Holy Spirit? On what specific evidence do you base your beliefs about the Holy Spirit?

4. What do you believe about Scripture? Is it error free? Is it the inspired Word of God? Which other books are just as important? Is Scripture relevant for people today? What is the purpose of Scripture for you, both personally and professionally? Be specific. On what evidence do you base your beliefs about Scripture?

5. What do you believe about the supernatural? To what degree does the supernatural affect what goes on here on earth? What role does the supernatural have in students' lives? How might the supernatural be evidenced in classrooms? On what evidence do you base your beliefs about the supernatural?

6. How might your beliefs about the above (choose one of questions 1–5) influence who you are and what you do in the classroom?

7. What do you believe about people? Where did they come from? Where are they going? Why are they here? What do people need? What do you believe about the uniqueness of individuals? Are people inherently good? If left to themselves, will they do what is right? What do you believe about the relationship between God and people? On what evidence do you base your beliefs about people?

8. What do you believe about how God works in history and in human lives? On what evidence do you base your beliefs about God's working in history and in human lives?

9. What do you believe about truth? Is it something to be discovered or something to be created? Is truth different for different people? Is there absolute truth? If so, what is it? Is knowledge different from truth? What do you believe about wisdom? What is real? Upon what evidence do you base your beliefs about truth, knowledge, wisdom, and reality?

10. What do you believe about meaningful interpersonal relationships? Is what you believe true for all people, for some people, or just for yourself? Is it true in certain situations and not in others? Is there a place for hierarchical interpersonal relationships, with some people having authority over other people? If so, explain. On what evidence do you base your beliefs about relationships?

11. How might your beliefs about the above (choose one of questions 7–10) influence who you are and what you do in the classroom?

For those of you who want to take this one step further, choose two characters from Scripture and analyze how their personalities, obedience to truth, beliefs, and responses to various leadership responsibilities and challenges affected their success in God's eyes. Consider how God's grace was critical in enabling them to lead. For example, the apostle Paul was steady and consistent in his faith, but sometimes he lacked the grace to give other people a second chance. Peter, on the other hand, was often impulsive, but he had a passionate heart for Christ that influenced others greatly.

Evaluating Your Foundation

What have you learned by identifying your foundation? Were you encouraged? Did you see gaping holes in your foundation? Do you know what you believe? Were you able to provide sufficient support for what you believe and articulate why you believe what you believe? Does your foundation enable you to address all aspects of life? What is missing? In what ways does your foundation differ from that of others around you? How does your foundation line up with Scripture? When faced with new information, new experiences, new relationships, new ministries, and new thoughts, how will you process them?

Does your foundation provide sufficient criteria by which to evaluate new information?

How Firm Is Your Foundation?

Take time now to evaluate your foundation using the following questions, which are based on work done by Arlie J. Hoover (1976, 48–53) and adapted by Ravi Zacharias. Hoover identified the first five questions, and Zacharias added the sixth (2006, 4–5).

- Is your worldview strongly rooted in correspondence? In other words, does it have factual support? Does it refuse that which is known to be false? Does it examine all areas of reality?

- Does your worldview have a high degree of coherence and internal consistency? Do some parts of your worldview contradict other parts?

- Does your worldview have explanatory power? Does it explain reality?

- Does your worldview avoid two extremes—is it neither too simplistic nor too complex?

- Does your worldview have more than one line of evidence to support it?

- Is your worldview able to refute, implicitly or explicitly, contrary worldviews?

To make it even simpler, Zacharias suggests the three-four-five grid. The three tests of logical consistency, empirical adequacy, and experiential relevance must be able to truthfully and consistently provide answers for our origin, meaning, morality, and destiny. These four areas will illuminate five topics: God, reality, knowledge, morality, and humankind.

Responding to Challenges to Your Worldview

How do you respond to challenges to your worldview? Problems arise in a society that manifests a plurality of worldviews. If a society does not have one dominant worldview, that particular society is a house divided against itself, and it will eventually disintegrate. On the other hand, if one worldview dominates, then that society must somehow deal with the minority world-views (Walsh and Middleton 1984, 22). According to Badley (1996, 27–28, 386–387), people can respond to differing worldviews along this continuum:

ANNIHILATION

ASSIMILATION

TOLERANCE

RESPECT

CELEBRATION

Badley explains these responses in the following ways:

Annihilation: making a determined attempt to eliminate differences

Assimilation: persuading the minority to act in ways the majority chooses

Tolerance: putting up with differences, allowing people whose opinions or ways of life differ from our own to express those opinions and live in different ways

Respect: recognizing that all of us come from "another culture" when viewed from another person's perspective

Celebration: viewing differences as enriching and worthy of celebration, welcoming the fact that we are not all alike

As Christian teachers, should we be celebrating differences? Is tolerance the most for which we can hope? Should we avoid annihilation at all costs? When might it be appropriate to assimilate people into the ways of the majority? When might it be appropriate to work to annihilate differences? Which of these responses are most likely to be followed in schools and in society today? Are all of these acceptable responses? Are some more acceptable than others? Which responses should not be considered acceptable? Which response is most in accord with your particular worldview? What does Scripture say?

Closing Thoughts on Building on a Firm Foundation

A final warning: It is possible for us to have a solid foundation built on God's Word and to have a strong, godly character and yet over time to grow complacent and to become weak. We must purpose in our hearts to present ourselves daily to God, renewing our commitment to obedience so that we don't become casualties in ministry. Consistency and perseverance in building rightly are critical if our ministry is to be effective and if it is to last.

QUESTIONS: BUILDING ON A FIRM FOUNDATION

1. Using Hoover and Zacharias' six questions, evaluate the firmness of your worldview.

2. Do foundations ever change? Should they change? If yes, when? If not, why not?

3. Do you have one foundation for your personal life and another foundation for your professional life? Is this a good situation? Why or why not?

4. Should Christian teachers have one foundation if they teach in public schools and another foundation if they teach in independent schools? Why or why not?

5. Where is your foundation weakest? Why? Where is it strongest? Why?

6. How can your foundation be strengthened?

CHAPTER THREE

EMBRACING GOD'S VISION

Then God said, "Let Us make man in Our image."
—Genesis 1:26

According to George Barna (1997, 47), "If you want to be a leader, vision is not an option; it is part of the standard equipment of a real leader." For Christian leaders, vision is something God gives them to show the direction that He wants them to go in. God-given vision is the basis from which leaders' lives and ministries should flow. For us to be the people and leaders that God would have us be, we must understand the vision that God has of people; we must know who *God* says we are. As I said in a previous chapter, many people do not have a grasp of the biblical truth about *who they are*, and they are therefore limited in *who they can become*. It is essential that we understand who God has created us to be. If we don't know who we are as God sees us, we will have the tendency to be overly influenced by others. We will be prone to do things to earn people's approval rather than God's approval. We may do things we normally wouldn't do in order to be liked by others. When we know the truth about who God created us to be, that truth will set us free. In this chapter, we will identify the biblical truth—the God-given vision of who God has made us to be and, by implication, who God has made our students to be.

Secular Views of the Person

One of the fundamental and all-encompassing visions we have, as people and as teachers, is our view of people—ourselves, our friends, our students. Our view of people will affect everything we do in life and in our classrooms. It will affect how much we need the approval of others, how much we let others intimidate us, and whether we doubt our abilities and giftedness. In our classrooms, it will affect how we teach academic content; what we expect in terms of students' behavior, learning, and interpersonal relationships; whether we involve students in developing classroom rules and procedures; how we arrange the classroom; if and how we discipline students; whether we use collaboration or competition in the classroom; and many other things.

Because our view of people is so crucial, we need to identify it. We must be able to articulate what we believe and why. Are people born good or bad? Are they passive recipients of knowledge, or are they active participants in the learning process? Can people guide themselves, or do they need guidance and structure from others? Are they "little gods"? Do all people have the same potential? On what do we base our responses to these questions?

Historically, according to Harro Van Brummelen (1998, 93–95), teachers have held four common views about children. They have thought of children as blank slates, trainable objects, unfolding plants, and primary agents of social change. A fifth common view, arising out of Van Brummelen's first two, is that children are products of their environment. A sixth is that children's success depends on self-esteem.

Children as Blank Slates

Teachers who believe that children are *blank slates,* or *banks* into which teachers deposit information, set up teacher-centered classrooms where the teacher is viewed as the "fount of all knowledge." Lecturing and encouraging the memorization of facts are techniques commonly used by teachers with this view of children. Academic content, defined as the accumulation of facts, is highly valued. This view of the child was evident in many classrooms up to the 1950s and early 1960s. Of course, at times there *is* value in having students memorize facts and listen to lectures. Sadly, however, some teachers still hold almost exclusively to this view, which tends to see children as passive recipients of knowledge rather than as active participants in their own learning.

A number of problems and questions emerge when teachers base their teaching on this view of children. The most obvious is this: If God is active and purposeful, why are students treated as passive and aimless?

Children as Trainable Objects

Teachers who view children as *trainable objects* value good behavior. Valuing good behavior is not wrong in and of itself, of course, but teachers who view children as trainable objects may train them to respond to stimuli, such as rewards and punishments, rather than lead them to have a heart change so that they take responsibility for their own behavior. The focus of such teachers is on rewarding or punishing students' behavior in order to maintain classroom order and control. It is argued that good behavior is necessary so that students will learn more effectively and efficiently. Many teachers who are in classrooms today were taught under such a system. There are some present-day classrooms with such elaborate reward and punishment systems that the attention given to the learning of academic content pales in comparison.

Behavior modification is no longer at its apex, although all recent textbooks on classroom management (from 1993 on) have devoted space to behavior modification, behavior management, or behaviorism. It certainly is politically correct to say you are against behavior modification today, yet it is still being used to some degree in many classrooms.

Again, this view of children raises numerous questions. Should teachers in classrooms today practice behavior modification, which uses rewards and punishments? Why is it politically correct to be against behavior modification? Why might teachers still make use of it in the classroom? Can something be effective and yet not appropriate? What is the difference?

Children as Products of Their Environment

A present-day view of people, accepted by both Christian and non-Christian teachers, flows out of the two views just mentioned. It is that people are simply *products of their environment*—victims of their circumstances. They can't really be held responsible for bad behavior. Others are to blame. Almost every current textbook on classroom management in education sets forth reasons why children behave the way they do: family composition, family socioeconomic level, violence in the media, abusive relationships, the availability of drugs, the unemployment rate, the negative impact of technology, and legislation that seems to favor young offenders. The authors of these books are saying that society is to blame—not the child. They believe that children cannot be held responsible for their own behavior when they are products of such circumstances.

No one would deny the importance of understanding and caring for every child regardless of background, but in many cases this knowledge and understanding has become synonymous with having lower and fewer expectations of students from difficult backgrounds. Commendably and appropriately, teachers are encouraged to know and understand their students' life circumstances. Teachers must know and accept students as they are in order to help them to become the persons God created them to be. However, too often, children who come from adverse family conditions (and who determines what is adverse?) are not challenged to "reach for the biggest and the best." They may be encouraged to "reach their full potential," but, consciously or subconsciously, many teachers see certain students as having limited potential because of their family backgrounds.

What is the truth? Are people simply products of their environment? What can teachers expect from children who have been abused? From children who come from dysfunctional families? How far can teachers expect a homeless child to advance in school?

The apostle Peter points out that God has given people all they need to live a life of godliness (2 Peter 1:3–11). He gives no indication that people's backgrounds can exempt them from doing the right thing—from being godly. That means that all people have the potential and responsibility for becoming godly. No one needs to be held back or negatively defined by background or environment. Every person *can* be godly regardless of past or present circumstances. As stated before, we must move beyond our past, and we must help our students to do the same. This truth offers hope to all people who have come from less-than-exemplary environments.

Children as Unfolding Plants

Teachers who view children as *unfolding plants* see the teacher's role as one of watering the plant and placing it in a position where it will grow naturally. This analogy has some merit. God compares His children to trees whose roots go down into the soil of His Word (Psalm 1).

However, at least two problems emerge with seeing children as only unfolding plants. First, the focus of this view is usually on preordained cognitive developmental levels to the exclusion of other equally valid human dimensions. Christ indicated that people are spirit, soul, and body (Mark 12:30). Therefore, focusing on only one of these dimensions is out of step with the scriptural view of people. Second, children are not plants. Children can make decisions about learning, but plants cannot. Children are not passive recipients of learning.

Nevertheless, this view is held in classrooms today, a fact that raises a number of questions. What is positive about the analogy? If children will develop and grow naturally, as plants do, what is the teacher's responsibility?

Children as Primary Agents of Social Change

Seeing children as *primary agents of social change* leads teachers to create an environment in which children can take on leadership roles and be actively involved in the democratic process. This view is extremely popular in classrooms today. In classrooms set up according to this philosophy, children are the center of attention. Children determine what they want to learn and to do. Children decide on classroom rules and the consequences for breaking them. Teachers are simply facilitators of students' learning.

All of this sounds like a worthy practice. However, underlying this view is the assumption that children are innately good and thus will choose to learn and to do what is best for them. This, of course, is in direct opposition to the teaching of Scripture that "all have sinned and fall short of the glory of God" (Romans 3:23. See also Jeremiah 17:9, Proverbs 22:6, and Deuteronomy 6:4–7.) Therefore, this approach also raises questions. How can students be active participants in their learning without being the center of attention in the classroom? What problems might arise in classrooms where this approach is used?

Children as People Who Require High Self-Esteem

Out of the view of children as agents of social change, another more recent view has emerged—the idea that the future of children depends primarily on whether they have high self-esteem. This humanistic philosophy regarding self-esteem was at its peak in the mid-1980s and early 1990s, but many still adhere to its tenets. In fact, this view of children seems to be the most common one in classrooms today! Sadly, it is a view held by both Christian and non-Christian teachers and in both public and independent schools. Basically, those who hold this view see almost all their students' problems as being caused by low self-esteem. Discipline problems, attitude problems, underachievement, and lack of motivation are all attributed to "low self-esteem." Teachers who view their students as those whose problems result from a lack of self-esteem focus much of their energy on developing self-esteem in children. Sadly, more focus appears to be on building positive self-esteem than on teaching academic content or on developing students' sense of responsibility for their own learning, attitudes, and behavior. When this philosophy is followed, report cards point out only positive things; teachers are more concerned about a student's happiness than the student's personal, spiritual, and academic growth; and school policies forbid failure and punishment.

What does Scripture say about self-esteem? Is it something to be desired or shunned? Self-esteem (the Bible calls it pride) is not something to be desired. If you react strongly against this statement, I encourage you to keep an open heart and mind as you read the discussion below on the biblical view of the person. Christian teachers need to get back to the biblical view.

Six Views

Which of these views of children do you agree with most? What are the ramifications of these views for children and teachers? How does our view of people enable or hinder us in building a meaningful, growth-producing community in our classrooms?

My desire is that as you read and reflect on who God created you to be, you will be gripped by the truth in such a way that you will be set free to live out the full reality of who you are in Christ. When you are transformed, you will be able to lead others into applying this glorious, freeing truth!

A Biblical View of the "Person"

What is the biblical view of the person? Jack Fennema (1977, 1–49) develops this topic in some detail in the first chapter of his book, and it would be worth your while to read that chapter. A brief summary is presented here. Fennema suggests that there are "four basic truths about the [person] which must be recognized, accepted, and acted upon by Christian teachers before they can deal effectively with their children in a manner which finds harmony with Scripture" (2). According to Scripture, Fennema says, a child (a) is created by God, (b) bears the image of God, (c) is a sinner, and (d) can become a new creature in Christ.

We Are Created by God

According to Fennema, there are three important aspects to the teaching that human beings have been created by God:

1. God created us as religious beings (Genesis 1:27, 2:7).

Scripture indicates that God breathed into the first human the breath of life, and thus humans became living beings. God gives us life. We continue to breathe the breath that God has given. Therefore, "We cannot live without a god, even if it is one of our own making. We need a center, an ultimate focus, a point of orientation for our lives" (Walsh and Middleton 1984, 61). What Fennema is suggesting is that as religious beings we have an intrinsic desire to worship—and not just at special times and in special places, but at all times, in everything we do, and in every part of our lives (1977, 3–4).

Whether our students are Christians or not, they have been created as religious beings. If they don't worship God, they *will worship* someone or something else because God created them to be worshippers. This is true about our students no matter where we are teaching. Every human thought, word, and action contains religious significance, whether it is directed toward God or another being or even toward an inanimate object. To overlook the importance of our students' need to worship someone or something would hinder us from understanding why certain things have such a grip on our students. In our teaching, we frequently find that they appear to be obsessed by certain things or people. And these obsessions are not just passing fancies; they seem to be consuming our students. We may wonder how or why anything or anyone can gain such a hold. Is it possible that we are viewing a child, a religious being, worshipping something or someone that God never intended him or her to worship? We will not be able to address this phenomenon in a lasting way until we realize that this strong desire to worship is part of who God created people to be. The problem is not with the *fact* of worship but with the *focus* of worship. Who or what is being worshipped? We need to understand this truth and to help our students understand it as well.

At the same time, we must evaluate our own worship. What or whom consumes our thoughts and our time? What are we worshipping that God never intended us to worship (such as possessions, grades, relationships, TV programs, experiences)? This evaluation should become a regular check of our hearts not just a one-time exercise. We need to guard our hearts!

2. We are created beings—different and separate from the Creator (Psalm 139).

We are not autonomous, nor are we created to be independent of the Creator. In a society that tells people that they are "little gods" or that they can become "god," it is important to note the distinction God makes between that which was created and the One who did the creating. We are not gods; and no matter how long we live, we will never become God. There is only one God (1 Timothy 2:5).

We, the created beings, gain our identity from our relationship with the Creator not our relationship with others. This is important! We must never get our identity from another person. We must never let other people define us. People will try to define us, often by one characteristic (an ability or disability) or one situation they've observed us in (a major success or failure). We must let God alone define us. He's the one who created us. No one else can give us a proper identity. No one else can esteem us as highly as the One who created us. We need to recognize this truth in our own lives and then actively teach it to our students. Living outside of this relationship (the created being with the Creator) is living a life out of perspective.

Sadly, society is so mixed up that many people worship created things rather than the Creator (Romans 1:25). (Remember, as religious beings, people will worship something.) Worshipping created beings rather than the Creator brings harsh judgment from God. Take the time to read Romans 1:18–32. You will think you are reading about our present-day society. Even though human beings are the crown of God's creation (Psalm 8), endowed with many talents and gifts, we are *not* the center of the universe.

The fact that we are the created ones rather than the Creator also suggests that we are dependent on the Creator for existence. Don't skip over this truth too quickly. All of us, Christians and non-Christians alike, are dependent on the Creator for our existence, whether or not we realize that dependency. The very breath we breathe—that which keeps us alive—is from the Creator.

Another implication of humanity's creaturely dependence on the Creator is that there are absolutes put forth by the Creator. The Creator, not the created, sets the absolute parameters. God's boundaries allow for order and creativity, and they are designed to build us up and benefit us. Submission to His standards will enable us to prosper.

Teachers who hold to this view will know their place in creation and will help students to understand and accept theirs. If Scripture says that students are dependent on God, other people, and the creation (and it does), why do so many teachers encourage students to be self-sufficient and autonomous? God created us to be interdependent—not self-sufficient and autonomous.

3. God created us as unique beings.

Every person is different from every other person. God has gifted each person with specific characteristics, talents, and abilities. Therefore, as teachers we need to allow for diversity within the unity of Christ. Does this truth demand that children receive different assignments in the classroom? Does it dictate that students study only the subjects in which they have natural ability? What does it mean to treat our students as unique persons? Is there a limit? How far should we be willing to go? Does being unique people ourselves affect how we teach? Given that God created us as unique beings and knit each one of us together in our mother's womb (Psalm 139), how is it that we dare to look at another person as inferior or bothersome or unworthy of time, attention, and love? Do we realize that each person is created uniquely? Do we also realize that his or her uniqueness may frustrate us at times—and even anger us? This uniqueness may pull a person in a different direction from the way we want him or her to go. It is at these times that we can choose a spirit of thankfulness for the uniqueness of the children we teach even while we encourage them to use their unique qualities for good and for the benefit of others.

Once we understand the biblical doctrine of human creation, we will no longer be plagued with doubts about our worth, with feelings of inadequacy, with the need for others' approval, or with the need to prove something to others.

Take the time to thank God that He created you as a religious being to worship Him. Thank Him that when you don't worship Him, you can know that something is not right. Thank Him that He, the Creator of all things, wants to be in relationship with you. Thank Him that you have been created as a unique being. Ask Him to show you how to express your uniqueness in ways that bring Him glory and that set you free to be the special person He created you to be. Please don't move forward until you have done this. The truth about who you are is foundational for becoming all that God intends you to become.

We Are Image Bearers (Genesis 1:27, 9:6; James 3:9)

According to the biblical view of the person, not only are we created by God but we are created in His image—we bear the image of God. An image is a representation of a person or thing. As a verb, *image* means "to imitate, to reflect, to mirror." This definition provides a vivid picture of who we are. What does it mean to imitate, reflect, and mirror God? Fennema (1977, 5–17) offers insight into this question when he explains that people are created to reflect God in who they are (their nature) and in what they do:

We are image bearers in who we are—our nature. You and I are the image bearers of God! And there are several implications of that fact.

First, as image bearers of God, we are a *unity*. We are more than the sum of our parts. We cannot be separated into parts. As God is, so each one of us exists as a total, unified, integrated person. This reality has implications for us as we interact with others, including our students. We must realize that our nature is created to mirror God as a unity (body, soul, and spirit)—not just body and soul (mind, will, emotion). Further, we have been created to live out this unity in community. Society wants to fracture that unity by trying to limit us, at least in public places, to just operating out of our body and soul, but this separation is not God's vision for us. We need to learn how to live as whole unities, and we need to invite others to live in relationship with us as well. We shouldn't leave one part of ourselves (our spirit) behind, no matter where we are or where we teach. We can't allow ourselves to become fragmented. God has created us with a nature in which our body, soul, and spirit are meant to work together in unity.

Second, as God's image bearers, we are created to be *rational*. We are able to think and understand, and we desire a logical and orderly environment to live in. We reflect the God who "took an earth that was without form and void and brought harmony and purpose out of chaos" (Fennema 1977, 11). Because we reflect God, we seek structure, organization, and patterns to make sense of created reality. This truth will have implications for us as we set up our classrooms. Every classroom that operates effectively will bring harmony and purpose out of chaos.

Third, being the image bearer of God means that we are *interactive*—always existing in relationship with God, with others, and with creation. This is a truth to reflect on: we are always in relationship with others, regardless of whether those relationships are broken or intact. God is triune, and He lives in relationship as the Father, Son, and Holy Spirit. "Not only is God in relationship within the Trinity, he also establishes relationships with his creatures. He is an interactive God, one who relates in a personal way.... The child too is interactive. He initiates actions and responds with actions" (Fennema 1977, 12).

But our ability to initiate action does not mean that we initiate *all* action and that we are therefore autonomous and independent. The fact that we are interactive means that we are also responsible—able to answer for our conduct. Being interactive means that we have the freedom to choose within the limits of our nature, the freedom that comes from accepting who we are before God and submitting to Jesus Christ and to the norms found in Scripture (1 Corinthians 7:22, Galatians 5:1, 1 Peter 2:16) (Fennema 1977, 13). Being interactive also means that we are accountable for our actions (Romans 3:19, Matthew

25:1–46). It means that we cannot blame others or our circumstances. Understanding that our students are created as interactive beings, we must ask ourselves why we often expect them to work and learn as individuals (even though doing so has its place at times). We have been created to live in community with others. Do we seek this interactive community? Are our classrooms communities of interactive, relational, and whole people?

Fourth, as image bearers, we have *moral awareness*—a conscience (Jeremiah 31:31–33, Hebrews 8:10, Romans 1). We can determine right from wrong, good from evil. Is this true of murderers, rapists, and child abusers? Yes. As image bearers, they are also created with a moral awareness. Our society would like to have us believe that there is no absolute right and wrong—no universal moral truth. Yet, the God who created us with a moral awareness of His standards is the God who created everyone else. No matter what people say, He created us with an inborn moral compass that is set to His standard. People can't get away from that innate compass. God makes very clear what happens when we choose to go against His standard (Romans 1).

Fifth, as image bearers of God, we are *creative*—we can copy an original, can create a new product, and can appreciate the beauty of God's creation. Think of classroom activities and assignments designed by teachers who truly believe in the creativity of individuals. What will they look like? No one should say, "I am not creative." As image bearers of God, we are created to be creative. Too often students are asked only to reproduce what has already been created by someone else. We can see the creativity God gave us in many areas of our nature. Creativity is not the same as being artistic. Those who are not artistic still have a creative nature that can express itself in other ways. As a teacher, you need to ask yourself these questions: Am I enhancing *my* God-given creativity? Am I stretching my students' God-given creativity?

I hope this section has convinced you that we are all image bearers. Take time once again to thank God for the truth regarding who you are—God's view of you. Be set free to live out the reality of who God has created you to be.

We are image bearers in what we do. As image bearers, we are created to bring glory to the Creator (Romans 11:36, 1 Corinthians 10:31). This is the purpose for our existence here on earth. Originally, we were given the task of taking charge of God's creation, of caring for it and not exploiting it, of unearthing the riches of creation and bringing them into the service of people for God's glory. Now we have also been given the responsibility of going and making disciples of all nations (Fennema 1977, 7). Because of sin, our broken relationship with God must be restored before we can live lives of service to God. We fulfill our responsibility by being: *prophets*—accepting God's revelation of truth and then sharing that truth with others; *priests*—interceding on behalf of persons separated from God and bringing such persons to God; and *kings*—reflecting God's perfect rule by administering the world God has created (8–10). As prophets, we set forth the truth about the subjects we teach; we show the order in the world as well as the ways and the reasons society is changing. As priests, we pray for our students and answer truthfully the questions they ask us; in turn, we ask our students worldview questions designed to make them think in ways that bring their values and morality to the forefront. As kings, we are the authority figures that God calls us to be in our classrooms.

We have been created to reflect the image of God, both in who we are and in what we do. Anything less is a distortion of God's image.

We Are Sinners

That we are created by God and that we are created as His image bearers are encouraging biblical truths, but believing only these two truths about ourselves would give us an incomplete view. It is true that we are gloriously created by God, created in His image to be His image bearers, but it is also true that we are sinners.

This view of the person flies in the face of the claims of many humanists, who view children as basically good and able to direct their own lives, and of behaviorists and many contemporary humanists, who view children as neutral—neither good nor bad. Scripture says that the hearts of people are inclined toward evil (Jeremiah 17:9). So even though we bear the image of God, sin has distorted and marred that image. We should not overlook this fact. It is crucial to our understanding of people. Each thought, word, and action has within it the taint of sin—total depravity. According to Fennema (1977, 20), the taint of sin is different from absolute depravity, the idea that every human thought, word, and action is so absolutely corrupted that it contains no redeeming feature whatsoever. Our rebellion has redirected our hearts and deeply tarnished the beauty of God's image within, but we are still people created by God and therefore worthy of being treated with dignity. The biblical view of people is balanced. On the one hand, we bear the image of God; but on the other hand, we are sinners in need of salvation. Christian teachers must remember that the image of God in human beings is polluted and perverted by sin but not destroyed. It is still there. Our hearts may be turned away from the Lord, but our hearts still direct all our beliefs and actions. Emphasizing the image of God while downplaying our sinfulness or emphasizing our sinfulness while downplaying the image of God—either extreme distorts the biblical view of persons.

We Can Be New Creatures in Christ

The biblical view of persons has one more essential component. "All children are created by God. All children bear the image of God. All children are sinners. But *not* all children are new creatures in Christ" (Fennema 1977, 21; italics in the original). These ideas are key to the biblical view of persons. Hopefully, you have found the truth and you know Jesus Christ as your Savior and Lord. If so, you may understand that all people *can* become new creatures in Christ but that some *will not* and will have no desire to. We who have been made new creatures in Christ have had our hearts changed, and the restoration of God's image within us has begun. Unless our hearts have been touched by the Holy Spirit, our attitudes will not be acceptable to God and often will not be acceptable to others either (22).

What can we expect from children who are not yet new creatures in Christ? How can we encourage them? What can we expect from children who *are* new creatures in Christ? How can we encourage them? Teaching truth is the beginning but is insufficient in itself. Building respectful, loving relationships with students is key to educating our students' hearts and opening doors to share our faith. Pushing students toward outward conformity without their undergoing inner transformation is futile. Herein lies our challenge! We want our students to move toward an inner transformation that will be reflected in their outward behavior, attitudes, and speech. We need to view all our students as individuals who can become new creatures in Christ. We must not give up on anyone! We need to pray that the Holy Spirit will get hold of each one of our students. God's Word says that He is not willing that any should perish but that all should come to repentance (2 Peter 3:9).

Closing Thoughts on Embracing God's Vision

Fennema enriches this discussion about the biblical view of a person by drawing attention to the fact that children are "beings" but they are also "becomings." Children are who they are right now, but they are also people in the process of becoming something else. We must keep this fact in mind if we are to view our students through the eyes of Scripture. Remember that we too are in the process of becoming.

QUESTIONS: EMBRACING GOD'S VISION

1. What four basic truths about the person must Christian teachers recognize, accept, and act upon before they can deal with the children in their classrooms in a way that is in harmony with Scripture? What does each of these four truths mean in a practical sense?

2. Which of the four basic truths about the person do you find the most difficult to believe with respect to your view of yourself? Why do you think this is the case? What or whom will you choose to believe?

3. How does what you believe about the child affect how and what you will teach? Be specific. For example, how would believing in the four basic biblical truths about children described above affect your teaching? What verbal and nonverbal techniques can you use to communicate these four basic truths about God's view of people to your students?

4. Fennema says that God equips people with a nature, made in the image of God, that allows them to fulfill the task that God has called them to. Describe the five characteristics of that nature and indicate what expectations teachers who believe in those characteristics would place on students. Also indicate some of the activities in which these teachers might involve students.

5. What point was Fennema making about children being prophets, priests, and kings? If children (and teachers) are prophets, priests, and kings, how might

you structure your classroom so that you and the children can manifest these functions?

6. What distinction was Fennema making between the person as "being" and the person as "becoming"? What are the implications of this distinction for you as a Christian teacher in dealing with your students? In what areas are you still "becoming"? Be specific.

7. As discussed in this chapter, people view students in different ways—as blank slates, as trainable objects, as products of their environment, as unfolding plants, as primary agents of social change, and as people primarily requiring high self-esteem. Evaluate each of these views in relation to the biblical view of the person.

8. As a teacher holding a biblical view of students, how will you make wise decisions concerning expectations, discipline, and instruction when you find that your view is in direct opposition to that of your students' parents?

CHAPTER FOUR

NURTURING TEACHER-STUDENT RELATIONSHIPS

The Teacher

Lord, who am I to teach the way
To little children day by day,
So prone myself to go astray?

I teach them knowledge, but I know
How faint the flicker and how low
The candles of my knowledge glow.

I teach them love for all mankind
And all God's creatures, but I find
My love comes lagging far behind.

Lord, if their guide I still must be,
Oh, let the little children see
Their teacher leaning hard on Thee.

—Leslie Pinckney Hill

As leaders in the classroom, our goal is to build Christlike communities of learners, communities that reflect how God expects us to live here on earth. Community is an idea that comes from God. He created us to be in interdependent relationships—to be working together, learning from each other, and sharing common interests. Such communities offer great opportunities for sharing Christ. They value diversity and encourage the development of the unique abilities of each community member. They hold everyone accountable for behavior, words, and attitudes. Community members genuinely care for one another, and everyone is welcomed, valued, and respected. These types of communities are supportive and growth-producing; they encourage ongoing learning. Christlike communities are places of grace and forgiveness. They have a positive effect on students' school attendance, classroom behavior, and academic achievement.

What is the teacher's role in building such communities? It begins with developing meaningful, professional, and growth-producing teacher-student relationships. Teachers will (and they should) spend much time and effort on this task, which is one of the most important and most difficult ones they face. Teachers who are warm, personal, and friendly affect students' behavior, attitudes, achievements, and feelings toward school in a positive way. They build community by building relationships with their students.

There are four teacher roles that have the potential to influence the teacher-student relationship in favorable ways. Teachers are to serve as models, authority figures, servants, and mentors/disciplers.

Teachers as Models

Certainly the concept of teacher as model is familiar to all who have studied Scripture. Christians are to be models of Christ for other Christians and non-Christians alike. Modeling theory states that children learn by watching others and can learn a great deal especially by watching adults (Jones and Jones 2004, 82). Young people today are more in need of adult models than ever before; therefore, we need to capitalize on that fact by serving as godly models for our students.

By definition, models offer a standard of excellence to be imitated. Christian teachers need to be godly models in all aspects of their lives— attire, attitudes, character, preparedness, orderliness, work ethic, creativity, establishment of classroom environment, and interactions with others. Healthy, hardworking, godly people will have a huge impact on their students.

Scripture gives many admonitions to Christians regarding the type of behavior and the attitudes that we should model for our students. Among other things, we are called to these:

- To live in harmony with others (Philippians 4:2)

- To speak no unwholesome words but only words that are edifying and that give grace to those who hear (Ephesians 4:29)

- To be kind, tender-hearted, and forgiving (Ephesians 4:32)

- To exemplify compassion, kindness, humility, gentleness, patience, and love; and to let the peace of Christ rule in our hearts and His Word dwell in our minds to give us wisdom (Colossians 3:12–17)

- To be reverent in our behavior (Titus 2:3–5)

- To be above reproach, not self-willed, not quick-tempered, not quarrelsome, but sensible, just, and self-controlled (Titus 1:7–9)

- To be kind to all, able to teach, patient when wronged, and gentle when correcting those who are in opposition (2 Timothy 2:24–26)

We are to teach with a vision of being part of the perpetual community of God, one more generation passing on the faith to the next generation of faithful hearts (Psalm 78:1–8). As Christians, we are called to live as children of light (Ephesians 4:17–5:21), as holy followers of Jesus (Colossians 3:1–17), and as godly people (2 Peter 1:1–11). Scripture provides guidelines for righteous living that will, if followed, mature us into the kind of godly people our students will benefit from modeling.

We do well to take time regularly to evaluate ourselves in light of the guidelines presented in Scripture and to pray for God's Holy Spirit to fill us and enable us to live according to those guidelines. We dare not hide behind the cop-out that "It's just the way we are." If there is something in "the way we are" that renders us ineffective or hinders the ministry to which God has called us, we need to let God change us! Being submissive and obedient to God as He makes us more Christlike is a powerful model for our students. We need to model the reality that we are still open to correction, partially by asking forgiveness when we are wrong. We need to submit to the messengers God uses to bring us to maturity in Christ. We should have a continually teachable and tender heart. In our classroom communities, we are called to model for our students genuine, supernaturally transformed lives—not just good lives that follow a set of standards, but lives that have been completely changed by the power of God (Romans 12:1–2).

Teachers as Authority Figures

Is there a place for authority and power in learning communities that reflect Christ? This issue is an important one that must be addressed within the context of building meaningful, positive teacher-student relationships. In an age when authority and power have been abused, much of contemporary society would like to do away with both authority and power. Sadly, this is the proverbial "throwing the baby out with the bath water"! It is obvious that some people who are in positions of authority abuse their authority and power, but the way to prevent further abuse is not to get rid of these positions but to return to a biblical understanding of authority and power.

According to Scripture, authority is God's idea. Authority is delegated to us by God, both directly and indirectly. God directly delegates authority to parents, pastors, and anyone else He has called to a special task such as teaching. God also indirectly delegates His authority to us as teachers through other people—the students' parents. We must not shirk our God-given responsibility when it comes to being authority figures in the classroom.

Biblical authority includes a balance between *dominion* (being in charge; being responsible for what's going on; taking initiative; giving leadership, guidance, and direction) and *service* (making our primary concern the welfare of those we lead). Dominion by itself is selfish and dictatorial. Service without dominion fails to provide the necessary leadership and direction (Fennema 1977, 96).

"Authority might be defined as the right to make decisions that affect the choices available to [other] people." When we have authority, we specify the goals that are most appropriate and we select the best means for attaining them. This type of authority is conferred; "it need not be earned by acting in ways that please the group over whom the authority is exercised." For instance, students have little choice but to accept the authority conferred on teachers by others (Froyen and Iverson 1999, 263). Another definition of authority is "the power to act which is given as a right to anyone by virtue of the position he holds"—it is legitimate or recognized power and "is always linked with a particular position or mandate" (Blendinger 1976, 601, 607). Robert Greenleaf (1998, 18, 44–45) discusses the *influence* (which assumes mutual knowledge and gives others the freedom to disagree) of a servant. He differentiates between *persuasion* (which encourages others to accept the rightness of a belief or action by their own intuition, conscious logic, and discernment) and *coercion* (which uses threats, penalties, or other forms of pressure to persuade others to accept a certain belief or action). He also contrasts *persuasion* with *manipulation* (which "guide[s] people into beliefs or actions that they do not fully understand"). Robert Pazmiño (1994, 20) concludes that proper authority uses influence and persuasion rather than manipulation and coercion.

Power, on the other hand, is "the inherent capacity of someone or something to carry out a task or an activity" (Pazmiño 1994, 18). Len Froyen and Annette Iverson (1999, 264–268) identify five types of power:

Attractive Power

Attractive power "is essentially relationship power, the power educators have because they are likeable and know how to cultivate human relationships." It is "earned by being personable and hospitable." What matters most is not what we say or what we do, but who we are.

Expert Power

Expert power is "the power that accrues to educators because they possess superior knowledge in one or more fields." Those who influence student behavior by relying on expert power "are often characterized as having great enthusiasm for their subject, enthusiasm that is often contagious." Teachers acquire expert power by imbuing a subject with significance. These teachers' power resides not only in expertise but also in the ability to convey that expertise to others.

Reward Power

Reward power often depends on attractive or expert power or both. It is the power to give praise, or "positive feedback that affirms the value of a student's effort" or the product of that effort.

Coercive Power

Coercive power "is the ability to mete out punishments when a student does not comply with a request or a demand. It is often used as a last resort because most educators do not like to make life miserable for students."

Legitimate Power

Legitimate power "emanates from the student's belief that the educator has a right to prescribe the requirements." It is similar to authority in that it permits us to make decisions. The difference is that this power is "not just the conferral of authority by those who hired the educator," but the acceptance by students of that authority, their recognition that we as the teachers are the rightful leaders of the classroom community.

According to Nicholas Burbules (1986) and John Smith (1977), if authority is to be effective, it must be backed up by power. But power becomes an issue only when students resist a teacher's authority. Ideally, teachers are able to show students the benefits of learning and the detriments of misbehaving without needing to use coercive power (Froyen and Iverson 1999, 264).

As we seek to build community in our classrooms, we must use our God-delegated authority, seeking always to balance dominion and service. Prevention of misbehavior through preparedness and organization, among other things, enables us to be the authority figures God calls us to be.

Teachers as Servants

The biblical perspective on leadership includes both authority and service. As servants, we go the extra mile and spend extra time and effort to build relationships with our students and their families. As servants, we become advocates for our students.

Using each letter in the word *servant*, the teacher-student relationship might be described as follows:

A Sustained Relationship

We can and should develop godly, professional relationships with our students. The process begins with developing a personal, vibrant, and growing relationship with Jesus Christ. Our relationship with Him needs to be our first priority. Unless we are growing closer to God, our relationships with others will not be as productive as He wants them to be.

The prophet Amos challenges people to "seek the Lord" and not Bethel, Gilgal, or Beersheba (5:4–7). This truth is important for today. What does it mean to seek the Lord rather than Bethel? *Bethel* means "the house of God." So many people today are drawn to a specific church (house of God) rather than drawn to the God of the house. It is not enough just to attend church. We must grow in our relationship with God; otherwise our church attendance will be hypocrisy and empty ritual. We are to seek *El-Bethel*—the God of the house of God.

What does it mean to seek the Lord rather than Gilgal? In the Old Testament, Gilgal was a place of past visitations from the Lord, a place where the Lord had once moved in power. It was a place where the sin of Israel had been rolled away, circumcision had been instituted, and Israel's covenant relationship with God had begun. The first Passover feast in the Promised Land had been celebrated at Gilgal. So why would Amos say not to come to Gilgal? The problem was that the people were glorying in their past religious experiences. They wanted to hold on to the past instead of moving forward with God. They no longer had a fresh, vibrant, living relationship with God. We too need to be reminded not to seek Gilgal but to seek the God of Gilgal—the God who can lead us into fresher and deeper experiences with Him.

What does it mean to seek the Lord rather than Beersheba? Beersheba was a place of great blessings in the Old Testament. It was the site of a well that provided refreshment and life-renewing water. Hagar, Ishmael, Abraham, and Jacob had all been blessed at Beersheba. However, we are encouraged not to seek God's blessings for their own sake. We are supposed to seek the One who blesses—God. We need to get to know Him and to grow in communion with Him.

As Christian teachers, we should be aware that our relationships with students can exert an impact on their lives for eternity. But this will happen only as we are in a growing, dynamic, genuine relationship with the God of Scripture. Our relationship with God and with our students needs to be sustained.

An Edifying Relationship

Our relationships with students need to be edifying. *Edifying* means "instructing, enlightening, building or improving morally or spiritually." One of the greatest things we can do for our students is to light within them a spiritual fire that inspires them to follow the Lord wholeheartedly. We can build up our students in love and truth. This means that along with saying things our students love to hear, we must also, in love, point out areas in which they need to grow. We can encourage students to be responsive to God and to go from simply *absorbing* spiritual truth to actively *choosing to live by* such truth. Students have a way of becoming what we encourage them to be rather than what we nag them to be. In our relationships with students, we can be encouragers, edifiers, and motivators who inspire students by challenging them. Remembering that life and death are in the power of the tongue, we must speak words that are life-giving to our students.

A Respectful Relationship

We need to earn respect by being persons worth respecting. Respect will not come because we demand it. If we want our students to respect us, then we need to respect our students and treat them with care. Each student should be treated as a special individual created in God's image. As teachers, we need to know each student's name within the first two days of school. At the same time, we must be careful not to become overly familiar with our students. Such a relationship often leads to disrespect. Respect creates warmth not familiarity. There will be days when our students may not like us, but they should still respect us. We must set healthy limits so that we do not create within students an emotional dependence on us. We must also get beyond wanting our students simply to conform to our rules; instead we should want them to be transformed by the power of God. Therefore, we must respect our students enough to wait for God's timing in their lives. No student is beyond the reach of God! We can't let ourselves escape our responsibility through doors marked "I can't reach everyone" or "What can I expect when he comes from a home like that?" or "There's no way she'll ever succeed."

A Valued Relationship

Relationships with our students should be valued, seen as highly important. God values each one of our students, and He has handpicked precisely who will be in our classes. God has created people to be relational beings and has chosen to work within the context of relationships. We need to value these relationships as God's gifts to us because in them and through them lives can be changed by the Holy Spirit. We are there to teach our students, but students are there to teach us as well. It will help if we realize that the student who is challenging us the most was handpicked by God to be in our class. God can teach us much about becoming more Christlike when we walk beside students who cause us problems! God is in these relationships for His glory and for the benefit of every one of us. Think of ways to demonstrate that you value the students entrusted to your care. Be creative.

An Affordable Relationship

Relationships take time. However, the *amount* of time we spend with students is not the most important thing. *How* we spend that time is the key. Being prepared for the day allows us to be free from "administrivia" and routine so that we can work with people. Do you see relationships with students as inconvenient interruptions of the daily routine? Would you rather spend time with certain students? Being a disciple of Christ will cost us. We must give ourselves fully to the ministry of building relationships with our students. Voluntarily denying ourselves will bring honor and glory to Christ. Teaching will cost us time, money, misunderstanding, disappointment, rejection, confrontation, and opposition—to name only a few of the related costs. Yet these costs pale in comparison to the cost Christ paid that we might have a relationship with Him.

A Nurtured Relationship

Those who nurture others promote their development. Nurturing others involves feeding, training, and educating them. Therefore, we should make a thorough study of our students' needs. Praying for students is another way we can nurture them. Taking time to sit in each student's desk before class begins and to pray for that specific student can change the direction of his or her life. Our personal relationship with God can naturally lead to our "feeding the sheep" as we share what God is doing in our lives. We will have many opportunities to nurture our students, to help them develop into the people God created them to be.

A Trusted Relationship

If we are to build Christlike communities in our classrooms, we cannot gossip or speak harshly about students. We must not belittle or mock them—even in the form of humor. Such things destroy trust. We cannot talk with students about other students. Arthur Nazigian (1983, 61) says that words are "emotional steps." He adds, "By using key words and experiences, you are building a set of stairs that take a student up … or down!" This is a good analogy. Are we taking students up or down by the words we speak? Again, life and death are in the power of the tongue. As we speak life-giving words to our students and life-giving words about our students to their parents, we are building relationships of trust.

Confidentiality is also a component of trust. Is it right to disclose information students share with us in private? Should teachers promise to keep confidences? How do teachers deal with these issues?

Teachers as Mentors/Disciplers

Mentors are wise, loyal advisers. Those who are wise see life situations from God's frame of reference. Those who are loyal confess that they are under obligation to defend or support those to whom they are loyal—and teachers should be advocates for their students. Advisers are those who counsel (give advice after careful deliberation of the matters involved), admonish (give gentle reproof and earnest advice concerning a fault or error), and caution or warn (give advice that puts others on guard against possible dangers or failures). Mentors, then, are advisers who can see life situations from God's perspective and can share this knowledge with those they have been called to support.

Today the mentor role of teachers seems limited to being encouragers, saying only positive things to students. We are often told not to say anything negative because such words may damage our students' self-esteem and leave permanent emotional scars. Too many Christian teachers have bought into this lie. As Christian teachers, we have the opportunity and responsibility to let students know that their worth is tied to Christ and to His view of them not to how well they do, what they do, what others tell them, or how others treat them. The only correct, undistorted view of them—the view that matters—is God's!

Disciplers take mentoring further. Teachers who disciple their students encourage them to become faithful disciples of God. First, to be disciplers of our students, we must check our focus. We should not focus on helping students "reach their full potential" but on moving them toward joyful and willing obedience to Jesus Christ as their Savior and Lord. Second, we must change our vocabulary. Having high expectations for students isn't being mean; letting students experience the consequences of their choices isn't being inflexible; and pointing out areas where students need to improve isn't being negative. Third, we must increase our involvement and go beyond simply teaching academics. We must get fully and actively involved in the mentoring-discipleship role—instructing, warning, giving consequences, counseling, and following up.

Just Do It

So how do we develop these types of relationships with our students? Here are five practical suggestions:

1. Build relationships with students systematically. Mentoring/discipling relationships don't just happen. Speak *personally* to each one every day, keeping track if necessary.

2. Be open, transparent, and genuine with students within appropriate professional boundaries.

3. Encourage your class to develop into a community of interdependent learners in such a way that students don't become dependent on you and that you don't become dependent on them to have your emotional or other needs met. The goal is to create an atmosphere that motivates everyone to encourage the others to grow.

4. Communicate high expectations in a community that celebrates students' growth, uniqueness, and creativity.

5. Take time to attend student activities outside of school. Eat lunch with students occasionally. Get feedback from students on issues that concern them. Show a personal interest in them.

Closing Thoughts on Nurturing Teacher-Student Relationships

To be leaders who are able to build Christlike communities of learners, we must model the behaviors, attitudes, words, and relationships that God desires. We must take seriously our God-given authority. We must walk humbly before God as servants concerned for the welfare of our students. Finally, we must embrace the role of mentoring/discipling our students as our highest privilege as a teacher. In this role, we walk alongside our students, doing whatever is necessary and appropriate for them to develop into the people God created them to be.

QUESTIONS: NURTURING TEACHER-STUDENT RELATIONSHIPS

1. Describe the characteristics of the teacher who most affected you and made a genuine difference in your life. What impact did that teacher have on you? Be specific.

2. Which of the following best describes the teacher you named in number 1: a model, an authority figure, a servant, a mentor/discipler? Provide a rationale for your answer.

3. How did each teacher role (model, authority figure, servant, mentor/discipler) impact you as a student?

4. To what degree and in what ways do you think your view of an effective teacher has been shaped by your experiences as a student? Be specific.

5. How did your former teachers build community in your classes? Which teacher role(s) mentioned in this chapter most facilitate(s) Christlike community in the classroom? Explain your answer.

6. How did your favorite teacher deal with the issue of power and authority?

7. Which types of power (Froyen and Iverson 1999) do you think are most effective? Which types are least effective? Why? How does your foundation affect your view of power? Which type of power do you have the most difficulty relating to?

8. Define the concepts of mentor/discipler, model, authority figure, and servant for your students. Record people who filled these roles in your life, and

explain how they did so. What specific truths about teacher-student relation-ships can you glean from the influence of these people?

9. What specific steps might you take to show individual students that they are special and unique and that they matter to you?

CHAPTER FIVE

ENCOURAGING PEER RELATIONSHIPS

There's a powerful transformative effect when you surround yourself with like-minded people. Peer pressure is a great thing when it helps you accomplish your goals instead of distracting you from them.

—Po Bronson

Chapter 4 focused on the importance of teacher-student relationships in building Christlike communities in our classrooms. This chapter will discuss the importance of building solid, meaningful, appropriate, and growth-producing peer relationships.

Our Inner Circle of Friends

Before discussing the teacher's role in developing peer relationships among your students, I want to challenge you to look at your own peers—the people with whom *you* are friends—and evaluate the influence they have on your life. Do you have an inner circle of people who are spurring you on in your relationship with God and others? Are your peers people who will move you toward being a Christlike leader in your classroom? According to John Maxwell, highly effective leaders surround themselves with a strong inner circle of friends. He uses the biblical example of King David, who brought alongside himself influential, nurturing, empowering, resourceful, character-driven, intuitive, responsible, and competent people. Inner-circle friends are valued not only for what they can do but also, and especially, for who they are. In your inner circle, you would do well to include an intercessor, a listener, a discerner, an implementer, a mentor, a thinker, and an encourager (2000, 178–185).

In 1970, when I had just begun teaching, I attended a conference that God used to radically change my life. The speaker said something that has guided me ever since. He said that in five years we would be the books we've read and the friends we've kept over that time period! I have found his words to be true, and they made me rethink my relationships and led me to make some hard but necessary decisions. God continues to help me develop an inner circle of people who keep me accountable and who move me closer to Him. For instance, He has given me an accountability partner; we pray together every week, we are very real with each other, and we are able to speak truth into each other's lives. If you haven't already done so, begin now to develop relationships that will encourage you to grow into Christlikeness.

According to the dictionary, a *peer* is a person of the same rank, value, quality, and ability. Our peer group consists of all the people around us who are about the same age, who have a similar status in society, and who have a common system of values. In light of the fact that it is important for us to have a good peer support group, consider how important it must be for our students. "When children enter school, they are required to negotiate two extremely important social-behavioral adjustments: teacher-related and peer-related" (Walker, Colvin, and Ramsey 1995, 7). Peer-related adjustment means forming friendships and other positive relationships with one's classmates, as individuals and in groups (Dodge 1993; Hollinger 1987; Patterson, Reid, and Dishion 1992).

Scriptural Guidance on Friendships

Scripture is full of examples of the tremendous influence peers can have on one another. No wonder parents and teachers encourage young people to pick friends wisely. Remember the saying "Don't follow the crowd" in doing something wrong? That was taken straight from Exodus 23:2.

Scripture shows that friends can have a positive influence on each other. Friends can sharpen each other as iron sharpens iron (Proverbs 27:17)—an analogy that suggests that even the friction in a friendship may be beneficial, leading to growth in both people's lives. Friends confront and wound at times to cause their friends to grow (Proverbs 27:6). True friends give wise counsel (Proverbs 27:9), help in troubled times (Proverbs 27:10), speak truth when others tell lies (Numbers 13:30–14:10), and love at all times (Proverbs 17:17). The characteristics of good friends are that they fear God and keep His laws (Psalm 119:63), that they are wise (Proverbs 13:20), and that they are pure in heart and are gracious speakers (Proverbs 22:11).

Scripture also sheds light on the results of having the wrong peers as friends. Many people in Scripture influenced friends and associates to do wrong. One man was encouraged to rape his half sister (2 Samuel 13:3–22). Another was encouraged to rape his father's concubines (2 Samuel 16:16–23). In another case, many people were killed because they supported those who had sinned (Numbers 16:1–35). Scripture also indicates that bad friends can corrupt good morals (1 Corinthians 15:33), cause a person to suffer harm (Proverbs 13:20), lead a person to humiliate a parent (Proverbs 28:7), and turn a person away from God (James 4:4). God makes it clear that those who befriend fools will suffer harm, and He describes fools as those who "despise wisdom and instruction" (Proverbs 1:7), reject their father's discipline (Proverbs 15:5), and always lose their temper (Proverbs 29:11).

The Importance of Peer Relationships in the Classroom

In the past, teachers have ignored or downplayed the importance of peer relationships in the classroom. Often teachers want to focus on academic learning and think that intentionally working toward developing peer relationships in the classroom is a waste of time. Traditionally, teachers have also focused attention on individual learners and have seen influencing students to behave appropriately as an issue primarily between the teacher and the student. Many teachers have neither acknowledged nor addressed the tremendous effect peers can have on determining the quality of the classroom community.

Yet, according to Richard and Patricia Schmuck (2001, 27), "Peers can be quite influential in shaping classroom group processes. They can provide emotional support as students attempt to break loose from dependency on their families and other adults. They can also threaten each other, making classroom life uncomfortable. The worst result of peer-group rejection is to feel lost as a social outcast and to want to lash back at those who have been hurtful. As students give and take information from one another, they learn ways of relating to others either with empathy and reciprocity or with aggressive hostility and social distance. Peers also help shape one another's attitudes, values, aspirations, and social behaviors."

The reality is that "When students feel liked by their peers and when interactions are characterized by thoughtfulness and helpfulness, students experience a sense of safety and security, belongingness and affection, significance, respect for others, and power. Students are then able to concentrate more fully on learning and are willing to take greater risks in attempting to master new skills" (Jones and Jones 2004, 122). Conversely, when children don't experience acceptance and belonging, the results can be disastrous. Recent media reports have shown that some students who have felt rejected at school and have been victims of taunting and bullying have sought a permanent solution to their misery by taking their own lives. We have also seen, at places such as Columbine High School, that students who felt rejected became violent and killed other students. Even for students who never go as far as suicide or murder, failure to be accepted by other students can cause mental, emotional, and social trauma that can have very negative effects. Some students who do not feel they belong with their peers in their classroom become involved in gangs: "Gang membership alluringly offers the promise of identity, belonging, protection, excitement, money, and sex. Membership springs from dysfunctional families, exposure to pervasive poverty, and crumbling social institutions" (Walker, Colvin, and Ramsey 1995, 27). Still other students withdraw from reality and create their own fantasy life—often with the help of the Internet.

This whole problem is well illustrated by a film made several years ago about a young boy who died. When his parents went to his school to get some idea of what had been going on there, very few teachers even knew who the child was. A good number of students in his class did not know him either. He had attended school, but apparently no one had ever talked to him. He had been totally ignored. Is it possible that a child could attend a school and yet not be known by the teachers and the other students? Unfortunately, experience shows that it is. What a sad commentary on what can happen in classrooms!

So we see that helping to develop positive peer relationships in our classrooms is no incidental concern. The impact that peers can have on our students can make the difference between life and death. We must take our students' peer relationships seriously.

"Some classrooms are characterized by feelings of belonging or togetherness of all the students, while others are characterized by tension, divisiveness, scapegoating, exclusive cliques, and destructive competition" (Kauffman et al. 2002, 94). What makes the difference? By now it should be apparent that effective teachers develop group awareness and learn to deal effectively and appropriately with groups of students. It takes time and intentional planning to get to know our group of students. It takes time and planning to provide ways for our students to get to know one another. It takes time and planning for us to become familiar with a particular group's dynamics. Many teachers do not realize that the time spent in developing community will be amply repaid in students' increased academic self-confidence and enjoyment of the class. Such results are worth the time spent in attaining them.

Children are created to be interdependent not independent and autonomous. They are supposed to become involved with others. Therefore, we as teachers "have an obligation to do what [we] can to make positive peer influence an important aspect of [our] students' lives in the classroom and to help students learn to make wise choices about peer relationships.... Peer pressure will be at work in the classroom whether [we harness] it or not" (Kauffman et al. 2002, 94). We are responsible to make *every* student feel loved, accepted, and needed in the classroom.

If we do not realize the importance of clarifying interpersonal peer issues within groups, we will have a classroom community that does not function effectively. More importantly, we will have students who are left outside the community, and the consequences of their disconnectedness can be serious. We must create a classroom climate in which positive, supportive peer inter-actions develop readily. According to Vernon and Louise Jones (2004, 136), "Group cohesiveness and a positive group identity do not develop simply because students spend time together. Rather, positive feelings about being a group member are developed by making the group seem attractive, distin-guishing it from other groups, involving the group in cooperative enterprises, and helping students view themselves as important components in the group."

Much of our teacher preparation in classroom management, discipline, and leadership has focused on teachers' interaction with individual students. This is as it should be. We should never lose sight of the fact that we are dealing with individual, special, and unique students. However, we cannot limit our interac-tions to individual students since many of our interactions are with groups of students. Just as an individual student has a personality that differs from that of other students, so different groups take on different group personalities. For example, when we are teaching mathematics to two different grade-seven classes, even though the teacher, the content, and the grade level are the same, the two classes may be completely different and may require different teaching methods and motivational strategies. The blending of students in a class creates a unique class "personality," which significantly affects student participation, achievement, and sense of belonging.

There is much research showing that peer relationships influence students in their attitudes, academic achievement, educational aspirations, school behavior, involvement in the learning process, and values. For these reasons, and because peers can help troubled students adjust to school (Schmuck and Schmuck 2001, 27), teachers are strongly advised to facilitate cohesive support structures within their classroom communities. They should do so early in the school year and should continue throughout the year.

Principles for Building Peer Communities

How do we build communities that foster healthy peer relationships? How do teachers create a climate of group cohesiveness such that students love to come to our classrooms and to participate with others and in learning? Teachers can build community in the classroom by developing positive peer relationships. To encourage and achieve such positive relationships, they should do the following:

- Create an atmosphere of support and acceptance in which hurtful comments, mocking, and put-downs are not allowed.

- Teach students how to understand the needs of others and to empathize with them.

- Prepare students for living interdependently.

- Deal with students' bad attitudes and prejudicial thoughts.

- Enlist student cooperation in working to encourage positive attitudes and behavior.

- Accept the loss of some instructional time to the task of creating positive peer relationships—because a classroom in which students feel safe and supported will significantly enhance learning.

Activities That Build Effective Peer Relationships

It is wise for teachers to develop a file of activities that can help students (a) get to know one another, (b) develop group cohesiveness, (c) understand diverse liking patterns, and (d) examine peer relations. Jones and Jones (2004) is a good resource for these activities. Teachers should include as many of these activities as possible, choosing ones that are suitable for the ages of their students. Usually, these activities are used only once for each class, often at the beginning of the school year.

There are also activities that continue throughout the school year. Some of these have proved effective in developing and maintaining meaningful and appropriate peer relationships. Following are some specific types of activities common in many classrooms today:

Observational Learning and Vicarious Consequences

Teachers can use observational learning and vicarious consequences to affect the behavior of their students. Basically, students whose conduct is appropriate model desirable behavior for misbehaving students. This method addresses many of the following problems: inattention, aggression, social withdrawal, lack of study skills, and specific academic difficulties. One major challenge is the choice of student models. Choosing the same one or two students regularly will quickly minimize the effectiveness of this strategy. Therefore, teachers must know which students are most likely to be imitated. First, choose models whom the target students see as attractive, competent, and similar to themselves in important ways (such as gender and academic ability). Clearly, the models will be different for different target students. Second, choose models who exhibit behavior that the target students are able to imitate successfully. The authors correctly identify the difficulty in trying this approach with older students, among whom pleasing the teacher might not be the thing to do. Therefore, this strategy may be used more effectively with younger children (Kauffman et al. 2002, 96–97).

Group Contingencies

Group contingencies can be used to create desirable peer pressure in our classrooms (Kauffman et al. 2002, 99–101). Four types of group contingencies are mentioned: (a) independent group contingencies, for which every member of the group must perform at the required level and the reward is given only to those who hit the target; (b) dependent group contingencies, for which rewards are given to the full group only when requirements are met by one member or a small number of members, usually ones that cause problems; (c) interdependent group contingencies, for which all members of the group receive the reward if their combined or total performance and behavior meet the specified target; and (d) cooperative learning, in which there is a combined use of independent and interdependent group contingencies.

Each type of contingency has the potential to encourage positive peer pressure. However, we must carefully manage contingencies so that they don't backfire and become negative peer pressure. We must make sure that our requirements are realistic and that the focus is on reward for appropriate performance rather than on punishment for undesirable behavior. At times, we may allow students to opt out of participating in certain activities (in which case we may choose to set up individual contingencies for them). We must also ensure that the students we put together in a group have about an equal chance of being successful.

Peer Tutoring

Peer tutoring has been shown to be effective in improving the academic performance of the tutor and the tutee as well as beneficial for developing communication skills and interpersonal relationships. However, before using peer tutors, we should know specifically what we expect peer tutoring to accomplish and should clearly spell out our objectives for it. Tutors can be either the same age as, or a substantially different age, from those they tutor. When choosing tutors, James Kauffman and others (2002, 104) suggest considering age, gender, social class, ethnicity, skill development, and behavioral characteristics. Robert and Mary Kay Zabel (1996, 145–147) present the following guidelines for developing peer tutoring programs:

• Tutors should have at least adequate skills in the material they teach.

• In addition to considerations of age, grade, and ability, some interpersonal skills are important for tutors. Some children may be too young, but many schools use cross-grade tutors (such as grade-six students assisting grade-one students with reading).

• Tutoring should be regularly and carefully scheduled.

• Tutors must be trained, and tutoring must be carefully monitored.

• It is important to provide feedback, encouragement, support, and recognition to tutors.

Peer Mediation

Peer mediation can be useful in resolving conflicts among peers. "The goal of [peer mediation] programs is to resolve conflicts peacefully, enabling all students to learn constructive approaches to handling problems and engendering acceptance of responsibility" (Emmer, Evertson, and Worsham 2006, 186). According to Hill Walker, Geoff Colvin, and Elizabeth Ramsey (1995, 205), peer mediation is "a voluntary method for resolving peer conflicts and disputes without resorting to coercion. The peer mediator must be an unbiased, empathic listener and respectful of all parties to the process. Mediators are expected to remain neutral and objective and to maintain confidentiality of information; those involved in the process are not allowed to interrupt when someone else is talking, and the parties involved must also agree to cooperate." David and Roger Johnson (1995, 73) list four steps in the peer mediation procedure: (a) end hostilities, (b) ensure that both students are committed to the mediation process, (c) help students negotiate successfully with each other, and (d) formalize the agreement. There are many advantages to using peer mediation in the classroom. These include that it helps children learn to understand their differences and that less adult time is spent in dealing with discipline problems. So peer mediation does have its place in classrooms, but it should not convey to children that adults do not understand or care about the students' problems, or that peers are the only ones who understand. We as teachers have an important role in helping students work through their problems. Adult support, adult oversight, and proper training of mediators are critical for peer mediation to be a valuable program in our classrooms.

Cooperative Learning

Cooperative learning skills increasingly need to be taught to students! Many children do not know how to interact and work effectively with others. David Johnson, Roger Johnson, and Edythe Johnson Holubec (1990, 9–13) suggest four "levels" of cooperative skills that students need to develop, including required student behaviors for each level: (a) *forming skills*—moving into groups quietly, staying in the group, using quiet voices, and encouraging everyone to participate; (b) *functioning skills*—staying focused, supporting others, asking questions, explaining, and clarifying; (c) *formulating skills*—summarizing key points, connecting ideas, seeking elaboration of ideas, determining ways to remember material more effectively, and checking ideas and understanding through articulation; and (d) *fermenting skills*—criticizing ideas without criticizing people, asking for justification, probing for more information, and extending other people's ideas. We must teach these skills to our students if we want them to benefit from their experiences in cooperative learning.

Taking Up the Challenge

Throughout our teaching career, we need to answer the following questions about building effective and meaningful peer relationships in the classroom:

- How can we harness peer pressure as an effective force for motivating our students to learn, grow, and become responsible citizens?

- How can we use peer relationships in our classrooms to improve our students' behavior and achievement?

- How can we encourage cooperation and caring among our students?

- How can we help students on the social fringes of our classes to become better accepted among their peers?

We need to be intentional about building community by developing positive peer relationships. Let's take up the challenge to build communities that focus on the whole person. In such communities, individuals should grow in the understanding and the living out of who they are—their giftedness, abilities, passions, and experiences. But they should also do so in ways that influence others in the community for good.

Closing Thoughts on Encouraging Peer Relationships

Building community means that we target all students, not just the select few who may be the natural leaders. Community means helping each person realize, appreciate, and celebrate the uniqueness and contribution of every other member. Community is a place for building up one another, not tearing one another down. It is a place where there is a desire to work harmoniously and collaboratively. Building community isn't just about accomplishing tasks; rather, it is about building meaningful and appropriate relationships among all the participants. It is about creating a place where each person feels safe, accepted, and eager to become all that God wants him or her to be. Building community takes time—but it is worth it!

QUESTIONS: ENCOURAGING PEER RELATIONSHIPS

1. Do you have an inner circle of people who are spurring you on in your relationship with God and others? If your answer is no, what steps will you take to develop one? What will you do now to develop relationships that will encourage you to grow into Christlikeness?

2. What aspects of your foundation will you draw upon in developing meaningful and appropriate peer relationships in your classroom? Be specific. How will you build upon those aspects of your foundation as you establish positive peer relationships in your classroom?

3. What three factors do you think are most important in developing group cohesiveness in your classroom? How will you deal with these factors?

4. Given your biblical foundation and your view of children, will you use all, some, or none of the group contingencies discussed in this chapter? Provide the rationale for your answer.

5. What drawbacks and concerns do you see in using peer tutors in the class-room? Might undesirable assumptions be implied about adults being unable or unwilling to help children? If so, how will you address, eliminate, or minimize those assumptions?

6. To what extent is it a teacher's responsibility to deal with peer relationships that affect student success in the classroom negatively? How involved should teachers become when friendships among students adversely affect students in ways *other* than academic learning? Should teachers inform parents of inappropriate peer relationships that are forming? Should teachers speak to students who are involved in inappropriate relationships if such relationships do not affect classroom learning? Give reasons for your answers.

7. How do the following verses inform the discussion on peer relationships: Proverbs 27:17; Ecclesiastes 4:9–10; 1 Corinthians 15:33; Proverbs 13:20; Psalm 1:1–2; Ephesians 5:11; Ephesians 4:29, 32; and Romans 12:4–8?

CHAPTER SIX

INVITING EFFECTIVE PARENT-TEACHER RELATIONSHIPS

Unity

I dreamed I stood in a studio
And watched two sculptors there.
The clay they used was a young child's mind,
And they fashioned it with care.
One was a teacher—the tools she used
Were books, music, and art.
The other, a parent, worked with a guiding hand
And a gentle, loving heart.
Day after day, the teacher worked with touch
That was deft and sure,
While the parent standing by her side
Polished and smoothed it o'er.
And when at last the task was done,
They were proud of what they had wrought,
For the things they had molded into the child
Could neither be sold nor bought.
And each agreed they would have failed
If each had worked alone,
For behind the parent stood the school
And behind the teacher, the home.

—Anonymous

Much has been written about the benefit of parents and teachers working closely together in the education of children. The impact parents have on their children's education is often the primary factor in determining their children's success in school.

Inviting Partnerships in Education

According to Scripture, God gives parents the primary responsibility for *nurturing* (Deuteronomy 6:6–9, 11:18–21; Ephesians 6:4), *teaching* (Deuteronomy 4:9, 6:7, 31:13), *training* (Proverbs 22:6), *providing for* (2 Corinthians 12:14), *controlling* (1 Timothy 3:4, 12), *loving* (Titus 2:4), and *correcting* their children (Proverbs 13:24, 19:18, 23:13). We should not ignore the fact that parents are responsible for their children's education.

Centuries ago, the family was the main agent for educating children. (This is still true for families in which the parents homeschool.) However, as society became more complex, many families requested help in educating their children, and they looked to the church and the school.

According to Harro Van Brummelen, the three main agencies of Christian nurture are the home, the church, and the school. The home provides the first educational experience for children as parents model Christian convictions and a Christian lifestyle to their children. Second, the church teaches what the Word of God says, how to apply it to life, and how people should function as part of the universal Body of Christ. Third, Christian schools teach children to develop thoroughly Christian minds in all areas of life as they study the various academic disciplines. These three agencies "form an educational tripod standing firm on the base of the Word of God and the flame of Christ's Spirit. All three need to work together to prepare children for the Christian life" (Van Brummelen 1988, 4). Bringing these three agencies into partnership does not absolve parents from being the ones who are primarily responsible for their children's education. Parents need to remain actively involved in shaping what is going on in their churches and in their children's schools and classrooms, and in the field of education generally, to make sure that their children are receiving an effective and appropriate education.

We as teachers need to take note! In God's scheme of things, we are responsible to our students' parents to educate their children. We do not stand *above* parents in the education of their children. We must therefore desire parents' input and listen to their suggestions. It is true that they have put their children into the hands of the educational "experts," and we should know what works and what doesn't work educationally; but again, that responsibility does not mean that hierarchically we are above parents. We have been called alongside parents to help them in the task that God has given them to do. We need to let them know that we care about their children and that we accept their primary role in their children's education. We must engender confidence in our ability to teach. We must be prepared to inform parents about their children's progress, using accurate records and evaluations, and we must speak with them honestly and graciously.

This parent-teacher partnership sounds doable if we are Christian teachers working with Christian parents whose children are Christians. But what if we are Christian teachers working with non-Christian parents and children? What is our responsibility to children who may not go to church and may not have a Christian home life? Is it our responsibility to nurture all children in the Lord, or only those children who live in Christian homes and who attend church? What if our students' parents don't uphold Judeo-Christian values? Do we believe that all children are created in the image of God and for His purpose—even those who aren't Christians? If parents aren't Christians, are they still responsible to parent according to scriptural principles? How will we work with parents who may be shirking their responsibilities? What will we do with those who are abusing their parental role? How might we interact with parents who are teaching their children things contrary to Scripture? Our answers to these questions will establish the framework for our relationships with our students' parents and will determine whether the communities we are building will embrace those who may be outside the faith. Remember, relationships are the key to building a growth-producing, Christ-centered, and Christlike community.

To what degree should parents become involved in their children's education? What obstacles hinder the development of effective parent-teacher relationships? How can teachers and parents overcome those obstacles? What framework of skills and attitudes should guide teachers' interactions with parents? What specific things might teachers do to enhance parent-teacher relationships and to make them more effective? What should teachers know about parent-teacher conferences? These are the questions addressed in this chapter.

Teachers who teach junior and senior high school students should not dismiss this topic as something relevant only to teachers of elementary school students. Parental involvement still has an impact on older students' attendance, achievement, attitude, and behavior. So if you teach at these higher levels, be sure to encourage the parents of your students to become involved.

Involving Parents in Their Children's Education

Why should parents be involved in their children's education? First, God said they should be. Second, many jurisdictions have enacted legislation that requires parents to be involved in schools "in advisory or decision-making roles" (BCCPAC et al. 1996, 6); thus parental involvement in education is mandated by law. Third, research shows the benefits of parents' involvement to teachers and students, as well as to the parents themselves.

Benefits to Parents and Teachers

Parents are legally responsible for their children, so they must know what is going on in their children's education. In turn, parents are valuable sources of information for teachers, especially with respect to their own children, and they can often provide insight into their children's classroom behavior. Parental insights and understandings "can enhance decision-making in schools" as they remind schools of "what is meaningful and relevant to their children." Parents also "can assist in increasing goodwill ... and in developing a sense of community within the school" (BCCPAC et al. 1996, 7). Informed and involved parents are more likely to be supportive of decisions made. By assisting in the classroom, parents can make classroom management easier for teachers.

By becoming involved with parents, teachers may learn what their students' home conditions are like, enabling them to understand and help the children more effectively.

We have much to gain from the parents of our students through building relationships with them!

Benefits to Students

Research shows that parents' involvement in their children's education has several benefits for students as well. First, the children's attendance, achievement, and behavior all improve. Second, since parents influence their children's attitudes about school, parental involvement often translates into student cooperation. Third, parental involvement minimizes the chance that children will be able to play the parents against the teacher—or the teacher against the parents. Fourth, children come to realize that they can learn from adults other than teachers.

Limits to the Development of Effective Parent-Teacher Relationships

Although much research suggests that there is a positive relationship between parents' involvement and their children's educational success, teachers do not always find it easy to get the parents involved. Three types of barriers to parent participation in school activities have been identified by Oliver Moles (1993, 30): limited skills and knowledge among parents and teachers, restricted opportunities for parents and teachers to interact, and psychological and cultural barriers between the home and the school.

Limited Skills and Knowledge

As teachers, we may have limited skills in working with parents because our teacher-training programs did not provide enough meaningful opportunities for us to learn how to work with them effectively. We teachers may also hold negative attitudes or stereotypes about parents' lack of willingness or ability to get involved. Parents, on the other hand, may lack fluency in English, may be unfamiliar with education, may not understand the schoolwork being assigned to their children, or may not know how to approach their children's teachers. Additionally, perceptions of a lack of competence on the part of both teachers and parents can interfere with good relationships between the home and the school.

Restricted Opportunities

Parental involvement may also be restricted because of administrative policies that schedule conferences and meetings during the day, when many parents are working. We often fail to consider the changing nature of the family when planning parent-teacher conferences. Increasing numbers of single-parent families, working parents, and recombined families as well as increasing social and economic struggles in the home leave many parents with little time or energy to become involved in their children's education. Also, with increasing numbers of school-aged children being placed in foster families, many adults in these homes do not know the educational background of the children they are caring for. Further, parents may not have the social support networks to provide babysitting and transportation services so that they can attend conferences.

Similarly, teachers may be overwhelmed with their personal responsibilities at home and may not feel they have time outside of school hours to work with parents. (We can help alleviate this problem by setting good limits and communicating to parents specific times when we will be available for discussion or involvement.) Additionally, there can be conflict between us as teachers, who are responsible for a whole group of students, and the parents, who are concerned about their individual children.

To overcome these barriers, we need to be approachable and not defensive, even when parents come in with a critical attitude. We also need to develop effective communication skills with our students' parents.

Psychological and Cultural Barriers

Psychological and cultural barriers also affect parents' involvement in their children's education. Some teachers may not want to get involved with parents because they fear that their professional competence will be questioned, and they fear parents' criticism. Other teachers may assume that low-income parents (or parents from other types of families) are indifferent and uninvolved in their child's education, and therefore these teachers do not think that trying to get these parents involved is worth their time. Teachers may avoid encouraging parental involvement because they recognize that many parents are already overextended and they do not want to place yet another burden on them. Some teachers are reluctant to get involved with parents because they have had negative experiences in the past.

Similarly, there are a number of reasons why parents may be reluctant to get involved with teachers. They may have had bad experiences with teachers in the past. Some prefer to leave their children's education "to the experts." Others are concerned that if they become more involved, teachers will shift more of the responsibility onto their shoulders. Parents may avoid questioning teachers because they fear negative reprisals against their children. Parents may fear criticism, or feel insecure around professionals, or feel guilty over problems they know their children are having. In the past, teachers may have contacted parents only when there were problems, and parents may want to avoid hearing any more bad news. Parents who feel inadequate because of teachers' misconceptions about their family status may avoid getting involved in their children's education.

Whatever the barriers are, we must work to overcome them!

Overcoming Barriers to Parental Involvement

Have you been struck by how many barriers and obstacles to developing solid parent-teacher relationships are caused by fear and ignorance? We must begin by addressing these problems.

Address Our Fears

We address our fears by realizing that our worth comes from God and not other people. As noted in chapter 3, God created us as unique people. Once we grasp this truth and apply it in our lives, we will be set free to reach out to parents and to value their input and involvement. We won't take their comments personally or become defensive, because we'll realize that parents' views of us don't define us. Rather, we will accept as valuable any parental input, even criticism, because we have the potential to grow through it. We will take this parental input to God and then let Him tell us what needs to be addressed in our lives. Knowing that God created us in a unique way for His special purpose can set us free from the need for people's approval and the tendency to let others intimidate us. The enemy brings the spirit of fear, and fear is not of God; therefore we must ask God to set us free from our fears.

Meanwhile, God often calls us to do things when we are afraid! That's what courage is all about. We cannot let fear paralyze us and keep us from doing what is right.

Change Our Thinking

God works through the renewing of our minds. If we come into parent-teacher relationships with the mind-set that parents are the enemy to overcome, our effectiveness with them will be hindered. If we want to build better relationships with our students' parents, we need to work with them collaboratively. God has put parents in their children's lives for a purpose. We dare not shut them out. We need to see them as God sees them.

Communicate with Families

Not only is it important to communicate with parents, but the timing of the communication is also important—we need to do it *early* and *regularly*. An additional caution is that we need to make sure that the parents have understood our communication. We should not assume that because we sent a note, the note was received, read, and understood. This caution is especially important when parents are not fluent in the language spoken at school. Many schools have parent volunteers who translate school newsletters into the languages that are spoken in students' homes (e.g., Spanish, French, Chinese, and Punjabi) so that parents receive communication in the language with which they are most comfortable. More detailed suggestions for communicating with families are presented later in this chapter.

Get Parents Involved in the School

One way to get parents involved is by encouraging them to attend school events, to volunteer in classrooms, or to share with the students about their jobs, hobbies, or cultural backgrounds. Other opportunities for parents include working with teachers on special theme days, representing other parents on the school's parent advisory council, helping with fund-raising, and collaborating with other community agencies interested in children. We need to make parents feel welcome in our schools and in our classrooms. We need to let them know about the myriad ways of supporting their children's education.

Encourage Parents to Get Involved in Learning Activities at Home

Learning activities in the home are critical to a child's education. Teachers need to encourage parents to involve their children in home activities right from the beginning of the school year. We should affirm parents for what they are already doing, emphasizing that even if they cannot volunteer in our classrooms, they still can be actively involved in their children's education at home. Most parents want to be involved, so it is helpful to compile a list of home activities and to make that list available to parents. Such activities include children reading to parents, parents reading to children, parents editing children's writing, parents supervising homework, and parents and children doing at home some of the activities students have done in class. We can encourage parents to provide children with a quiet place to do their homework. Also, we can let parents know what topics we are currently teaching so that they can help their children visit related Internet sites.

Help Families Fulfill Their Basic Obligations

We can also help families fulfill their basic obligations by encouraging our schools to offer workshops on child development and parenting skills. We can help parents form parent support groups, and we can provide resources for them. Toy-lending libraries will help some parents. We should be able and willing to refer parents to community agencies. It is good to have a list of referral agencies' contact people, phone numbers, and addresses that we can make available to parents. We can also run training sessions for our students' parents so that they understand the expectations in our classes.

Guiding Our Interactions with Parents

What framework of skills and attitudes should guide teachers' interactions with parents? What key pointers do we need to consider when building relationships with parents? C. M. Charles (1999, 249) discusses four human relations skills that teachers would be wise to embrace when working with parents: (1) communicate regularly, (2) communicate clearly, (3) describe expectations, and (4) emphasize progress. Again, *early* contact with parents is important! We must begin to build solid relationships with parents from the beginning of the school year, even though that time is incredibly busy. Doing so will definitely benefit the community we are trying to build within our classrooms.

Len Froyen and Annette Iverson (1999, 290–292) provide insight into the skills and attitudes that should guide our interaction with parents. First, we should identify parents' expectations of teachers. What do parents want from us? Parents usually want teachers who are concerned about the individual child, who teach and inspire the child, who stimulate the child's achievements, who encourage the child's aspirations, and who help the child become self-disciplined. Second, we should examine our attitudes toward parents' expectations. Are parents' expectations too high? Not high enough? Not reasonable? We should talk with parents honestly and graciously about our perspective on their expectations. Third, we should determine our own expectations and have confidence that those expectations are appropriate. We need to decide what we are willing to do and know why we are doing it. Fourth, we should identify the specific types of parent-teacher contacts we wish to use. We should also have a plan to encourage cooperation from reluctant or negligent parents since parental cooperation is critical for student success. Additionally, we should know the differing needs of parents and the differing levels of interaction necessary to meet those needs.

Reaching Out to Parents

Introductory Letter

In a letter sent at the beginning of the school year, we should introduce ourselves to our students' parents—where we come from, our educational background, our teaching experience, our goals for the school year, and anything else we think parents would be interested in knowing. Sharing our faith journey is critical because it lets them know that our faith is important to us; however, some teachers may prefer to do so later at the back-to-school night. In this letter, we may want to tell parents the room number of the classroom, the number of children in the class, the students' gender, and the class's ethnic, or cultural, makeup. In the introductory letter, we should invite parents to orientation night (see Back-to-School Night below) and give them a brief overview of the year's curriculum content. We can include the school's telephone number, the best times to contact us, any extra fees they will be charged, a list of necessary student supplies, and a list of available home helps. We should also indicate how we will be communicating with parents. Finally, we may want to include a brief survey for parents to complete, one that provides information about their children.

Teachers must be sensitive about what is appropriate to tell parents. (If you are a first-year teacher, you might check with your principal or a veteran colleague for tips about your introductory letter.)

Telephone Conversations

Telephone conversations are for short, timely updates on students' behavior and achievements. We should be cautious when using the phone to inform parents about problems: "Because telltale nonverbal reactions cannot be used on the telephone, it is wise to talk about classroom activities and ways in which children have demonstrated growth; a negative comment by the teacher may cause a child to be punished unnecessarily as a consequence of a misunderstood comment" (Lemlech 1988, 232). When parents phone us, we should be prompt in returning their calls. We should start making phone calls early in the year, asking how the child is responding to school. We may also ask for parents' perceptions of recent classroom assignments and activities. Some schools require teachers to phone two parents a day. If we do this with a class of thirty, we will phone the home of every student every three weeks. In these calls, we must make sure that our comments are genuine and meaningful. Just phoning parents with "fluffy warm fuzzies" does not benefit anyone—student, parent, or teacher.

When we phone parents, we must remember God's view of a child and the biblical injunction to parents to educate their children. These ideas will influence what we say, when we say it, and how we say it.

We should document each phone call briefly in case there is a need to refer to it later. Our notes should indicate the date and time, the person who made the call, the person to whom we spoke, and the content of the call.

Newsletters/Calendars

It is a good idea to send home monthly newsletters detailing scheduled activities, curriculum information, future special speakers, upcoming field trips, and assignment and test dates. These newsletters will help parents prepare their children for learning. They also provide us with an opportunity to be salt and light to our students' parents. Homework planners or home-to-school notebooks are also helpful.

E-mail

Many parents are connected to e-mail. Using it to send notices home or to keep parents informed about what is happening at school will save paper and will ensure that parents do in fact receive the newsletters.

Good News Notes

Good news notes are brief notes, indicating children's accomplishments and special contributions and commenting on both academic achievement and behavior, that are sent to parents. You can use your attendance record to keep track of these notes. As you write them, you may want to start a file to provide ideas for future notes (Walker, Colvin, and Ramsey 1995, 276). Be sincere. Don't say a student is doing well in a specific area if he or she is not.

Report Cards

One helpful thing to remember when sending out report cards is that they are communication tools not score cards. Thinking about this distinction will make a difference in how we look at report cards. They need to be designed and written in such a way that parents understand what is being communicated. Report cards should give snapshots of academic progress based on objective, documented data. In addition to sending the cards out, we need to give parents an opportunity to ask specific questions about them. One way to do this is to develop a comment sheet to send home with the report cards, a way to make it easy for parents to write back with their own ideas and concerns (Weinstein and Mignano 2003, 133). The comment section of report cards also helps parents because it adds meaning to percentages or letter grades. Parents should never receive bad news about their children's progress for the first time through report cards. As soon as we realize that a child needs additional support, or as soon as we have concerns about a child, we should contact the parents—not wait until we issue report cards.

Sending Student Work Home

Teachers should send student work home once a week in a designated student work folder, enabling parents to see the type and quality of their children's work. We should also send a sheet indicating how many pages of work are included in the folder, thus minimizing the possibility that children will remove their lower quality work. Parents should sign the sheets, indicating that they have seen the work, and students should return the signed sheets in a timely manner. The sheets should include a space for parents to write any comments they may have. Once parents know that every Friday this folder will come home, they will begin to look for it.

Home Learning Activities

Parents want to know how they can help their children study at home. Sending home ideas for home study in our monthly newsletter is one way to provide the help they need. It is also important to have ideas readily available to give to parents whenever the need arises. Especially in the younger grades, in which home practice grows and changes constantly, the monthly newsletters should provide updates on different types of home learning. By providing resources for parents, we can help them parent more effectively.

Home Visits

Home visits by teachers are not common anymore, although some teachers at the kindergarten and primary school levels still do them. Home visits give teachers an opportunity to see the children and the parents in their own environment. Teachers can discuss with parents how their children benefit when the home and the school work together. Teachers learn about the parents' worldview and how it might influence their children's success in school.

Home visits should be made before the school year begins. Before each visit, the teacher should make an effort to find out something about the community and the home. Many kindergarten teachers use home visits to build rapport with young children, thus easing their transition from home to school life.

Bringing Parents into School

Back-to-School Night

A back-to-school night is an opportunity for us as teachers to meet our students' parents (as a group, not individually) and for them to meet us. First impressions are important, so we must make sure that we and our rooms are organized and prepared. Some teachers do not rely solely on the introductory letter to invite parents to this meeting; they also have their students create personalized invitations for the parents. Students can also put their names on their desks so that the parents can see where their children sit. We should greet the parents when they arrive and make sure we speak to all the parents, even if just during a brief greeting. In most cases, that is all there will be time for at this meeting. During the meeting, we can discuss our approach to instruction, to classroom management, and to discipline, and we can convey our genuine love and concern for the children. This meeting is a time for parents to ask questions, so we need to give them an opportunity to do so. However, we must not let one parent monopolize the time. If we need to speak to certain parents individually, we should arrange to meet them the next day or soon thereafter. Vernon and Louise Jones (2004, 161–162) offer a good outline of content to cover during this orientation meeting.

Another helpful practice is to give all the parents a folder containing information on topics such as the curriculum, the class schedule, and the characteristics of children at that particular age level, as well as on our general background and teaching experience. The folder could also include a handout containing information about convenient times to meet with us and about volunteer opportunities for parents (when to come, how often, and in what capacity). It's a good idea to collect this handout at the end of the meeting because it can then serve as a sign-up sheet for parental involvement.

Parents-at-School Day

Another good idea is to invite parents to watch a lesson on a specific day of school or to spend an entire day with their children at school. Instead of "Take your child to work day," have a "Bring your parents to school" day.

Informal Contact at Extracurricular Events

By attending extracurricular events, teachers gain great opportunities to have more relaxed times with parents. Watching school sports teams, attending music concerts, and becoming involved in community activities give teachers and parents opportunities to interact informally. Don't underestimate the importance of this type of contact. These events are great ways to reach out and minister to parents.

Volunteering

We should make parents feel welcome in the school environment. We should provide diverse opportunities for them to participate in their children's education, and we should also ask them how they want to be involved. The school should have written policies, developed with parental input, that clearly define guidelines for parental involvement in the school and the classroom. Before parent volunteers serve in our classrooms, we need to let them know what we expect regarding confidentiality, professionalism, and interpersonal relationships with us and with the children. Of course, we must be sure to follow any existing school policies with respect to classroom volunteers.

Parental Support Resources

Recently more schools are beginning to offer workshops for parents on child development, parenting skills, family management techniques, and curricular support for home reading programs. Many schools provide a parent room in the school where parents can meet with other parents and can find literature on key parental concerns. Schools can provide a toy-lending library, or teachers can inform parents where to locate one. Schools also have the responsibility to connect parents to community resources outside of school. For instance, public libraries often offer homework resources, as well as workshops for parents, via the Internet.

The area of parent support is receiving increasing attention, but much remains to be done. How can we motivate parents to attend parent-help workshops? What can we do to minimize any stigma attached to either the workshops or to those who attend?

Parent Advisory Councils

In many jurisdictions, parents have the right and the responsibility, often mandated by law, to advise the school board, the principal, and the teachers respecting any matter relating to the school. Often these parent advisory councils meet regularly to consider school issues and to organize parent education. They may choose to invite the principal and a staff liaison person to the meetings. These advisory groups provide parents with opportunities to shape and support the goals of the school. Teachers should not minimize the importance of such parental input. Parents often have something worthwhile to offer, and teachers should encourage those who want to have an increased say in their children's education.

Conferencing with Parents

One of the main opportunities for formal contact with parents is a parent-teacher conference. Because of the importance of this type of conference to parent-teacher-student relationships, a separate section is included here to give practical suggestions on how to conduct an effective one. When parents cannot make it to a parent-teacher interview, we can arrange to meet them at an alternative time (perhaps by phone or e-mail) to discuss their children's progress.

Preplanning and preparing for conferences is the key to making them successful. Students, parents, and teachers must all be prepared.

Preparing Students

Allow students to choose a number of work samples that they want their parents to see. You may reserve the right to add more samples. Have the students evaluate their own work on a form you provide. You should evaluate each student's work on this same form. In this way, parents will be able to see how the student's evaluation compares with your evaluation of each piece of work.

Preparing Parents

By this time, you should already have had several positive contacts with parents, so you should have a good rate of attendance at the conferences, providing you are willing to work around the parents' schedules. Make sure you send a note in advance reminding parents of the conference, possibly including a tentative general agenda and giving parents an opportunity to have input. Encourage all parents to come, even if just to hear how well their children are doing. It encourages parents to hear once again that their children are doing well. Having all parents attend conferences helps you to intersperse the "heavier" conferences (with parents of students who are not doing well) with some "lighter" ones (with parents of students who are doing well).

Preparing Teachers

As the teacher, you need to carefully think through the logistics of each parent-teacher conference: What is the purpose? Where should it be held? When should it be held? How can I encourage both parents, if applicable, to be there?

Also, you should determine whether students will be invited. It is a good idea to schedule the meetings in a small conference room where distractions are minimal. Your focus should be on the parents not on yourself. If you do all you can to make the parents feel welcome and at ease, you will feel more at ease yourself.

It is a good idea to prepare an agenda that specifies the purpose of the conference, a sequence of topics to be discussed, and the times when the meeting will begin and end. Compile data about students' behavior, feelings, and academic work ahead of time, and be ready to describe each student's strengths and needs. Data objectify the discussion and protect the teacher, so document what you are going to say. Be sure to highlight key curricular and behavioral concerns, but also find something positive to say about each child. Anticipate questions the parents might ask.

Meeting with Parents

Once all the preparations have been made, give careful attention to the conference itself. Following are some practical guidelines for ensuring that the conference will achieve its purpose:

- Provide a copy of the agenda to each person in attendance—and follow it! Let parents know if there is a time limit and what happens if you don't finish in the time allotted.

- Create a warm, relaxed atmosphere. Use everyday language. Approach parents as team members, for you truly are in this task together. Show your appreciation that the parents took time to meet with you (Evertson, Emmer, and Worsham 2006, 162). Sit side by side rather than across from each other (Charles 1999, 250) so that the parents will feel more relaxed. Put yourself in their shoes and ask yourself how you would be feeling.

- Ask the parents to read their student's self-evaluation and to look at their child's work samples. Parents can often read these self-evaluations in advance.

- Discuss academic progress first, and then behavior, attitude, and peer relationships. Keep the *whole* child in mind.

- Share positive, personal qualities about the child. "Stick to descriptions of behavior rather than characterizations of students [e.g., "Abigail calls other children names," rather than "Abigail is mean"]" (Evertson, Emmer, and Worsham 2006, 162). Avoid characterizations and personality judgments. Convey a clear, consistent message regarding the value of the child.

- Ask the parents some key questions about the child: their perception of the child's strengths and weaknesses, something they would like you to know about the child; and the level of contentment they have regarding the child's school experiences. Encourage the parents to ask questions and make comments. Respect and value the parents' knowledge of their child. Demonstrate an authentic interest in their goals for the child. Do not argue or criticize. Don't ever put parents on the defensive. Pay careful attention as you actively listen and ask clarifying questions.

- Learn from each other during the meeting. Pick up ideas for working with the student more effectively.

- Make a plan of action, and set up a date for follow-up.

- Offer resources to the parents. Public libraries in some jurisdictions have pamphlets on school subjects with a list of books, Internet sites, and other resources related to the subject area and the grade level.

- Ask the parents if you may share confidential information, if necessary, with the child's counselor and other teachers. Ask how they want you to share the information.

- Make notes on the conference and keep them in a confidential place. Focus on needs, goals, and plans for accomplishing goals. When possible, these notes should be written immediately after the conference and before your next parent-teacher conference. Often conferences are scheduled back-to-back, so time is scarce; you might want to jot down brief reminders of what you discussed and how you said you'd respond. Take as few notes as possible during the conference, however, since some parents may be intimidated when they see you writing. File your notes immediately and systematically. Don't forget to follow through on everything you agreed to do.

- Keep in mind the following: avoid blaming parents; admit when you are wrong and when you don't know the answer to their questions; accept the family as it is; be cognizant of cultural differences between you and the parents; find something positive to say about both the child and the parents, but be sincere.

Handling Criticism

Handling criticism, mentioned briefly before, deserves further attention. Be aware that confrontation and criticism will inevitably come. Welcome them. Listen actively to what parents and others have to say, and be genuinely interested. When you sense that you are becoming defensive, that feeling is a clue that you may not be open to hearing parental input. But parents have perspectives that you need as their children's teacher. Always take any kind of personal criticism and confrontation to the Lord, letting *Him* tell you what you need to hear. Don't dismiss parents' criticism by saying, "Consider the source." Don't put up walls to keep yourself from hearing what you need to hear. Value others' input into your life and your work even if they don't give it in the most desirable way. God speaks through many people who speak in many different ways and with many different emotions attached. Be sure to listen.

Developing Strong Relationships with Parents

Parents are integral members of the school community. Do everything you can to build bridges to them. Affirm and encourage them in their parenting. Make them know that they are essential partners with you in the education and development of their children. As teachers, we build community by being people of godly character, firmly rooted in God's Word; by having God's vision of the people He has called us to lead; and by prayerfully and intentionally taking time to build relationships with God, our peers, our students, and our students' parents.

Closing Thoughts on Inviting Effective Parent-Teacher Relationships

There are no gimmicks or strategies or communication techniques that can take the place of genuinely loving our students, taking a sincere interest in them, and being enthusiastic about teaching them. The sacred trust given to us should fill us with awe, excitement, and a sense of responsibility. Parents will see through a front of put-on professionalism. If we are fulfilling our vocation with joy, working as unto the Lord, keeping our lives above reproach, and pursuing excellence, parents will usually respond to us. Be encouraged.

QUESTIONS: INVITING EFFECTIVE PARENT-TEACHER RELATIONSHIPS

1. How much do you think parents should be involved in their children's education? Provide a rationale for your answer.

2. Which of the obstacles to developing effective parent-teacher relationships do you think you will have the most difficulty addressing? Make sure it is an obstacle that you can do something about. Why will this obstacle be the most difficult for you? What specific things can you work on *now* to overcome it?

3. In what ten specific ways will you be salt and light to your students' parents? Answering this question will require much wisdom and direction from God. Begin to reflect on the kinds of things you can do.

4. What should you do if a parent challenges you on one of your teaching methods? What if this person has no teaching experience but disagrees with your methods? What do you say? How do you treat that parent?

PART TWO

All teachers long to teach in classroom communities in which students are motivated to learn—and in which they experience satisfaction in their learning; develop as unique individuals; support and encourage one another; and grow in their thinking, attitudes, and behavior. But how do teachers go about setting up such positive classroom communities? What type of organizational and management strategies will enable them to do so?

Christian teachers should envision classroom communities that (a) encourage the development of Christian maturity in the teacher and the students, (b) give Christ the preeminence and allow the Holy Spirit to work fully, (c) teach children to accept and appreciate who they are according to God's standards, (d) encourage acceptance of others, (e) encourage the pursuit of excellence, (f) promote personal responsibility so that students realize there are consequences for their choices, and (g) teach children to work interdependently. Each of these components is essential for properly functioning classroom communities—in public schools as well as independent schools. Yet too many teachers just "go with the flow" and create classroom environments that adhere to the popular theories of the day. Rather than following such fads, Christian teachers should base their vision for the classroom on God's idea of community.

As a Christian teacher—no matter how well grounded you are in your subject matter, no matter how much training or how many education courses you have taken, no matter how many lesson plans you have written, and no matter how dedicated you are—until you learn how to build an appropriate, effective, and inspiring classroom environment in which students are motivated to learn and grow, your students will be hindered from fully achieving their God-given potential.

CHAPTER SEVEN

MOTIVATING BY MANAGING WELL

Students benefit from knowing that their motivation and behavior in a
classroom will be influenced by their confidence in their ability to complete the work
(expectation), the degree to which they find value in the work (value), and the quality
of peer and teacher-student relationships in the classroom (climate).
—Vernon and Louise Jones, *Comprehensive Classroom Management*

The Challenge Before Us

Many teachers do not realize how important motivation is in a classroom. Yet, as a teacher, I would place stimulating motivation in the top four emphases teachers must have—along with building relationships, preventing problems, and teaching subject matter!

Amazingly, most preservice teachers have never even been exposed to the topic of motivation in their teacher preparation programs. In contrast, these programs give much time and emphasis to controlling student behavior, resolving conflict, and responding to student violations when they occur. The focus is on *controlling students' performance* rather than on *stimulating students' motivation*. As a result, teachers use incentives, rewards, penalties, and grades to get their students to meet the teachers' goals. They give little or no attention to stimulating students to generate their own goals and to do whatever it takes to reach those goals.

Many teachers have mistakenly focused on *control* in their classrooms. What a tragedy! By having the wrong focus, teachers end up spending an inordinate amount of time and energy just trying to make students behave. How many teachers want to spend the school day doing that? Is wanting to control students or make them behave the reason you went into teaching? Hopefully not.

Is student misbehavior a big concern? Are you worried that you will be unable to control your students? If you answered yes, you are not alone! Student misbehavior is a major concern of new teachers. It is also increasingly a concern of more seasoned teachers because of the needs of the children who are now in their classrooms. Teachers are dealing with disruptive students, unmotivated students, children who are angry at the adult world, students who are discouraged, and students experiencing emotional stress. Today's teachers face increased violence, increased cultural diversity, larger class sizes, a lack of basic resources, a wider range of student abilities, and the inclusion of children with special needs in their classrooms. Many students come from backgrounds that include poverty, crime, unemployment, family disruption, addiction, and abuse. An increasing number of students are coming to school unprepared to follow rules, cooperate, or respect adult authority. Sin is taking its toll.

Because of this challenging situation, some teachers assume that student misbehavior is inevitable. But it doesn't have to be so. It may be true that you have some hurting and needy children in your classroom, but God has handpicked them for you. Much student misbehavior presently happening in classrooms can be prevented—by teachers who learn to motivate their students to take responsibility for their own learning and behavior. The question you need to answer is, What focus do I want in my classroom—control or motivation?

Teachers who catch the vision to motivate each student in their classroom find that it revolutionizes their teaching—especially if they were previously bound by the *control* mind-set. It is possible to make your classroom an exciting place that you and your students look forward to going to each day.

Here is why focusing on motivation works. When our emphasis is control, we tend to be focused on what students do wrong and how we can stop that behavior. On the other hand, when our emphasis is on motivation, we look for the positive things that students do. Years ago, in the very early years of my teaching career, Stacey, one of my sixth-grade students, said to me: "You are so positive in so many areas in our classroom, but giving demerit points for misbehavior is so negative because you are focusing on what we do wrong. Why don't you, instead, give responsibility points, because then you will be focused on what we do right?" Out of the mouth of babes comes wisdom (Matthew 21:16). What Stacey taught me made an incredible difference in my classroom. In essence, she was telling me to focus on motivating my students instead of trying to control them.

It should come as no surprise that students who are motivated to learn cause fewer disruptions in the classroom. Why then don't teachers focus on motivating students and capitalizing on students who are motivated to learn? Too much emphasis in classrooms today is placed on the "average" student. In our teaching, we are told to go as fast or as slow as the average student, or the middle group, can understand—and perhaps to focus any remaining time and attention on students of low ability. Why? Why would we want to do this? Is it even possible? I have been in classrooms long enough to know that it is difficult to identify average students. I also know that by gearing teaching to those students, we will bore the academically more advanced students and go beyond the limit of some of our academically lower-level students. So what's the answer?

Let me suggest an alternative. It's one I adopted many years ago—and I know it works! Why not focus on the *motivated* students (regardless of their ability or their speed) and become familiar with the different organizational and management strategies that will keep these students motivated? When I tried this approach, I found that the attitudes of the unmotivated students changed dramatically as they saw the excitement and enthusiasm for learning in the motivated students. Previously unmotivated students *wanted* to get on board. I've seen it happen over and over again! Motivated students are like trains going downhill. They are hard to stop. As their teachers, we need to help these students by simply laying the track—and then letting them run on it. We need to let these motivated students help set the climate for learning in the classroom.

Focusing on the motivated students will dramatically influence the atmosphere of our classrooms. Students will want to be there and to be involved in learning. They will want to be part of a productive community. They will be excited. They will participate. They will go beyond the expectations we have for them. They will see that their efforts are paying off. The whole tone of the classroom will exude enthusiasm, excitement, productivity, support, and cooperation.

This chapter will give some practical suggestions on how to gain and maintain student motivation. It will discuss eight principles of motivation, the different types of motivation, strategies for enhancing *individual* student motivation, strategies for enhancing *group* motivation, strategies for helping students with special needs, and strategies for addressing personal and cultural differences.

Principles of Motivation

The following eight principles provide the strategic framework for motivating students to take the initiative and responsibility for their own learning, growth, attitude, and behavior:

1. Teachers should understand and take into consideration the factors motivating students to behave as they do (Levin and Nolan 2004, 1).

2. Teachers should organize and manage their classrooms as efficient learning communities. Students need opportunities to be actively engaged with the material and to interact positively with their peers (Good and Brophy 2003, 212).

3. Teachers should provide opportunities for students to be successful in completing tasks they value and see as challenging (Good and Brophy 2003, 213). Teachers who are intentional about involving students in goal setting and self-assessment will enhance students' motivation to learn.

4. Teachers should have worthwhile academic objectives in mind when they select activities. (Good and Brophy 2003, 213).

5. Teachers should systematically encourage students to replace their negative thinking about themselves with positive truths about themselves. This kind of encouragement can transform students by helping them renew their minds. Too many students and teachers focus on what students do wrong and on what they can't do, and this kind of thinking becomes a self-fulfilling prophecy. Students will never succeed if their minds are full of thoughts such as "I'm no good," "I can't do math," "Everybody is better than I am," and "Nobody likes me." How students think about themselves determines what they will become.

6. Teachers should help students recognize the relationship between effort and outcome. When students put forth a lot of effort, they want to know that there will be a payoff. But what should teachers help students see as the most important payoff for their effort? Is the reward something extrinsic (candy or stickers) or something intrinsic (feeling good about themselves for working hard) (Good and Brophy 2003, 214)?

7. Teachers should show moderation and variation in using motivational strategies (Good and Brophy 2003, 214).

8. Teachers should relate lessons to students' lives, model interest and enthusiasm in learning, and include novelty and variety in their lessons. They do so by setting the stage, getting students' attention, teaching with focus and enthusiasm, and changing activities to keep students motivated. Lessons must be well thought out to accomplish these things (Good and Brophy 2003, 235).

Types of Motivation

Most information on motivation divides the topic into two types: *extrinsic motivation*, in which students perform in order to obtain some reward or avoid some punishment external to the activity itself, such as grades, stickers, or teacher approval; and *intrinsic motivation*, in which students undertake an activity for its own sake—for the enjoyment it provides, the learning it permits, or the feelings of accomplishment it evokes. "Motivation refers to an inner drive that focuses behavior on a particular goal or task and causes the individual to be persistent in trying to achieve the goal or complete the task successfully" (Levin and Nolan 2004, 107).

Much teacher attention is focused on extrinsic motivation—the giving of rewards or punishment. Should rewards be used? If so, how might we incorporate extrinsic motivation into our classrooms? What rewards are effective for the ages, personalities, and abilities of particular students? Should we use punishment? If so, what penalties/consequences are appropriate and effective? Often extrinsic motivation is more effective at the lower grade levels but less effective in the older grades, especially after students' intrinsic motivation has developed. Be aware that using *extrinsic* motivation on students who are already *intrinsically* motivated will lessen these students' intrinsic motivation—an unfortunate outcome. We must be careful how we use extrinsic motivation in our classrooms.

Intrinsic motivation is the most desirable type because it does not rely on an outside source. Classroom communities composed of intrinsically motivated students are exciting places to be! In these kinds of classrooms, students *want* to learn and *take responsibility* to learn.

Some would say that it is possible to motivate someone else extrinsically but not intrinsically. However, teachers can create classrooms with the following intrinsic motivation appeals (Rinne 1997, 29–37):

- Novelty ("This is different.")

- Security ("I can do this.")

- Completion ("I can do this and use it later in this lesson.")

- Application ("I can do this and use it outside the lesson.")

- Anticipation ("Watch for …" "What next?")

- Surprise ("Something unexpected will happen.")

- Challenge ("See if I can …")

- Feedback ("I will know how well I am doing.")

- Identification projection ("This is just like me.")

- Achievement ("I will have done this myself.")

- Ownership ("This will be my very own.")

- Belonging ("I know I belong here.")

- Competition ("I can be the winner.")

We can lead a horse to water, *and* we can make the horse so thirsty that he will drink the water that we lead him to! Our job is to make our students "thirsty" so that they will want to "drink the water" when we lead them to it. This task is within our realm of capability.

From experience, I can tell you that it is exciting to continue to learn about what motivates my students. It's always changing. What motivated students twenty years ago seldom motivates students today. What motivates certain students may not motivate others. And what motivates certain students today may not motivate those same students tomorrow. That is what I like about teaching: it challenges me to keep on learning!

Strategies for Enhancing Individual Students' Motivation

Julius Kuhl (1982, 125) suggests that motivation equals expectation (the extent to which students believe they can be successful at the task) times value (the degree to which they value the task and its rewards). Vernon and Louse Jones (2004, 192–193) add a third variable, climate ("the quality of relationships within the task setting during the time the people are engaged in the task"). Combining Kuhl's work with that of Jones and Jones gives us this formula:

$$\text{motivation} = \text{expectation x value x climate}$$

Students will be motivated to complete a task if they expect that they can accomplish it successfully, if they find value in it, and if they can complete it in an environment (climate) supportive of their basic personal needs. Note that this formula describes motivation in terms of multiplication, suggesting that students will *not* be motivated unless all three components are present: anything multiplied by zero equals zero. Thus, if one is missing, motivation will not occur. This fact—that teachers need to develop strategies to motivate students in all three areas—is basic to our understanding of how to motivate our students.

Expectation

For students to be motivated, they must know that they have the ability and the resources to accomplish a task successfully. Therefore, we need to collect the necessary resources ahead of time and organize them systematically so they are easily accessible. It is imperative that we think through the logistics of how to engage students with these resources while allowing only the least possible amount of disruption.

Unless students know that they can successfully complete the task, they may not even begin. For this reason, we may need to make modifications and adaptations for students with special needs. Not all students can handle the same level of difficulty. For example, in a grade-three class, one student may be able to write coherent essays with ease, while others struggle to write even one logical paragraph. In these cases, we need to provide "scaffolds" to help the struggling students complete the entire assignment.

Jones and Jones (2004, 195) have identified specific ways of helping our students know they will be successful:

Help students understand what is expected of them. We must be very specific and not just tell students to "do their best work." We must show them what "best" looks like by keeping samples of (1) work that does not meet expectations, (2) work that minimally meets expectations, (3) work that meets expectations fully, and (4) work that exceeds expectations. We can have students compare their work with these samples and analyze their own work before handing it in for grading. It is also good for students to keep their own work so that they can see their growth over time.

Provide students with opportunities to experience success. Often students who have experienced a great deal of failure tend to think they can't do anything, and so they give up. Our challenge is to help students rethink past failures and provide them with new activities that they can succeed in. We must challenge them to move beyond their level of comfort. Here is a case in point: Many elementary teachers do not like math. They had bad experiences with it when they were students, and so they have come to believe that they are "just not good in math." The sad part is that many of their bad experiences may have been due to the poor teaching they received in math rather than their own inability to do math. If these teachers don't recognize this reality for what it is, they may pass their attitudes toward math on to their students. As teachers, we need to give our students every opportunity to succeed, beginning with our own attitudes toward the subject matter we teach. We also need to be aware of students' attitudes, behaviors, and self-doubts, as well as the students' understanding of the material. Just because a student is in grade six doesn't mean that he understands all the math content from grade five. Review, teach, reteach, demonstrate, practice, and help students get past their fears and inadequacies. Take this problem as a challenge.

Provide assignments and activities that are at an appropriate level. If students find assignments too easy or too difficult, their motivation may decrease. Let me give another example from math (my favorite subject to teach). Teachers often assign all the students the same questions for homework or practice. One day it may be the odd numbers and the next day, the even. Sound familiar? Why not instead give students the opportunity to choose which five or six questions they want to tackle? (First explain how the math textbook is set up, with the easy questions first, those of medium difficulty second, and the most difficult last.) I've seldom found students choosing to work below their level of ability when they have been given the opportunity to choose their own level of learning. On the contrary, I've found that they rise to the challenge and try some questions that really stretch them!

I gave the manuscript of this book to a number of teachers to get their feedback before the book went to publication. One of them read the above suggestion and thought she would try it. She was skeptical that something so simple would work. Yet when she phoned me a few days after trying this strategy, she said she was absolutely blown away by the eager response of her students. Even her teacher aide couldn't believe the excitement of the students about doing math. Every student got involved. Some wanted to continue to work after they had done the six questions they had chosen. The exciting thing was that the students were excited to get back to math the next day. Amazing! The beauty of this successful experience is that now this teacher is highly motivated to find other strategies that work.

Give students time to integrate learning. I've heard many teachers say that they don't have time to teach math "for understanding" because it takes more time. Yes, it does, but once the concepts are learned and understood, they are rarely forgotten. We must remember that there is *conceptual* knowledge and *procedural* knowledge. We can rush through the teaching of procedural knowledge, but teaching conceptually takes more time. We need to give our students time to fit new information into their existing framework of knowledge. We need to give them time to absorb things. If students don't have time to make the connections between what they already know and what they are learning, they will be less motivated to learn. New knowledge is integrated and remembered only when it is linked to past experience or a perceived future need. Therefore, we need to review, to ask questions, and to help students see the relationships between the new concepts and their existing knowledge.

Show students that there is a predictable relationship between the level of effort invested in a task and the level of success. We can help students understand that the outcome is up to them, that they have the ability to do better on a task if they choose to invest the necessary effort.

Help students understand the difference between being evaluated on the completion of an assignment and being evaluated on the quality of the product. Too many older students think that completing all components of an assignment automatically earns them an A. Handing in a completed assignment is only the first stage. The quality of the completed assignment could still be unsatisfactory. We need to help students value quality as well as completion.

Value

In order to be motivated, students must also see value in their assignments. Jones and Jones (2004, 195) have identified specific ways we can help our students value the tasks we give them:

Actively involve students in the learning process. Students aren't easily fooled. They know the difference between a valuable learning activity and busywork. Learning opportunities should be interaction oriented. Students who have the opportunity to be actively involved will be more highly motivated to learn. Therefore, it is a good idea to invite students' input on finding different ways to demonstrate their learning. Give them the opportunity to show evidence of their learning in the way that is best for them (recognizing the reality of multiple intelligences) within the boundaries that you provide. You'll be amazed at how much they have learned, and they'll be excited to show you! Let me give you two examples from my own teaching experience:

1. Early in my teaching career, I had a young boy in my sixth-grade class who had been severely abused as an infant and had been placed in and out of foster homes. He lived in such fear that when he came into the classroom, he would hide under the table. He came into my classroom for social studies ... so that he could try to learn to interact socially with his peers. At the beginning of the year, I think almost every time he was in the classroom, he was under the table. I continued to teach even while trying to build a relationship with this young boy. My principal asked me how I was going to test whether he had learned anything. I told her that I couldn't test him because he couldn't read or write. (At that time, I hadn't yet realized that there were other acceptable ways of determining what students had learned.) She suggested that I just ask him the questions orally. I must admit that I thought she didn't understand how pro- foundly "challenged" this boy was, but because she was the principal, I decided to give it a try. Was I ever surprised! This boy, who seemed as if he wasn't pay- ing attention at all, and who seemed in many ways incapable of understanding the lesson, gave me the correct answer to almost every question. I would never have realized this boy's potential had I not moved away from doing things the way I normally did them.

2. Here's another example. When I was teaching eighth-grade American his- tory at a missionary kids' school in Malaysia, I told my students that there would be a quiz the next day on the chapter that we had just completed. When I arrived at school the next day, I remembered that I was supposed to have a test ready for them—but I had forgotten. (That was the only time in my teach- ing career I forgot a test. I learned!) I knew my students well enough to know that they had studied for the test and would have been quite upset not to have one that day. (Missionary children have time set aside by their dorm parents to do their homework.) What could I do? I didn't have time to type out a test and copy it for each student.

Here's what I did. I put a blank piece of paper on each student's desk, and then I rummaged in my desk and everywhere else inside and outside the classroom to come up with items that I had enough of to give to each student (such as erasers, scissors, elastic bands, stickers, and dirt). Just to let you know how "crazy" this was, I actually put pencil shavings on each desk. By then, I was having a great time being creative! When the students came in, I told them the test was to use what was on their desks to show me what they had learned from the chapter. The only words they could write were their names. I learned a lot that day—and so did my students. Some of my strongest academic students sat the entire class period wondering what in the world pencil shavings, dirt, and stickers had to do with what we had just studied in American history. Jenny was one of those students. Other students, who normally had difficulty writing the usual kinds of tests, started immediately and created incredible representations of what they had learned. I was moved to tears and was forever changed when my top student (Jenny, who usually scored at least 95 percent on written tests) came up and thanked me for doing this. For the first time in her schooling, she said, she realized how other students felt when they sat before a test and drew a blank. It had an incredibly positive effect on building supportive relationships in our classroom community. We need to give our students the opportunity to show us in a variety of ways what they've learned.

Help students understand and value the learning goals. We need to help students understand why it is important for them to learn specific material and why it is important that they be involved in specific activities related to this material. We need to build relevance into everything we teach. We can encourage students to rephrase the question "When will I ever use this stuff again?" to "How will this assignment change me if I let it?" We need to help them ask the right questions. We can help them understand that if they don't allow their schooling to change them, they won't truly get an education. Education is about being changed. Students need to understand that even though they have received the highest grades in the class, if their lives haven't been changed for the better, then they haven't truly gained an education. We need to help students remain open to being changed by new ideas.

Relate subject matter to students' lives. When students can relate course content to their own lives, they value the information more highly and they are more likely to remember it. Students' motivation is greatly increased when they see a useful purpose for what they are learning. On the other hand, although we can make student learning relevant, we must be careful not to encourage self-centeredness. For example, many historical events may not appear to be connected to anything in students' lives at present. Still, students must learn about those events because that knowledge helps them understand the bigger picture of how God has worked in history and continues to work today.

Provide opportunities for students to set learning goals and follow their own interests. Student learning should not be limited to just what is required in the curriculum. Encourage students to thoroughly research a specific topic of interest within a general curriculum area.

Model learning as an exciting and rewarding activity. We can demonstrate the emotional responses that we want students to have regarding certain tasks. How often I have heard teachers start lessons by saying, "This is boring, but we have to cover it, so let's go quickly and get it over with"! Students pick up our attitudes toward specific subjects or lessons. Many elementary children have been turned off math or science because they've had teachers who either didn't like the subject or were afraid of it.

Teach more than facts. Facts are the basic information. But we also need to teach concepts (the relationships between the facts and the major themes associated with the facts), generalizations (using facts and concepts to solve problems or interpret situations), and personal applications (relating learning to students' own beliefs, feelings, and behaviors) (Jones and Jones 2004, 200). Students are more likely to be motivated when they are required not just to learn basic facts but to use those facts to solve problems, draw conclusions, and discover applications for their own lives.

Help students understand that although not all tasks seem valuable to them at the moment, they are all still necessary. In other words, even when the motivation isn't there, the students still need to complete the tasks! We can do our best to make learning relevant for them, but if a student doesn't value a particular task, it doesn't mean that the task has no value. Some things are necessary to learn even when the learner can see no value in them. For example, learning the rules of grammar is tedious for some students. We can do our best to make it more appealing, but still not all students will come to value learning grammar. Motivation helps students do tasks more enjoyably, but lack of motivation doesn't mean that they don't have to do the tasks.

Climate

The third part of the motivation formula is the climate, tone, or emotional atmosphere in the classroom (Levin and Nolan 2004, 109). Tone refers to how we interact with students, how students interact with us, and how students interact with each other. We as teachers have the potential to set a tone in our classrooms "that directs and re-directs [our students] and ourselves into walking in God's way of truth and uprightntess" (Van Brummelen 1998, 39). Setting and keeping a positive tone in the classroom involves us in making wise choices every day.

Following are specific suggestions for creating classroom communities that enhance students' motivation to learn:

- Set up the classroom in ways that invite students to feel accepted, safe, and eager to learn. This includes desk arrangements, use of wall space, and the presence of plants or animals. We should also provide every student with his or her own personal space. (For more information on this topic, see chapter 9.)

- Establish a climate of inclusion, in which every student feels respected by and connected to other students (Wlodkowski and Ginsberg 1995, 19). Students have a wide variety of abilities and disabilities. Therefore, we must know how much time our group of students needs to spend in cooperative activities and in individual activities. The amount of time needed will vary, depending on our students.

- Incorporate standards that provide students with safety (from both physical danger and embarrassment), involvement (giving them a meaningful stake in what's going on), care (because students respond positively to being liked, accepted, and respected members of the class), and best instructional practices.

- Set up a goal-oriented and structured classroom. "In general, classroom life, and in particular, academic learning, will tend to go better when the norms [goals] of the peer group support cooperation, helpfulness, supportiveness, and interpersonal empathy" (Schmuck and Schmuck 2001, 208).

- Vary instructional strategies, and use these differing techniques in moderation. We must plan, organize, and understand what our students need by way of classroom tone. We can gear activities to the times of the day and week. Teaching art first thing in the morning may not be effective in setting an appropriate tone for the rest of the day. Yet, sometimes it is wise to shake things up by interchanging predictable activities with novel and creative activities.

- Engender competence. Create "an understanding that students are effective in learning something they value" (Wlodkowski and Ginsberg 1995, 19).

- Create a positive interpersonal atmosphere. (See chapters 4 and 5 on peer relationships and teacher-student relationships.)

- Provide students with realistic and immediate feedback. (See chapter 10 on managing student work.) A recent book suggests that we "feed forward" instead of giving feedback (Sanborn 2006, 67–68)! What the author says is that we should give our students input that will make them successful in moving forward.

- Speak words that give life and hope. We should look for qualities in our students and their work that we can genuinely affirm. We can let them know when we see improvement in their attitude, behavior, or quality of work.

- Actively listen to the students. We need to take time to ask them what is going on in their lives.

- Intentionally observe the students. Who is hurting? Who is tired and hungry? Which students are fighting with each other? We can come alongside these students and let them know that we see and we care.

- Pray! This is the single most important thing we can do in setting the tone in our classrooms. We can invite God's Holy Spirit to be present and active in our classrooms, in our lives, and in the lives of our students.

Strategies for Enhancing Group/Class Motivation

Almost all classes are heterogeneous. This means that the class has not only a wide range of academic abilities but also a range in the number of students at each level. What works to motivate one student may not work to motivate another. When it comes to academics, it is impossible for every student to have an individualized program. However, we can make modifications to the regular classroom instruction to meet the needs of all the students in our class and to have the highest possible level of motivation and productivity. The modifications required may be extreme or minor, depending on the students' needs.

There are several strategies that can be used to meet the needs of the group or class and thus enhance students' motivation to learn:

Team Teaching

In this scenario, more than one teacher teaches the same group of students. Usually teachers will teach in their areas of expertise.

Peer Tutoring

When expectations and objectives are known, it is sometimes a good idea to have students help one another. This method can work in two ways: (1) students of the same ability spur each other on and (2) more advanced students help those who are having difficulty.

Pull-Out Instruction

In this case, students needing extra help can be pulled out of the classroom for a short time to work with a learning-assistance or resource teacher on specific learning needs.

Small-Group Instruction

The makeup of such groups can be determined by ability, interest, or topic. Students need to know that they have the opportunity to move into different groups and will not be stuck in the "lowest" group all the time. Students can move into different ability groups when we form the groups according to interest level rather than ability level. Sometimes we can simply group friends together.

Individualized Instruction

There are some reading programs available that enable students to work on their own at their own level of ability.

Strategies for Helping Students with Special Needs

Students who are achieving two or more levels below grade level can benefit when we employ strategies for teaching students with special needs. Before going any further in this section, it must be said that there are students with learning disabilities who nevertheless display determination, perseverance, and an incredible work ethic. These are not the students referred to here. This section is about students whose special needs have affected their behavior in such negative ways that they seem trapped in a cycle of defeat and discouragement, almost a learned helplessness. Many of these students readily accept failure, and they are easily discouraged. At times, they are apathetic or belligerent, or they become class clowns. They might frequently be absent or late (especially in high school), and they may see grades as being assigned arbitrarily. They may have poor study habits, poor reading ability, short attention spans, and a low perception of their ability.

Students with special needs require extra management, organization, and care. Teachers must establish and maintain a solid management system, monitor student behavior carefully, and manage student work carefully (see chapter 10). With special needs students, we can modify the system by teaching content in shorter segments that include frequent student input to gauge comprehension, by using appropriate and sometimes simpler wording, by using several cycles of content development and seatwork rather than one long lecture, by being conscious of pacing, by making smoother transitions, and by teaching school survival skills.

When students' needs cannot be well met in a regular classroom, teachers may also opt for supplementary or pull-out instruction. This kind of instruction might be employed for students who are deficient in certain basic skills, are easily distracted by other students, are learning a new language, or even are uniquely gifted.

Strategies for Addressing Personal and Cultural Differences

How well students do in school, both academically and behaviorally, is partly a reflection of the culture of their homes and communities. Hawaiian children, for example, are highly peer oriented—collaboration and cooperation are commonplace in their natal Hawaiian culture. Navajo children, on the other hand, are often content to be alone, and they tend to be self-sufficient; so they do not regard separation from other students as a punishment (Tharp 1989, 350–351).

We need to learn motivational strategies that will be effective with the different students in our classes. What an incredible challenge! We will quickly realize that some students are motivated in certain settings but not in others. There are times when a student just won't value learning on a particular day.

At the same time, we expect students to master the material whether they are motivated or not, because the material is deemed beneficial and desirable. For example, babies who are fed a multitude of different foods before age two will like a wider range of foods when they are older. Children may value ice cream and Pop-Tarts, but a loving parent makes them eat healthy foods such as carrots, potatoes, and fruit even when they don't value these foods. Children who value video games often find it difficult to value the hard work involved in accomplishing more meaningful academic goals. Sometimes students can't assess value, and sometimes they simply won't value anything that seems like hard work, that is unknown, or that is uncomfortable. We must help students move beyond valuing only what they like and what they are already good at.

Closing Thoughts on Motivating by Managing Well

It is important for teachers to become experts at motivating their students within the context of a caring and diverse community. Educational books are available in this area. Student motivation is a key component to teachers' effectiveness in bringing about student learning. It is one of the four areas of expertise a teacher should have, along with teaching subject matter, building relationships, and preventing problems.

QUESTIONS: MOTIVATING BY MANAGING WELL

1. Discuss the difference between controlling students and motivating students.

2. To what extent do you think it is necessary or advisable to use extrinsic motivational approaches in the classroom? If you intend to use extrinsic approaches, how do you plan to minimize their undesirable effects?

3. How would you respond to unmotivated students who genuinely want to know why they are asked to study Shakespeare's sonnets or the history of ancient Greece?

4. According to your view of the child, what type of motivation do children need? Support your response.

5. Consider the debate about the value of extrinsic motivation versus intrinsic motivation. Which type of motivation do you support and why? Would a blend of the two be valuable? In what specific ways will you foster and encourage student motivation? How will your treatment of learning styles and multiple intelligences affect student motivation in your classroom? How will you know whether you are just paying lip service to the reality of different learning styles and not actually incorporating them into your classroom? In other words, how will your assessment of classroom learning be influenced by your awareness of different learning styles and multiple intelligences?

CHAPTER EIGHT

GETTING OFF TO A GREAT START

In my beginning is my end.
—Thomas Stearns Eliot, "East Coker"

Good teachers realize the value of the first day of class with respect to motivating students and building a caring, supportive, and productive classroom community. This first day is often the time when we have the highest percentage of motivated students in our classrooms, so we need to capitalize on it. We can make the most of it by having everything ready to go and by giving students everything they need so that every student who wishes to do so may begin organizing for success. What we do during the first day and the first week of class is important because it is at this time that students learn the behaviors, attitudes, and work habits that will affect them and their peers throughout the year. To a great extent, the first day will determine whether our students are committed to being active and effective participants in the classroom learning community.

Thus, we need to consider many things with respect to getting off to a good start. We need to organize our classrooms, materials, resources, activities, and students. This challenge is certainly not one for the fainthearted.

Remember that the focus of this section is on motivating our students within the context of the classroom community. How can we use our advance planning, the first day of class, and the first week and month of the school year to motivate our students to learn and grow?

Before We Begin

To get off to a great start, we need to consider what our students are concerned about on the first day of school. By doing so, we will be more effective in motivating them and building a safe, caring, and productive classroom community.

What concerns and motivates students on the first day? Is it having a new start and a clean slate? Meeting their new teachers? Being back with their friends? Dreaming of new possibilities? Having new clothes and new school supplies? Being involved again in sports, music, or art? What motivated you on the first day of school?

What fears or concerns do students have on the first day of school? Do they fear that this year will be the same as last year? Do they fear being bullied? Do they fear that they won't measure up to the teacher's expectations? Do they fear that the teacher won't like them or even notice them? Do they fear having no friends and being alone? Do they fear being separated from their friends from last year? Do they fear getting a "bad" teacher? What concerned you when you were a student starting a new school year?

On the basis of these first-day concerns and motivations, take the time to write down five messages you want to convey to your students before they leave your classroom on the first day of school. Do this now. Please don't read any farther than the next two sentences. This exercise should take only a few minutes. Then we will build on it later on in the chapter.

Scriptural Guidance

As we begin to look in more detail at using the beginning of the school year to motivate our students, consider the picture the apostle Paul used of a runner who enters a race: "Do you not know that in a race all the runners run, but only one gets the prize? Run in such a way as to get the prize. Everyone who competes in the games goes into strict training. They do it to get a crown that will not last; but we do it to get a crown that will last forever. Therefore I do not run like a man running aimlessly" (1 Corinthians 9:24–26, NIV). This portion of Scripture provides food for thought (and action) about planning for the new school year and beginning the year well. Let's consider some of the key phrases in these verses:

All Runners Run

Everyone is actively involved in the race; everyone who has stepped onto the track is running—yet only one receives the prize. Why is that? Weren't all the runners aiming for the finish line? Were some going in a different direction? Were they just not fast enough? How might this relate to motivating students and getting off to a great start in teaching? Our teaching credentials (degrees or certifications) only get us into the arena (or school). They do not guarantee that we will be successful in our race.

Everyone Who Competes ... Goes into Strict Training

When we think about Olympic athletes and their training regimens, we realize how much time, effort, and focus they put in, long before they get to the actual race. God will lead some to compete in marathons, others in sprints, others in hurdles, and still others in relays. Preparing for a marathon takes completely different preparation than preparing for a sprint does. Athletes need to know their race and the special skills they will need to compete successfully in it. For us, this "strict training" relates to the importance of planning and preparing before we ever step into our classrooms. The more we prepare ourselves (and our formal teacher preparation program is only the beginning), the better able we will be to win the prize. The prize in this case is being the teachers God created us to be—and creating the atmosphere and building the relationships that will enable our students to become the people God created them to be.

They Do It to Get a Crown

They do it to get a crown that will not last, but we do it to get a crown that will last forever. I trust that our purpose for teaching is based on God's eternal perspective. We are not competing to receive "Teacher of the Year" awards or any other rewards or accolades that people may give us. We are competing for the cause of Christ—and to hear Him say, "Well done, good and faithful servant" (Matthew 25:21, 23, NIV). We are not in competition with other teachers. The person that we are now is competing to become the person that God wants us to be. God has given us the gifts, talents, and abilities that we need to run the race He has assigned to us and to finish it well. We must use all He has given us for His glory.

I Do Not Run Aimlessly

Therefore I do not run like a man running aimlessly. As a new school year begins, we need to have purpose and direction. Running aimlessly, no matter how fast, will never win the prize. "If any one competes as an athlete, he does not win the prize unless he competes according to the rules" (2 Timothy 2:5). The same is true in teaching. There are boundaries, expectations, and a code of ethics for teachers that we must follow if we are to perform our task successfully. If He has called us into teaching, the Holy Spirit has chosen us to be His "athletes." He is willing to coach and advise us as we prepare for and "run with endurance the race that is set before us" (Hebrews 12:1).

What an exciting ministry God has called us to—teaching! It's so much more than a job; it truly is a ministry. In the flyleaf of my Bible, I have this quotation from John A. Holt (2007): "Ministry is ... giving when you feel like keeping, praying for others when you need prayer, feeding others when your soul is hungry, hurting with others when your own hurt can't be spoken, keeping your word when it is not convenient, being faithful when your soul wants to run away."

Teaching—influencing the hearts and minds of young people—is an incredible privilege, yet it is a heavy responsibility. All we do, say, and think—all we are—will convey either a direct or an indirect message to our students. Therefore, we must ensure that we consistently and purposefully base all these things on the solid foundation of who Christ is and who we are in Christ.

Scripture gives many examples of the importance of planning before we start a job. One such example is found in Luke 14:28–30: "Which one of you, when he wants to build a tower, does not first sit down and calculate the cost to see if he has enough to complete it? Otherwise, when he has laid a foundation and is not able to finish, all who observe it begin to ridicule him, saying, 'This man began to build and was not able to finish.' " What builder does not first count the cost? What teacher does not first do some advance planning?

Nehemiah's story also shows the importance of preplanning to get a job done—in his case, rebuilding the walls of Jerusalem. He asked the king for permission to go to Judah (Nehemiah 2:5), requested letters for a safe passage (2:7), requested materials to use in building (2:8), inspected the walls before rebuilding (2:13–15), planned for success (2:20), and finished the task of rebuilding Jerusalem's walls (6:15). What can we do that will motivate our students to join with us as active builders of our classroom community?

The Advance Plan (*PLAN*)

What type of advance planning will help us get off to a great start? New teachers, in particular, need to begin preparing early, because preparation tends to take longer when you're new to it. When you **PLAN**, there are four things you should do: **P**ray. **L**earn as much as you can as quickly as you can. **A**rrange the details. And then **N**avigate according to your plan.

Pray

Daily personal Bible reading and prayer are two practices that should be treasured by all Christian teachers. Begin each day quietly in the presence of your heavenly Father, seeking His direction, hearing His truth, sharing your concerns, being strengthened in your spirit, committing your day to Him, and choosing to walk in obedience to Him. Remember to pray for each of your students by name even before the year begins. Continue to do this throughout the year. As you get to know your students, you will know how to pray for them more specifically. Praying for the school administrators, your colleagues, and yourself will help you see things from God's perspective. There may be other Christian teachers on staff who would love to pray weekly with you. Begin to consider a group prayer time as a possibility; it's already happening in many schools. We need to ask God for wisdom, discretion, and discernment. We need to have eyes and ears to see and hear from His perspective. We need to ask Him to show us His divine appointments and purposes.

Remember that God's Word is a light to let us know where we are and a lamp to show us which way to go. God's Word sheds light on our world. But God speaks most clearly when our hearts are quiet. We can't hope to hear Him if we fill every moment with busyness and noise. "In quietness and trust is your strength" (Isaiah 30:15). "Those who wait for the Lord will gain new strength; they will mount up with wings like eagles, they will run and not get tired, they will walk and not become weary" (Isaiah 40:31). "Be anxious for nothing, but in everything by prayer and supplication with thanksgiving let your requests be made known to God" (Philippians 4:6). "Trust in the Lord with all your heart and do not lean on your own understanding. In all your ways acknowledge Him, and He will make your paths straight" (Proverbs 3:5–6). Let Him show you His vision for your classroom. Fix your eyes on Jesus.

Learn as Much as You Can as Quickly as You Can

Before school begins, teachers should become familiar with their school, their community, and their students.

Become familiar with district and school rules, policies, and procedures, including any handbooks for students, teachers, and parents. Most schools have specific procedures for teachers' administrative duties, such as recording attendance, collecting fees, distributing newsletters, making referrals, requesting field trips, and reporting child abuse. You should know what these procedures are before the first day of school. You should also know school policies relating to the use of the various areas of the school and the movement of classes between them. You need to find answers to these questions: What are the school policies regarding students who forget their lunch money, miss the bus, stay for detention, participate in after-school activities, get sick, have seizures, or need medications? What are the procedures for fire drills, tornado drills, and other disaster drills? What school rules and policies will you need to present to your students? What are the procedures for obtaining classroom books and for checking them out to students? What audiovisual materials and equipment are available, and what are the procedures for obtaining them? What is the required paperwork for the first day of school?

Become familiar with the community. What resources are available in the community around the school? Where can you take your students for field studies? What people are able to come in as guest speakers? What businesses might you work closely with? What community services are available to you, your students, and their parents? In what community volunteer jobs can students participate? Begin a list of names and addresses of contact people. As you prepare overviews of your units and school year, book these people to come at the appropriate times. Most of them should be booked before the school year begins.

Become familiar with the school. You should learn the layout of the school building so you know where everything is: office, nurse's room, washrooms, art supply room, equipment room, library, bus loading area, lunchroom, book supply room, music room, and gymnasium. Where do you get the keys to your classroom and other rooms you may need to use? How can you get additional furniture for your room? Will you have a teacher's aide assigned to work in your classroom? When will your students have music, recess, physical education, lunch, computer lab, and library? It is beneficial to have this information written down and displayed in a prominent place. It is helpful to make yourself a form with the names and contact information (room numbers) of your school administrators, the teachers at each grade level, the school nurse, the counselors, the teachers of specialty areas, the librarian, the teacher's aides, and the special education teachers. Do the same for the school district—you should know the names and contact numbers of the superintendent, assistant superintendent, curriculum director, personnel director, instructional materials center, and substitute teacher (teacher-on-call) line.

Learn the roles and responsibilities of your colleagues. You should take the time to get to know the resource room teacher(s), the librarian(s), the special needs teacher(s), the counselor(s), the principal(s), the nurse(s), the custodian(s), the art teacher(s), the drama teacher(s), the music teacher(s), and the physical education teacher(s). Find out what services and resources they can offer you as a classroom teacher and how you and your class can make their job and ministry easier.

Learn about your students. How much should you know about your students before the start of school? If you know too much, there might be a tendency to be biased, or prejudiced. Do you need to know that a student was a "troublemaker" last year? Do you need to know that a student did poorly in math last year? However, there are some things you should know before the school year begins. You should know and understand the basic *general* needs and abilities of students in the age range that you will be teaching. You should also know of any diagnosed medical conditions of individual students, especially if those students need special care. You need to know who has custody of each child so that you will know to whom and with whom you can send the child home. You also might be interested in knowing your students' birthdays and recording them on a classroom calendar.

Here is some other information you may want to know about your incoming students: their names (and pictures) so that you can learn their names before the first day of class, whether they are new to the school, and anything that is positive or that will help you to motivate your students from the moment they arrive. Otherwise, you should excuse yourself from conversations when former teachers want to tell you how "bad" or "challenging" a particular student was. You should be aware that students seldom respond the same way to different teachers. I had one student who had caused her previous teacher no end of anguish, and yet I had very little trouble with her (because I happened to coach the sports teams that she wanted to be on). In fact, she probably was the most well-rounded student I've ever taught. Be careful of being influenced negatively by another teacher or even by your own experience of having taught a sibling of an incoming student. You should give each student a clean slate— even if you taught that same student last year. You should also remember that a student who struggles in one area may not be challenged in another area. Be careful not to treat your students according to their weaknesses. Remember that *one* characteristic can never define a student. Students are complex people. As teachers, we get to start each year with a clean slate. And so should our students! In fact, as much as possible, we and our students should start each *day* with a clean slate.

Plan your classroom rules and procedures. You should write down the type of behavior that you would like to see in the classroom. Will you involve your students in developing the rules? If so, you should plan what questions you need to ask to get meaningful input from your students. As teachers, we must be people of integrity, so we must not involve our students in developing rules if we are going to manipulate them into coming up with the rules we want. (This kind of planning will be discussed at length in another chapter.)

Arrange the Details

Make a checklist. The value of making a checklist of things that must be considered before the first day of teaching cannot be overestimated. It will serve you well to develop this checklist even if you are still in university or college and are reading this book before you become a teacher. An excellent resource for such a list is the work done by Leo Schell and Paul Burden (1992) called *Countdown to the First Day of School: A 60-Day Get-Ready Checklist for; Beginning Elementary Teachers, Teacher Transfers, Student Teachers, Teacher Mentors, Induction-Program Administrators, Teacher Educators.* Headings on your checklist might include (a) organization of the classroom and materials; (b) classroom supplies; (c) room arrangements; (d) routines, procedures, and discipline management; (e) problems and ethical concerns; (f) parent-teacher communication aids; (g) school information (mailing address, phone number, layout of school); (h) information on administration and colleagues; (i) important dates; (j) school policies; (k) playground duty, lunchroom duty, and other responsibilities; (l) equipment available in classrooms; (m) student files; (n) personal preparation; (o) administrative tasks; (p) curriculum materials; (q) instructional strategies; (r) evaluation policies; (s) students with special needs; (t) learning centers; (u) health and safety concerns; and (v) resource contact list.

Prepare for the unexpected. What will you do if you get unexpected students on the first day of school? Will you be making name tags for your students? If so, will you have extra ones for unexpected students? Will you be handing out textbooks? If so, will you have an extra set or two? Will you also have two or more extra desks? How does your classroom show that you are prepared for students with special needs?

Dress professionally. Look your best, but at the same time be comfortable. You will feel confident and will make a good impression on students, parents, and colleagues.

Navigate According to Your Vision

Prepare your classroom. Your classroom should be completely ready for the first day of school. Preparation includes having enough student desks of appropriate size (with at least two extras), a list of class rules posted, a place for listing daily assignments, decorative displays to catch students' interest (such as a "Welcome Back!" sign or bulletin board, or a list of student names), and a classroom calendar (Evertson, Emmer, and Worsham 2006, 5). You should have enough textbooks for all students, enough places for students to keep their personal belongings (cubbyholes, desks, or lockers), and a place for your supplies. In the primary grades, bins of teaching manipulatives (teaching tools) and other supplies should be organized and ready to use.

Communicate with your students' parents as early as possible. An initial newsletter should be available for parents to pick up at the school before the first day of school. It should explain essential information such as your vision for the school year, the supplies your students will need, your contact information, the report card days, the conference times, and possible curriculum themes for the first month of school. The newsletter must be clear, accurate, and easy to read.

Convey your priorities. Before proceeding any further, take your list of five messages you wanted to convey to your students on the first day of school (the list you made at the beginning of this chapter), and for each message identify at least three ways you will convey that message *without* speaking it. Why is this exercise an important step? Identifying ways of conveying messages to students without speaking them will encourage you to use everything at your disposal—not just words. The hallways outside your classroom, the arrangement of the desks, the bulletin boards, the ceiling, the walls, the planned activities, the spots where you tend to stand in the classroom, the student cubbyholes, and the cloakroom—all these can be used to convey messages. The list is endless. Check with other teachers to find out what messages they want to convey to their students on the first day. You may be amazed at their creativity and motivated to come up with more of your own ideas—and more of your own ways of conveying specific messages without speaking them.

The First Day (*BUILD*)

What will you do on day one? What should you be considering? Here's how I suggest you **BUILD** the first day of school: Begin to **B**uild a community. **U**se the unexpected to model peace and calm. **I**nvite students into the classroom community. **L**et students know your vision and expectations. And **D**escribe the first day.

Build a Community

Creating a community that is positive and welcoming is a key part of starting the year off well. How can you establish a positive atmosphere in the classroom? Here are some suggestions: (a) Establish rules to follow, and be consistent in enforcing them. (b) Make each student feel welcome by personally welcoming him or her to class. (c) Have a name tag for every student. (d) Decide ahead of time whether you want to prearrange seating or let students choose their own places. (What message do you want to give them through the seating arrangement?) (e) Give small expressions of appreciation that you are happy that the students are in your class.

What other things help create a positive learning environment in the classroom? What about getting in touch with parents? Again, a parent newsletter should be available before the first day of school, but it is also a good idea to connect with at least some of the parents face-to-face. Also, allow your students to interact and introduce themselves so that they feel they belong.

By now you can see the importance of the first day, the first week, and the first month of a new school year. The goals for the first day should include setting a good working environment and helping students to eagerly anticipate the coming school year. On that first day, it is helpful to focus on interesting learning activities that will build a climate for learning. If you can show students how the year will go and let them experience some exciting learning on that first day, they will come to school eager to learn on subsequent days. The first day's activities should involve the whole class rather than just individual students.

Throughout the first week and the first month of school, you should pay particular attention to students who need extra help in following class rules and procedures or who need extra help and encouragement in order to hand in quality work. Now is not the time to be lowering your standards. It is a time for making your standards clear and making sure your students meet them.

By the end of the first month of school, everything should be moving in the desired direction. Students should be busy learning and cooperating well with the teacher and with their peers. There may be one or two students who will need more time. However, the majority should be actively and responsibly involved in their own learning.

Use the Unexpected to Model Peace and Calm

Teachers must be ready for unexpected events during the first day and week of school. New and unexpected students may show up, some students may arrive an hour late, some parents may wish to speak with you (the beginning of the first day is not a good time), or the principal may call an unscheduled assembly. Something unexpected *will* happen. You can count on it. Preplanning, however, will enable you to deal with surprises.

Invite Students into the Classroom Community

One way to invite students into the classroom community is to make sure you are standing by the classroom door to welcome your students as they enter. And you should continue this practice throughout the school year—yes, even with high school students. You can find out a lot by watching them enter the classroom. Who is tired? Who is enthusiastic about being here? Who is angry? Who is hyper? This practice also gives you a brief chance to talk with individual students. Look into their eyes to get a glimpse of what is going on within them. Use their names if possible. You might make it your goal to speak personally with every student every day. You can't always speak with each one at length, but a brief question or comment, sincerely given, is important. So is listening to the responses! What a positive impact this practice makes on building community in the classroom! As teachers, we must make *all* our students feel welcome and show them that we are glad they are in our class. And we must show genuine enthusiasm about the new school year!

It is important that from the outset students learn their teachers' names, that the teachers learn the students' names, and that the students learn one another's names. Don't hide behind the excuse that you can't remember names or that you have two hundred names to learn. Learning names shows students that you care about them. Learn them as quickly as possible! It is a great compliment to students to know all their names by the end of the first day. Some teachers take pictures of their students and print them (on a computer printer) before the end of the day so that students can put their names on their pictures.

It is wise to get student information on cards, including the names and phone numbers of parents or guardians and the names and phone numbers of the persons to contact when an emergency arises and a parent or guardian cannot be reached.

You should decide ahead of time how much you will tell the students about yourself. To begin, you should put your name on the board and pronounce it for the students. How much else you say depends on your philosophy of teaching. However, it is a good idea to share at least something personal and something professional.

Get-acquainted activities. There are websites that offer great activities for the first day(s) of school. Get-acquainted activities should be designed to help students feel comfortable in the classroom. They should focus on fostering class cohesiveness. If a whole-class focus is maintained rather than a focus on individuals, students will readily become involved and will stay involved. The activities should be such that everyone gets to know everyone else's name by the end of the day. Finding out interesting things about each student is informative and fun, and is helpful in building community.

Pair interviews. Among the many available activities, a lively and helpful one is to have pairs of students interview each other. Give them a list of questions to ask. The questions should be nonthreatening, they should have a positive focus, and they should seldom be personal. For example, nonthreatening questions might ask about students' favorite colors, favorite things about school, names of pets, favorite hobbies, or clubs the students attend or hope to attend. Potentially threatening questions might ask about the names of students' parents (if the last names differ), the students' height or weight, or the names of students' best friends.

Circle name game. Print each student's name on a piece of paper, and have each student draw someone else's name. The object is for students to stand or sit next to the person whose name they drew and to form a circle. The game is not complete until everyone is correctly placed in the circle. To make it more interesting, have teams compete to see which one can arrange its circle first. The goals are to help the students learn one another's names, to teach them to work together, and to create a positive learning environment.

Poster and explanation. The poster idea is simple. Give these directions to your students: "From the magazines provided, cut out pictures that represent part of your life. (For example, if you own a dog, cut out a picture of a dog.) When you have all the pictures you want, glue them onto your poster board." Then ask students to present their posters to the rest of the class and to explain the pictures they used. Similarities among students will emerge. The objective of this activity is to create an atmosphere of understanding. It will also help to build unity in the class.

Untangle game. This simple, fun game promotes cooperation and helps students get to know one another. The game starts with all class members facing each other in a circle, their hands outstretched. Each person then connects hands with two different people until all the hands are connected and everyone is tangled up. The object of the game is to untangle the mess and form a circle without letting go of the hands. This can be done as one large group or as a competition between groups. To make it more interesting, add the requirement that nobody talks.

Welcome bags. Giving out welcome bags to the students is a creative and fun way to emphasize important classroom concepts. Items in the bag are to symbolize what you believe is important for building community in the classroom. Things to include are an eraser (it's okay to make mistakes—just learn from them), a gem (you are valuable), a heart (this classroom is a safe and caring place), a star sticker (we always shine and grow), a pack of gum (we all stick together), and some Smarties (there are many different kinds of "smart"). You can come up with even better ideas, I'm sure.

Giant puzzle. Make a giant puzzle with as many pieces as there are students in the classroom. Ask the students to creatively "draw" their names on their own pieces and to add interesting information about themselves. Then they can come together to make the puzzle and read what everyone else wrote.

Singing name game. This activity is great for the younger grades. Make up songs to familiar tunes, songs that contain the names of all the students as well as a fun characteristic of each one.

Partner assignment. You may wish to assign each student a partner so that when one partner is absent, the other can collect handouts and assignments for the absent one. This plan helps students get to know each other early in the year, and it also helps them develop responsibility and accountability.

Let Students Know Your Position and Expectations

Getting off to a good start includes explaining your teaching rules and procedures. You must make your expectations clear, presenting the rules and procedures on the first day of school. When you teach the rules and procedures, keep them simple and don't overwhelm students with a long list. Follow these four steps to teach rules and procedures: (a) describe each rule and procedure and demonstrate the required behavior; (b) give the rationale for all rules and procedures; (c) rehearse them; and (d) provide feedback on how students are doing. Carol Weinstein and Andrew Mignano Jr. (2003, 68) say that teachers should teach rules and procedures "as deliberately and thoroughly as [they] would teach academic content." They make a good point. Discussing the rules and procedures communicates a great deal about the climate and relationships desired in the classroom. Teachers must deal not only with the *disciplinary* aspect of the rules but also the *emotional* aspects (Fennimore 1995, 190).

Include school rules as well as classroom rules. Be sure to post the rules for all to see and discuss the consequences for breaking them. At this time, you might also describe the room arrangement and the function of specific places in the classroom, such as the reading corner, the learning centers, the teacher's desk area, and the art area. (See chapter 13, which deals with using rules and procedures in discipline.)

Determine the Messages You Want to Convey

The first day of school is a great opportunity for you to convey special messages to your students. What do you want students to know about you, your expectations, the classroom, and the subject(s) they will study? What messages will the following convey to your students: the seating arrangement, the classroom organization, the decor, the bulletin boards, the first-day activities, the way you are dressed, and the way you greet the students? You can use these opportunities to pass along messages to your students.

Begin the Year (*INHABIT*)

The things we do at the beginning of the year will set precedents and establish habits that will determine how the rest of the year goes. Here are some things you can do as you begin the school year: **I**nterest yourself in getting to know your students. **N**otice what works with individual students. **H**elp students learn the rules and procedures. **A**dminister everything carefully. **B**egin teaching content. **I**ntegrate your foundation, or worldview. And **T**each for growth.

Interest Yourself in Getting to Know Your Students

As early as possible, you need to get to know who your students are. What do they like? What do they struggle with? Which students are friends? Which students seem to be on the outside? A good idea is to have your students write "keys for a successful year"—a letter telling you the things they want you to know about them.

Notice What Works with Individual Students

Get to know how your students learn. Plan how you will assess your students' learning styles, and then gather the information. These assessments will guide your teaching for the rest of the year.

Help Students Learn the Rules and Procedures

Model these and stick to them. It is important to enforce them consistently from the very beginning. Practice and reinforce often.

Administer Everything Carefully

Distribute textbooks and other supplies in an organized manner. Before you distribute the textbooks, number each one. Record the number of each child's book. For example, all of Sharon's texts will be 1; all of Bill's texts will be 2. In this way, students will know at a glance whose book is whose. I've been in a classroom where even the chairs were numbered to correspond with the students sitting in them.

It is almost certain that you will be required to do some administrative paperwork in the first day and week of school. To minimize the disruption, try if possible to put off some of your paperwork until after school is dismissed.

If the paperwork requires getting information from individual students, you might want to plan some interesting activity that other students can work on at their desks while you work with individual students. This activity could be making their own name tags or desk tags, writing a story about a "rusty old key" they found, reading a book, or listing three rules they think should be used in the classroom.

For the first days of school, it is wise to plan extra activities in case students complete those you planned faster than you had anticipated and then have extra time with nothing to do. Until you know how much time your class takes to complete activities, you would be wise to have extra, meaningful learning activities on hand. It is always better to overprepare than to underprepare.

Begin Teaching Content

Present an overview of what you will teach during the year. Get students excited about what is to come. Have activities planned that spark student interest.

On the first day of school, you should begin teaching academic content. Giving students something to learn on the first day will set the stage for a year of learning. You do not need to plan a lecture, but you should create an opportunity for students to learn academic content, either in groups, at learning centers, or individually at their desks.

Integrate Your Foundation, or Worldview

You must evaluate all you do in the classroom in the light of your foundational beliefs. What do you believe about teaching and learning? How do you view your students? What is God's role in your classroom? You need to put those beliefs into practice, allowing them to guide everything you do.

Teach for Growth

You shouldn't simply fill time at the beginning of the school year. Rather, you should make sure that all your activities are worthwhile and meaningful right from the start. You should never lose sight of the goal of helping your students grow into all that God intends them to be.

Closing Thoughts on Getting Off to a Great Start

If you have done all you can to plan ahead, if you have begun to build well on the first day, and if you have used the first few days to begin to inhabit the classroom, you can be confident that you have laid the foundation for a successful school year. You have prevented many problems from occurring and have established a positive classroom climate.

QUESTIONS: GETTING OFF TO A GREAT START

1. Discuss *whether* you agree or disagree with the following statement, and *why*: "Teachers should not be seeking the submission of children; they should be constructing an environment in which appropriate structure frees children to develop competence and self-direction" (Fennimore 1995, 191).

2. How much information about individual students do you think teachers should have before the beginning of the school year? Give reasons for your answer.

3. What concerns you most about the preplanning required for the beginning of a new school year? Why? What can you do now to address these concerns?

4. How much should students be involved in developing classroom rules? Provide a rationale for your answer.

5. In what specific ways is getting off to a good start related to effective classroom management?

6. Research and develop a bank of first-day activities that will help you get to know your students and help you build community, taking into consideration the grade level you are teaching.

7. Make a beginning-of-the-year checklist of the things you want to have prepared before the first day of school. (See the "Arrange the Details" section in this chapter.)

CHAPTER NINE

ARRANGING THE CLASSROOM PURPOSEFULLY

When environmental conditions are appropriate for learning,
the likelihood of disruptive behavior is minimized.
—James Levin and James F. Nolan, *Principles of Classroom Management*

For many years, researchers have said that classroom environments can have a considerable effect on students' attitudes and conduct. According to Carol Weinstein and Andrew Mignano Jr., effective teachers are aware of the physical environment and its impact on student motivation, and they have the ability to use the environment to meet their goals. Teachers who have this environmental competence "can plan spatial arrangements that support their instructional plans. They are sensitive to the messages communicated by the physical setting. They know how to evaluate the effectiveness of a classroom environment. They are alert to instances when physical factors might be contributing to behavioral problems, and they can modify the classroom environment when the need arises" (2003, 31). Therefore, all teachers need to learn how to create a classroom environment that encourages positive attitudes and conduct. Arranging a classroom is of primary importance in developing a desirable classroom community because the physical environment is the first thing students will see at the beginning of the year. Unfortunately, it also happens to be one aspect of building community and motivating students that is often overlooked.

When considering how to design the physical classroom, consider Fred Steele's listing (1973, ix) of the six functions of caring classroom communities and their physical settings: (a) shelter and security, (b) social contact, (c) symbolic identification, (d) task instrumentality, (e) pleasure, and (f) growth. This chapter will explain these functions in depth, showing how each function has the potential to influence the motivation of the individual students and the development of a caring community of learning.

Shelter and Security

The physical arrangement of the classroom should be such that all students are sheltered from noise, bad weather, extreme heat or cold, and noxious odors (Weinstein and Mignano 2003, 32). All students should feel physically, psychologically, and spiritually safe. Classrooms should be encouraging places where children develop and grow into all that God wants them to be.

When planning the physical layout of the classroom, teachers need to make it a priority to keep high-traffic areas free of congestion (Evertson, Emmer, and Worsham 2006, 4). The first step is to identify the high-traffic areas: group work areas, pencil sharpeners, trash cans, water fountains, bookshelves, storage areas, computer stations, student desks, and teacher desk. To keep those areas free of congestion, we must make sure that they are easily accessible and that they have plenty of space around them. To make the best use of the floor space, we should arrange everything carefully: student desks, teacher desk, file cabinets, overhead projector, TV/DVD player, bookcases, work areas, work centers, pets, plants, aquariums, and other items.

For security, teachers should be able to see all their students easily at all times (Evertson, Emmer, and Worsham 2006, 4). Knowing where the students are and what they are doing is an important management task. Teachers need to pay attention to the placement of bookshelves, file cabinets, and other furniture that can block their line of vision. When students know that their teachers can see them, they are less likely to get off task and distract other students.

Also, it is important to give students a place to keep their belongings. This point is often overlooked in discussions of room arrangement, and yet, in order to build a sense of community in our classrooms, we need to ensure that students feel they belong and that they have a specific place to keep their things. Often that place is their desks. However, in classrooms where tables are used exclusively, students are usually provided with cubbyholes or lockers. Bookshelves divided and labeled with masking tape can also suffice (Epanchin, Townsend, and Stoddard 1994, 100–101). You might consider establishing some guidelines for protecting everyone's personal possessions. Can students go into your desk? Can they go into other students' desks?

Social Contact

A classroom should encourage meaningful and caring interaction among students and between teacher and students. How much interaction among students is desirable? That depends partly on the age and ability level of the students. Are times and places set aside for group work, for working in pairs, and for independent work? What level of distraction will you permit? How will you use social contacts to build a community that actively and effectively encourages acceptance of and support for others—and to build a community that encourages personal responsibility and teaches students that there are consequences for their choices?

You should take care to keep incompatible activities separated. Quiet reading corners should be separated from active group work centers. Individual workstations should be separated from areas that invite interaction. Where will you conduct whole-class instruction, and where will you have small-group discussions or activities? Having carpet on the floor may be good for reading areas but not so good for an art center where students will be painting.

What types of seating arrangements encourage interaction among students? Will you use pods or clusters, circles, and tables? What seating arrangements discourage interaction and encourage independent work? Will you have rows and desks spread out individually around the room? When the students are sitting in a circle and you want everyone to participate, not just the few talkative ones, where will you place the most talkative students? Perhaps on either side of you? Where will you place the students who seldom participate in classroom discussion? Directly opposite you so that you will have eye contact with them? How can the seating arrangement facilitate full-class discussion? Would this discussion be most productive in settings in which no one's back is turned to another student and students have eye contact with one another? Don't underestimate the strong impact of seating arrangements on the classroom culture.

Symbolic Identification

Symbolic identification is a term that "refers to the information provided by a setting about the people who spend time there. The key questions are: What does this classroom tell us about the students—their interests, activities, backgrounds, accomplishments, and preferences? And what does the classroom tell us about the teacher's goals, values, and beliefs about education?" (Weinstein and Mignano 2003, 39). How might you develop an environment in which Christ has preeminence and the Holy Spirit is free to work fully in your life and in the lives of your students? How might you change negative aspects of the layout into positive ones? How will the classroom layout reflect your biblical foundation in some meaningful way? How will it reflect your desire to mentor and disciple your students?

Symbolic identification is closely related to the general atmosphere of the classroom. You can change the classroom atmosphere by adding personal touches and art objects, and perhaps even background music during periods of relaxation and independent work. You can vary the setting with warm and cool colors; open areas and small, cozy corners; and hard and soft surfaces. Although too much variation can lead to chaos and feelings of anxiety, too little is more often the case. For example, if your classroom, like many, has no soft surfaces at all, you should consider adding some softness, such as rugs, stuffed chairs, and pillows.

Don't overlook the more mundane aspects of classroom layout either. Post class rules, daily assignments, and local newspaper articles mentioning specific students. Create decorative displays to capture students' interest. Don't spend a lot of time making displays, but rather encourage student involvement in creating them. Display student work and contributions, but don't fill every space with them. Try not to overdecorate or clutter.

Task Instrumentality

The term *task instrumentality* refers to setting up the classroom environment in such a way that you are able to carry out the tasks you need to accomplish. How will your classroom encourage the pursuit of excellence? How can you create an environment in which children work interdependently toward completing their tasks? The keys to effective room arrangement mentioned below will help you set up your classroom in such a way that learning will occur.

Len Froyen and Annette Iverson (1999, 50–52) and Carolyn Evertson, Edmund Emmer, and Murray Worsham (2006, 4) suggest keeping frequently used classroom materials and student supplies readily accessible and in good condition. Frequently used materials include textbooks, the teacher's instructional materials, the students' personal and school supplies, and in some class-rooms, the TV/DVD player and the overhead projector. Organizing shelves and storage areas so that it is clear where these materials belong minimizes the time spent in retrieving them and in cleaning up afterward, a benefit that allows students to remain attentive and engaged in learning. Organizing and storing instructional charts in the order that you will use them in also saves time. Materials that serve a special learning outcome and those that are used only for short periods of time should not occupy prime space in the classroom.

Another key is to not store anything that will go bad or attract "creatures." You should label the supplies so that they don't get mixed up. Set firm standards for the cleanup of materials, and then enforce them. Take the time to throw away supplies or pass them on to someone else if you haven't used them for over two years. Use reusable plastic containers for storing tacks, game pieces, and puzzles, and be sure to label each container.

Be certain that students can easily see the instructional area without having to move their desks or chairs or to crane their necks (Evertson, Emmer, and Worsham 2006, 4). When students can't see what is happening, they will often tune you out and may quickly become management challenges. Be especially aware of this problem when you use the chalkboard or an overhead. Make sure you are not standing in a place where you are blocking a student's view.

Be aware that there is an action zone (front and center) where most student participation occurs. You need to move around the classroom to change the location of the action zone. "You can control the patterns of student participation in your classroom simply by moving around the room occasionally as you teach" (Rinne 1997, 113).

According to James Levin and James Nolan (2004, 135), seating arrangements also should be flexible. They should allow teachers to have close proximity to all students without disturbing others, and they should enable students to see the instructional area without facing distractions such as windows and hall-ways. You should familiarize yourself with the pros and cons of various types of seating arrangements and how they are related to the purpose of instruc-tion. Should you have students sitting by themselves? How can the seating arrangement in a classroom motivate some students and distract others? How will you deal with this problem? You need to know your goals with respect to your seating arrangements and then choose the appropriate arrangement for a particular lesson.

Pleasure

Is your classroom attractive and pleasing to both teacher and students? Attractive classrooms have a positive effect, helping keep students on task, improving attendance, solidifying group cohesion, and increasing student participation. Do you use a variety of colors and textures in your classroom? Are your bulletin boards pleasing to the eyes? What about having plants and animals in the classroom? Are pleasurable activities available for students when they finish their work? Use classroom space meaningfully, but don't overdo it. You need to take a good look at your classroom and analyze it to see what appeals and what doesn't. You can learn much simply by stepping back and taking a good look. One excellent professional development activity is to visit other classrooms and schools to observe various layouts and uses of space. Taking pictures of things you like will help you as you furnish and arrange your own classroom later.

Growth

Does your classroom encourage students to grow? Are *all* students invited to explore, observe, test, discover, and get involved in their learning? You should stock your classroom with a variety of materials that encourage student learning. Garage sales provide many educational materials at almost no cost. How will you use the arrangement of your classroom to encourage and develop Christian maturity in your life and in the lives of your students? What personal goals have you set for continued growth in yourself and your students?

Closing Thoughts on Arranging the Classroom Purposefully

How you arrange your classroom speaks volumes about your philosophy of teaching and learning. How you arrange your classroom indicates what you believe about motivating students and building community.

One final caution is that you should never stick to one seating arrangement for the entire year! The seating arrangement should be adjusted to suit the particular task at hand, the age of the students, their ability to focus on a task, the social context of the particular class, the best learning methods for specific students, and the functions of the classroom. Too often teachers use seating arrangements to control their students; as noted before, our focus should not be on controlling students but on motivating them. What classroom arrangements would do more to motivate your students? Take time to think about your answer.

QUESTIONS: ARRANGING THE CLASSROOM PURPOSEFULLY

1. What does the way you arrange and decorate your classroom say about your philosophy of teaching and learning? About your view of the child? About your view of knowledge and truth? Give specific examples.

2. Will you have a student-centered, teacher-centered, Christ-centered, or other-centered classroom? How will that choice influence the way you arrange and decorate your classroom?

3. What role does the classroom environment play in student learning? How does the classroom environment influence the choices students make and their sense of having a personal responsibility to learn?

4. Consider the six functions of a classroom. What would your room look like if you took into consideration each of the six functions? Go beyond the suggestions given in this chapter. Make a classroom map, and label the areas that help fulfill each function:

• Shelter and security. Which areas offer the students physical and psychological security?

• Social contact. Which areas promote interaction among students and between teacher and students?

- Symbolic identification. Which areas reveal the interests, activities, backgrounds, accomplishments, and preferences of the students? Which areas reveal the values, goals, and educational beliefs of you, the teacher?

- Task instrumentality. Which areas are especially helpful to you and the students in carrying out the tasks you need to accomplish?

- Pleasure. Which areas of the classroom are particularly attractive and pleasing? Which are not? What needs to be changed?

- Growth. Which areas invite the students to get involved in their own learning?

5. How could you use the seating arrangement in your classroom to *control* students? How could you use the seating arrangement to *motivate* students? Give specific examples.

6. Striving to create an appropriate, effective, inspirational, and outstanding classroom community reflects the belief that people's environment influences them. Does it? How much responsibility do students have for their own learning? How much is the responsibility of the teacher? Are people simply products of their environment? Elaborate.

7. Assume that you have twenty-four students in your classroom. Use your computer to design a seating arrangement for the class that maximizes on-task behavior and minimizes disruptions. Include areas for teacher lectures, small-group discussions, whole-class discussions, and individual seatwork.

8. One class learns in a classroom where there is nothing but a chalkboard, the teacher desk, the student desks, and two bookshelves. Another class has all of these, but it also has some workstations, several colorful posters, and a downtime area where students can relax. How will learning differ in each classroom? What should be added to or removed from each classroom to bring it more into line with your philosophy of teaching and learning?

9. Visit the classroom of a teacher you respect. Observe the classroom in relation to the content of this chapter. Ask the teacher if you can take pictures of areas you want to remember. What elements of the classroom environment appear to function well? What ideas would you not use? Why? What ideas for your own classroom did your visit spark?

CHAPTER TEN

MANAGING STUDENT WORK WITH INTEGRITY

As we discuss student work procedures, it is easy to focus on the products students will create: completed assignments, test scores, and so on. After all, these are the tangible, measurable outcomes of the activities you will engage in with students each day. It is important, nevertheless, not to lose sight of your goal as a teacher: to facilitate student learning. Your system for managing student work should lead you and your students to examine their learning and the learning process in which they are engaged.

—Edmund T. Emmer, Carolyn M. Evertson, and Murray E. Worsham,
Classroom Management for Middle and High School Teachers

Why is managing student work so important? How can we manage student work in a way that motivates students and keeps potential problems from developing? Should we be more concerned about managing students' work or about managing students' behavior, attitudes, relationships, and motivations? Or might managing students' work provide the opportunity to work on all these other areas?

Managing students' work is often seen as the least desirable aspect of teaching. It is often the thing that weighs down teachers. Considering everything else we have to do, when do we have time to grade assignments? Often ungraded assignments are piling up somewhere in our classrooms, in the trunks of our cars, or in our homes! It's always on our mind that we "aren't keeping up." Although I hope that your situation is different, I've taught long enough to know that management problems are a reality in many classrooms.

Scriptural Guidance for Managing Student Work

Before we discuss the specifics of managing student work, consider six scriptural topics that should influence how we manage student work:

Accountability

First, as Christian teachers, we are accountable before God for our actions (James 3:13, 1 Corinthians 3:11–15), attitudes (Philippians 2:5–11), words (James 3:1–12), thoughts (Hebrews 4:12), and motives (Proverbs 16:2). It is interesting to note that James, the brother of Jesus, advises, "Let not many of you become teachers, my brethren, knowing that as such we will incur a stricter judgment" (James 3:1). This calling of teachers to a higher standard of accountability is said in the context of the passage on taming the tongue. How fitting! Much of what we do is related to using the tongue. The way we speak to students is important. The way we speak about how our students are doing is critical. Christ calls all Christians, and that includes Christian teachers, to a high standard of excellence: "Whatever you do, do your work heartily, as for the Lord rather than for men, knowing that from the Lord you will receive the reward of the inheritance. It is the Lord Christ whom you serve" (Colossians 3:23–24). We are to do our managing of student work for God's approval and not for people's approval. In every aspect of our teaching, God is our boss. We are accountable to Him.

Christ showed His strong love for children by warning people that "whoever causes one of these little ones who believe in Me to stumble, it would be better for him to have a heavy millstone hung around his neck, and to be drowned in the depth of the sea" (Matthew 18:6). Is there anything in our handling of student work that might cause our students to stumble or that might push them away from God?

Authority

Second, our view of authority will shape if, how, and to what degree we manage student work. If we understand the biblical teaching on authority, we cannot shirk this responsibility. Biblical authority involves both dominion and service. Understanding our God-given authority in our classrooms will enable us to say the hard things that students need to hear and do to grow into the people God has created them to be. Biblical authority challenges us to say things that for the moment may hurt a student but will eventually bring necessary change if the student learns from them. We must say these things in the right manner, in the right spirit, and for the right purpose, but we should never shrink from saying the hard things when we think it is necessary to do so.

Salt and Light

Third, Scripture calls us to be salt and light. Salt must remain salty if it is to do its work. Salt without taste is useless (Matthew 5:13). Similarly, a bright light is useless if it is covered; it must be placed on a stand where everyone can see it. Only then will it help people to see. Our light is to shine in darkness so that people will be drawn to Christ (Matthew 5:14–16). The way we manage student work will give evidence of whether our salt has lost its saltiness and whether our light is covered and ineffective. Remember that the purpose of salt and light is to enrich people's lives. Our goal is to manage students' work in a way that will enrich their lives—by speaking truth to them in love, by showing them the ways they went wrong, by affirming what they did right, and by directing them toward ways to do better.

Favoritism

Fourth, Scripture condemns favoritism (James 2:1–10). We are to be impartial with our students, and we should manage their work without favoritism. As Peter learned, God does not show partiality (Acts 10:34), and we shouldn't either. We should not honor some because they dress well or shun others because they are less "put together." Unlike God, we don't know our students' hearts, so we shouldn't judge them by their "outward appearance" (1 Samuel 16:7). This teaching is crucial because we are called to evaluate our students' work all the time. Our own prejudices should not enter into our evaluation, and our evaluation of a student's work must not be an evaluation of the person. We must help our students understand this distinction as well.

View of People

Fifth, Scripture shows people to be *sinful* (Romans 3:23, Jeremiah 17:9), *needful of structure and guidance* (Psalm 119:105, Ephesians 6:1, Proverbs 22:6), *creative and unique* (Psalm 139:1–18, 1 Corinthians 7:7, Romans 12:4–8), *accountable* (Romans 3:19, Matthew 25:1–46), *morally aware* (Jeremiah 31:31–33, Hebrews 8:10), and *bearers of the image of God* (Genesis 1:26–27). God sees us as people of inestimable worth who are not yet perfect but are in the process of being perfected. Each of these aspects has ramifications for how we manage student work in our classrooms.

God's Messengers

Last, God often uses others, including teachers, to work in a person's life. We must be ready and willing to be used by God in this way. Many times, managing student work brings opportunities to share with students openly and honestly about areas in which they need to grow.

Overarching Principles

Several overarching principles give direction, perspective, and context for managing student work:

Building Relationships

Managing student work gives us prime opportunities to build relationships with our students. Many opportunities arise for us to interact with them on a deeper and more personal level. Management involves more than just giving a grade on an assignment. Students communicate a lot to us when they hand in their work—or don't hand it in. We need to see the completed assignments of our students as their direct communication to us. In over three decades of teaching, I have come to realize that managing students' work presents the most significant opportunity to help students grow personally, academically, and even spiritually.

When managing student work, we must often face issues related to how students view themselves. The need for other people's approval consumes some students. Helping them see that they aren't defined by their grades or by other people's approval or disapproval can set them free to be the people God created them to be. Often we will also have opportunities to help students deal with past "baggage" or to let them present family concerns that affect them in the classroom. The opportunities are there, but we need to look for them so that we can interact with our students in deeply meaningful ways. Following are some specific aspects of building relationships through managing students' work:

Managing students' work shows students that we care. Years ago, when I was teaching in middle school, some former students told me that another teacher didn't like them. I asked them what they were basing their conclusion on. Their response totally surprised me. They said something to this effect: "Our teacher doesn't mark our homework. If he really cared about us, he'd go over our homework to see if we understood the material." Who would have thought that, for some students, managing their work is a tangible sign that we care about them? Until that time I hadn't connected the two.

Managing students' work can identify potentially negative attitudes and home problems. These kinds of problems are especially noticeable when students consistently fail to complete assignments, when they are habitually late in handing in assignments, or when they show a major change in the quality of work they submit. We must take the time necessary to discern the real reasons behind their negative attitudes and behaviors. As a result of doing so, we may be able to provide meaningful support, understanding, and guidance.

Managing students' work keeps students accountable. When we know at a glance whether students have handed in their assignments and how well they are doing on them, we are able to hold them accountable for their learning. We will know how to communicate with each student. Unless students know they will be held accountable for their work, they are not likely to use their class time productively, and their failure to make good use of their class time is the source of many problems in management and discipline. Our students need to know that we care about them and that we are holding them accountable for their learning, behavior, attitudes, and words. Therefore, we need to have a system in place that tells them so.

Commit to Integrity

Integrity moves us to do a thorough job according to a stated standard, in ways that treat all students with fairness. Here are some ways we can show integrity in managing student work:

We are able to show why we gave a certain grade. We should be able to explain how we arrived at the grade each student earned.

We record completion of assignments. If assignments are worth giving, they are worth the time it takes to make sure that students have done them. If students are to learn and grow, they need to be consistent and accurate in completing their assignments. However, we should make sure students know that completed assignments are only the beginning. They will also be graded on the quality of their completed work and eventually on how much they learned by doing it.

We detect students who are having difficulty. Teachers who effectively monitor student work are able to detect students who are having difficulty in organization, time management, attitude, or comprehension of the task or the material. Initially, we may be able to identify only that certain students are having some kind of problem. As we work at it, though, we will be able to identify what the problem is. When we do, we must make sure that we follow through with appropriate helps for individual students.

We give a variety of assignments in a systematic manner over a period of time. We need to spread our assignments over the term. We should not have everything due a week or two before report cards go out. Also, we need to give a variety of assignments that reflect our students' varied learning styles in order to make a valid and reliable assessment of student learning. It is helpful as well to consider choosing assignments that we will enjoy reading and grading. For example, when we want our students to do a book review, we can give them an opportunity to be creative in choosing the format.

When I was teaching future teachers, I assigned a critique of some teacher videos. I asked the students to do one as a newspaper report (developing a newsletter is a skill they'd use as future teachers) and another as a report card (making tables is also a skill that teachers use). On the days these assignments were due, I gave students the opportunity to look at what the others had done. They were encouraged by what they saw. One young woman said to me, "Now I know why you enjoy reading our assignments so much. They are so interesting. You design assignments that you will want to grade." And interestingly, two former students gave me the ideas for the newspaper reports and the report cards! (Thank you, Kaisu and Candace.)

Motivate Students

Managing student work gives us opportunities to motivate our students to grow personally, academically, and spiritually by choosing tasks that they will value and that will challenge them. Many students are not motivated by grades, but most are motivated by assignments that capture their interest. We should always look at the big picture. How can we use the management of their work to motivate students to become the people that God wants them to be?

We can provide students with meaningful feedback. The purpose of providing feedback is to give our students opportunities to grow and improve and to do so without interruption. Students should be growing continually. Research shows that feedback having a positive to negative ratio of five to one is the most effective. Overwhelming students with negative feedback will not motivate them. We must give them feedback that will build them up because it is helpful to them. Meaningful feedback shows them what they did well and what they need to work on. It gives them specific ways they can improve.

We can measure whether learning has occurred. The students' learning may be about subject matter, organization of supplies, management of time, social interactions, self-discipline, or personal responsibility for learning. We must go beyond looking only at scores and grades. Managing student work is so much bigger than just grading assignments and keeping our grade book up-to-date. We also need to use assessments to adjust and guide our instruction. We must remember to seek input from our students about how we taught. What worked for them? What didn't? We can glean some important information from actual assignments. If everyone made a mistake on a certain part of an assignment, it may be that we didn't teach it well or explain it clearly.

We can encourage students to reach their goals and to keep working. We encourage them when we take in assignments regularly and give meaningful feedback promptly.

Managing student work with integrity invites us to build relationships with our students in ways that will enhance their growth.

Advice

At the beginning of my teaching career, I don't think I realized how important managing student work was in developing an effective and inviting learning community. But fortunately, when I first began teaching, my principal gave me three pieces of advice that I never forgot and that shaped my practice throughout my teaching career. Following this advice has saved me thousands of hours of emotional upset. Here is what Kathy, my principal, told me:

The Number One Motivator Is Feedback

Feedback on student work provides one of the greatest opportunities to build meaningfully into students' lives. Therefore, we should always return assignments the next day, or the next class period. I have followed that advice in elementary school, high school, and university. It works! In my years of teaching, I have been late in returning assignments fewer than ten times, and I can tell you that each of those times I had to expend a great amount of emotional energy trying to carve out enough time to grade them. When I followed Kathy's advice, I planned ahead of time when assignments would be due and slotted in the time required to grade them immediately afterward.

I can follow this procedure because I have a no-late-assignments policy. Because all assignments are submitted on the due date, I am able to grade them before the next class. If you don't have such a policy, you may run into problems handing back some graded assignments before all the assignments have been submitted. The solution is to make sure that all papers are handed in on time so that students who have met the deadline don't get penalized by not getting their graded assignments returned by the next class period. This practice will help keep your motivated students motivated.

If You're Doing What You Should, Few Elementary Students Should Have Homework

Kathy instituted a no-homework policy in the school. "Teachers," she said, "should be able to create an environment in which all students wish to learn and are successful in learning during school hours." She believed that students have lives outside of school that shouldn't be taken from them just because a teacher fails to make them work while they're in school. Because of this policy, only rarely did any student take work home. Now I'm glad she had that policy, although I didn't totally agree with it at the time. Because of it, I had to learn how to motivate my students to work during school hours. In time, I found that I loved the challenge! I was teaching sixth-grade students at the time, but that "rule" was for all teachers of grades one through eight. (Kathy did allow us to give one major assignment that, at the sixth-grade level, could extend no longer than three weeks—and we had to have checkpoints along the way to make the project manageable for students and make it possible for teachers to monitor student progress.) Because of the no-homework policy, I learned at the outset of my teaching career to use class time effectively and to create an effective and inviting learning environment.

Two caveats: First, home reading programs may be an exception to the rule in today's society. Second, because of the nature of high school and university teaching, this no-homework policy is neither practical nor wise at those levels.

Professionals Should Always Have Reasons for What They Do

Kathy said that teachers should not be "flying by the seat of their pants" nor doing things by trial and error. This piece of advice caused me, right from the beginning of my teaching career, to use sound reasoning in planning and organizing what goes on in the classroom. This practice has proved invaluable in my teaching career.

What we believe about each of these three pieces of advice will influence how we manage our students' work.

One Concern

One concern is worth mentioning before giving specific strategies for managing student work. This concern is based on one of the key educational philosophies undergirding today's teaching practice: the assumption that students always need to "feel good about themselves and feel happy." In my view, this philosophy undermines quality teaching and goes completely against what God calls us to do. As teachers, we must address the issue. If we are always primarily concerned with making children feel good about themselves and feel happy, we will not always give them an honest appraisal of their work. Sometimes the hard things that teachers share with students, the things students don't necessarily want to hear, will not make students feel good or happy about themselves—at least not for the moment. In the long run, however, if they learn from what they hear and if they act upon it, they will benefit and grow. What we believe about students' sense of worth and pursuit of happiness will influence our management of student work.

Strategies for Managing Student Work

Communicating Your Expectations

Managing student work begins with clearly communicating our expectations to our students. Here are some specific ideas:

Instructions for assignments. We should explain all requirements and features of assignments in written form. Some teachers do this by listing assignments on the board or in a class assignment notebook. Even though we give written instructions for assignments, we should also go over them orally, providing students with some examples from previous years so that they have some framework to guide them. (However, be careful. Sometimes I wonder if seeing too many examples limits their creativity.) It is advantageous to have one or two students repeat the instructions in their own words. You may be surprised at how they will interpret your instructions. You can ask questions to make sure they understand; but don't ask questions that require just a yes or no response. It's obvious that if students don't understand what they are supposed to do, they're likely to do something else. Students who know what is expected of them are able, more often than not, to meet those expectations. They are also more likely to work productively in class and thus contribute to the classroom learning environment.

Standards for form and neatness. When I first started teaching, I was frustrated during the first two weeks of school by the lack of quality in the work students were submitting. I knew they *wanted* to show me their best work. I could already tell that they respected me. What was the problem? Hadn't I told them to hand in their "best" work? Then why did I have assignments written in three different colors of ink, on torn pages of differing sizes, with lines drawn without a ruler, and without names at the top? I talked with Kathy about it. She said that I had to be specific in what standards I wanted. It was not good enough to say, "Do your best." I needed to explain what "best" looked like. It is very important that our standards for type and quality of product are clear to students. I had to tell them that "best work" meant using a ruler to draw lines, using the same size paper for every page, and using the same color of ink throughout. (I started teaching in 1970 before personal computers became common.) It meant putting their names and other relevant information in the top right corner of the first sheet and identifying any sources they used. I learned that teachers need to develop a standard set of instructions for all written work: Are students to include headings? What and where should these headings be? Should students number the pages? Should they write or type on both sides of the paper? Should they single-space or double-space their work? Do they cross out, white out, or erase errors? Does it matter what size and color the paper is? Should the paper be lined or unlined? Do they need to use rulers to draw lines? Do they need a cover sheet? What information should they include on the cover sheet? Should they use pen or pencil, or must assignments be typed? When they use pen or pencil, should the lead and ink be a certain color? Will the finished product be put together with staples or paper clips, or will it be coil-bound? Have you shown them the correct format for a completed assignment?

I can hear some of you saying, "Give me a break! Who cares about all that? Content is what is important." From experience, I can tell you that attention to detail in the format and presentation of their work usually helps students to be more conscientious about the systematic development of the content and thus improves the overall quality of the work. However, I've also seen assignments that had incredible color and formatting—all the bells and whistles imaginable—yet the content was lacking. Those students had bought into our culture's emphasis on *form without substance*. Looking at it another way, you could reason that having specific requirements will cause the students' work to meet an acceptable minimum standard. It is more likely then that we can focus on the content of the work and not its format.

We can't accept anything less than quality work. We must make students redo their work until it meets an acceptable standard. We should make these requirements clear as early in the school year as possible. It is important that we give a small assignment that is due in the first week—the sooner, the better. If the assignment is small, having the students redo it until it meets an acceptable level of quality will not be overly burdensome for them, and they will learn that work must meet a specified standard of quality. Having an assignment due early in the school year will enable students to know where they stand in meeting our expectations and will enable them to settle more quickly into the classroom learning environment. We should make our feedback as detailed as possible. We will be doing them a favor by showing them how to be successful from that point forward. After the fact (after our students have handed in their first assignment, having done their best work, and we have graded and returned it), we may choose to discount their grade and give them a clean slate. When working with younger students, we must take into consideration their current motor skills. We need to have high standards, but we also need to help our students succeed.

Due dates. This section concerns longer assignments, mainly in the upper grades. It is wise to notify our students of due dates far enough in advance to enable them to plan their time. Many high school students today have jobs that cut into the time they have to do schoolwork outside of school hours. Others have so many extracurricular activities that their outside-of-school time is taken up as well. In most cases, major assignments and test or exam due dates should be planned before the start of the course or term. They should be included on the course syllabus that we distribute during the first class period. Elementary teachers should have these dates written in their day planners. Due dates for assignments should be set so that students have enough time to do a good job. Younger students working on a unit project should have periodic checkpoints in which they hand in small, completed portions of the project. They should be given feedback on their progress at each stage.

One important issue related to due dates is that of late assignments. We need to develop a written policy about handing assignments in late, including the consequences. This policy should be included on the course syllabi. Consistency in adhering to our policy is crucial. Extending assignment deadlines is seldom a good thing to do. One life skill that students need to have is time management. They can learn powerful, personal life lessons when we stick to our due dates and enforce consequences for handing in late assignments.

Absent students. Some teachers meet with absent students to make sure these students know what they have missed, though doing so is not always possible. Other teachers have a classroom homework notebook that absentees returning to the class can check to see what assignments they missed. In any case, we need to establish a routine for handling makeup work. It is wise to give students a deadline for making up their work based on the number of days they were absent. Students must learn that it is their responsibility to find out and complete what they missed. Classmates may be helpful in providing information about the assignments. Makeup work that needs our time and attention can be done before or after school, during recess, or over the lunch hour. Additionally, before we distribute a handout, it is best to copy the exact number we need and put the name(s) of absent students on the remaining handouts so that we can give them to these students when they return. Alternatively, we can put them into a folder from which absentee students, when they return to school, can pick up any handout that has their name on it. We can have a student who sits next to an absent student collect all the handouts, put them into the folder, and, on a form provided, record assignments that need to be completed.

Monitoring Work in Progress

The purpose in monitoring students' work in progress is that we are aware of all students, not just those who need extra help. Some students will need encouragement to begin work. Others will need help in setting goals. Still others will need extra motivation, gentle nudging, or correction of their errors. Students who are doing the work correctly can be affirmed. Those who are using their time wisely can be encouraged. Those who misunderstand a concept can be identified and helped.

Following are some suggestions to monitor student work in progress effectively. Usually, this is work that is being done during a class period.

Beginning class with a whole-class activity. Once we have given students specific directions and provided examples of appropriate responses to the assigned task, we should make sure that all students understand the directions and that they are working. Then we can circulate throughout the room, making sure we don't get overly involved with one student to the exclusion of the rest. We can use this time to periodically check notebooks or assignments by going around to students' desks. Of course, we must make sure that we give students something to do while they are waiting for us to see their work. Classrooms quickly become chaotic if students are left doing nothing while the teacher is busy checking homework.

If you have any thought about sitting at your desk, forget it! Today's teachers seldom sit at their desks—or anywhere else, for that matter. Classrooms are active places of learning. Gone are the days when teachers would sit and deal with individual students lined up beside their desks.

As you know, some students will finish assignments before others. If we are monitoring their progress, we will soon be able to estimate how long specific students take to complete the work. We may have to make a time adjustment. Eventually, we will know our class well enough to estimate how long a particular assignment will take the students to finish. Even then, though, we can allot only a certain amount of time for them to work during school hours. Remember that we as teachers are ultimately responsible for how quickly and how well students move through the material. We may have to learn more effective instructional, motivational, and disciplinary strategies to help our students pick up the pace.

We should have procedures in place for determining what students can do when they have completed their work. We need to have meaningful activities ready for students to do when their work is complete, and we must make sure that work is worth doing and relatively easy to plan, organize, and monitor. For example, reading supplementary material makes valuable use of extra time. Planning quiet learning games is another option. Also, we can set up centers (listening centers, crossword puzzles, or project work) that students can go to when they have completed their classroom work.

Dealing with small groups. We must deal with the issue of what we will do when we are working with a small group of children while others are supposed to be working independently, but they aren't. What rules and procedures will we have in place for student behavior and interaction? Can students come to the small group to ask us questions? Will there be a buddy system that allows students who are having trouble to ask questions of their buddy? One effective strategy to minimize disruption and make good use of class time is having the small group we are going to work with begin something that does not require direct supervision. Then we can get the other students working individually and circulate throughout the room briefly until we know that all the students have understood what they should do and have begun to do it. Then we can go back to work with the small group.

Handling guided reading sessions. It is very important during guided reading sessions to set up policies for emergencies. We need to teach students to differentiate between emergencies that require them to interrupt us and those problems or challenges that occur regularly and can wait until we are free.

Monitoring Completion and Handing In of Assignments

Many teachers are ill-prepared for the responsibility of monitoring the completion and handing in of assignments. Teachers must have a monitoring system in place. We should not have students put their assignments under our office door (if we are fortunate enough to have an office). It's also unwise to have students put completed work in a basket without our knowing it. The key to monitoring the completion and handing in of assignments is to know *at a glance* who has and who has not completed and handed in the work. Finding out only at the end of the day is not good enough; you can't help students who have already left for the day.

How might we record whether students have handed in their work? Here is one suggestion. I use a separate record sheet for each subject I teach. Each sheet records students' names written in a column down the left-hand side of the page. The names of the assignments are written in separate columns across the top of the page (including the number of marks or the percentage of the final grade each assignment is worth). Thus each student will have a "cell" indicating what he or she scored on each assignment. When students hand in an assignment (always at the beginning of the class period), I place a small dot in the bottom left corner of the student's cell, indicating that (a) the student has handed in that specific assignment, (b) I have seen the completed work, and (c) I am now responsible for it. My students make sure I put a dot in the relevant cell by their names because a cell without a dot means that they have not handed in the assignment. The dot doesn't take up too much space in the cell, so I can still put their grades in the box. This method also takes no more than two minutes at the beginning of the class period. If some students do not have a dot next to their names, I ask them if they are handing the assignment in later that day. In this way, I know within two minutes who has handed in the assignment, and I have heard specifically from those who have not. If possible, I try to take a few minutes within the class period to speak with those students who have not handed in their assignments. Students need to know that I have a system and to know what it is!

Teachers should *never* lose students' assignments. Students quickly lose respect for teachers who don't respect their students' work and who show it by losing assignments, returning them with coffee stains on them, or returning them with little or no comment.

The need to monitor student work touches on the area of trust in the teacher-student relationship. As discussed in a previous chapter, the teacher-student relationship is based on trust. Failure to monitor student work can break that trust. Let me give you an example. I was teaching eighth grade, and a major assignment was due. I'd already implemented the system of putting a dot in my grade book when assignments were handed in, but I'd failed to inform the students that I was doing so. One young man did not hand in an assignment, and when I asked him about it, he told me he had already handed it in. Knowing he hadn't, I called his bluff. Fortunately, he backed down and said he had lied. It occurred to me then that I never wanted to be in that situation again, nor did I wish to have any of my future students in that situation. It wasn't good for the student, nor was it good for me. Because of that incident, I made it a policy to always explain my monitoring system to my students. As teachers, we are in a no-win position when students say that they've handed in their work and we can't find it. If they are telling the truth, they are not impressed that we've lost their assignments. If they are lying (and we can't prove it), they are not impressed that we are such "easy targets." Our record keeping can help us to sustain the trust we've established in our students.

Additionally, we might consider using an *ab* for "absent" in the appropriate cell when students are absent the day a particular assignment is due. However, when I was teaching future teachers, they were responsible for getting their assignments to me the day they were due even if they weren't going to be there, since teachers have to have their lesson plans at school even if they are going to be away.

How much student work will we record? We know that we should *mark* (look at and at least give informal feedback on) all assignments—but will we record the *grade* for all assignments? What about math homework? Probably every day in class we will go over (mark) students' homework, but will we record a daily grade for each student? Or will we record just the results of quizzes, tests, and exams? Some teachers believe that some work is only for practice and a grade should not be recorded for it. They believe that assignments should be checked at random and feedback given as appropriate. Others just want to check assignments for completion. Still others say that *most* assignments should be marked but *all* should have the possibility of assessment and that students should be held accountable for them all. I stand by my belief that if every assignment I give is worth the students' time and effort to complete, then every assignment is worth my time and effort to mark—though not necessarily grade.

Managing Paperwork

There are at least two types of paperwork: administrative paperwork (such as attendance forms, lunch money forms, insurance forms, legal forms, field studies forms, and referral forms) and student work. This chapter deals with only the second type. Still, it is important that we organize and stay on top of the administrative paperwork so that we can give full attention to managing student work.

I hope you won't see grading student work as drudgery or as a necessary evil that you simply tolerate. If we care about our students, we will care about how they are doing and how we might help them to improve. This paperwork and grading of assignments is all about communication—it is an opportunity for individual students to communicate directly with us. That is why I have never had teaching assistants grade my students' assignments or tests. By doing my own grading, I learn much about my instructional effectiveness and about my students' creativity, abilities, attitudes, and achievement levels. If, at the beginning of the course or the year, we have marked on a calendar all assignment due dates and have set aside time to mark each assignment, grading student work actually has the potential of becoming quite an enjoyable teacher task!

Another way to make this type of paperwork enjoyable is not to have any assignment due on the last day of the term. We should not crowd all our assignments into the week before report cards are due; instead we should spread them out over the term. With the pressure of finishing the term, we don't need the additional work of grading student assignments. At the high school and maybe the middle school levels, it is important that students know by the last day of the course what grade they have as they go into the final exam. All assignments should be graded and handed back before then. We will have enough to do during the final few days of school without loading ourselves down with last-minute marking. The emotional turmoil we avoid is worth every bit of the effort we'll put into accomplishing this task. Additionally, at any point throughout the course or the school year, students should have tangible evidence of how well they are doing in the specific course. Student conferences, self-assessment, and work samples are all useful here. Portfolios with dated samples of work can demonstrate the students' growth.

As mentioned before, one way to manage the paperwork is to grade students' assignments and tests before the next class period—we should never give ourselves an out. This way, the students will have their assignments and tests marked before they start anything else, and they can begin to make the necessary adjustments right away. However, handing back assignments promptly will not just happen. We must carefully plan when assignments will be due. This works especially well in middle school and high school, levels at which assignments are longer. Before the year begins, it is helpful to develop a calendar based on our long-range planning. The calendar should include the dates when specific assignments are due and the specific time we have set aside for grading them.

It is also helpful to color-code our course files or binders and grading sheets. This step can save a lot of time—even though we may get mocked by our colleagues! A color-coded box for each subject or class we teach provides a place to put assignments once we have checked off that they have been handed in and until we return them to our students. Even handouts can be color-coded to a specific course. Then when you find, for example, a yellow handout on your desk, you'll know it's a math worksheet.

By now you are probably familiar with and are using computer programs to do your grade sheets. If not, my question to you is, In what other ways are you not keeping current in your teaching?

Giving Feedback to Students

"Good monitoring procedures are essential for providing quality feedback to students" (Evertson, Emmer, and Worsham 2006, 50). "Because it provides both information that can be used to improve performance and a yardstick or criterion by which progress can be measured, feedback also increases motivation" (Levin and Nolan 2004, 109–110). Feedback is sometimes best given during instruction. There are several aspects to feedback that need to be considered:

Objectivity. Students should understand that *teachers do not give grades to students.* Teachers simply record the quality of work students have submitted. One teacher I know tells his classes that students indicate the grade they have earned somewhere within the assignment. His job is to find that grade and put it on the front page of the student's paper.

Fairness and transparency. At any point throughout the year, teachers must be able to justify their grading system to the students, the parents, and the school administration. To do so, they should have in written form the criteria for marking assignments, the answer keys to exams, and the formula for determining the final grade (the weighting for each assignment).

Systematic feedback. Feedback to students should be frequent, specific, regular, prompt, forward-looking, and honest. In this way, students will know how they can improve. I mentioned before a book that said we should be talking about "feed forward" rather than feedback. Good point. Feed-forward input implies that it will help students do well on the next assignment and not just know how well they did on the last one.

Peer evaluation. An effective method of providing students with additional feedback is peer evaluation. However, we need to teach students how to evaluate their peers' work by providing examples of acceptable and unacceptable feedback. Often peers can devastate a fellow student—by what they say or how they say it. We must be able to monitor student work and eliminate any negative potential in this method. Peer evaluation is probably more effective in the upper grade levels.

Self-evaluation. Students can also gather information about their work through self-evaluation. Here the most important thing is honesty. Students need to be secure enough in who they are that they can give an honest and accurate account of their own progress. They should be given opportunities to keep a record of their own progress. Checklists can show completion of the assignments, and charts can show the quality of the work. Not all students will do "A" work on any given assignment. We must gently and graciously help our students to understand and accept that fact. Students also need to know that their worth isn't tied to the grades they earn, nor is the teacher's relationship better with the students who get the highest grades.

Group checks. We can also use group checks for work completed in learning centers. The group can check each student's work for completeness, and then students can share the best or their favorite piece of work with the teacher at a specified time during the day.

Returned assignments. It is wise to hand back graded assignments at the *end* of the class period. If we distribute them at the beginning, students will focus on their grades and not on what we intend to have them learn and do. Certain students may display attitude problems because of the grades they received. Another policy we might consider implementing is not to discuss with the students the grade they earned on an assignment on the same day we return it. Students may be too emotional, and we teachers may tend to get defensive when students are emotional. Students need to know that from the day after we return the assignment until the end of the week we are open and willing to discuss their grades. Any problems concerning a grade should be discussed and finalized within that week. When we hand back tests or exams in class, we often want to go over the answers with the class. As we do, we should indicate what the acceptable responses were for each question. Then, if students have concerns about the grading of a particular question, they should mark that question and come in the next day to discuss their concern. This policy is helpful in building and maintaining trust and respect in teacher-student relationships.

Closing Thoughts on Managing Student Work with Integrity

I hope that this chapter has motivated you to see managing student work in a positive light—as a way of building relationships with your students and motivating them to be the best that God created them to be. Managing student work is a challenge, to be sure, but if you meet the challenge, you will find that it pays great dividends.

QUESTIONS: MANAGING STUDENT WORK WITH INTEGRITY

1. In what ways should Christian teachers be called to a higher standard of accountability? Make sure you support your response.

2. How does your view of authority shape if, how, and to what degree you manage student work?

3. How does managing student work provide you with opportunities to be salt and light in your classroom? Be specific.

4. What specific steps will you take to ensure that favoritism does not happen in your classroom? Relate your answer specifically to managing student work.

5. Give specific examples of how your view of children might influence how you manage student work.

6. On the basis of your worldview, or foundational beliefs, respond briefly to the following statements:

   a. God often uses others (including teachers) to work in a person's life. Many times the responsibility of managing student work brings opportunities to share openly and honestly with students about areas in which they need to grow.

   b. We should always have reasons for what we do in our classrooms. We should not "fly by the seat of our pants," nor do things by trial and error.

7. After reading this chapter, what systems will you set in place to help you organize, manage, and stay current with student assessment and feedback? What personal standards will you set for monitoring student work?

8. What do you want to accomplish by marking and recording the areas in which students are succeeding and those in which they need help? How will you allow this information to guide your teaching and your relationship and communication with students?

9. What methods of assessment do you plan to use? What methods of assessment do you need to learn more about?

10. Interview respected teachers at the grade level(s) you teach or the level(s) you are interested in teaching, and ask them to show you how they monitor student work. Be prepared to ask them key questions. Compare their responses with information from this chapter.

CHAPTER ELEVEN

INSTRUCTING EFFECTIVELY

The single most important factor in determining the learning environment is teacher behavior. Intentionally or unintentionally, teachers' verbal and nonverbal behaviors influence student behaviors. Teachers have the professional responsibility for assuming the role of instructional leader, which involves employing techniques that maximize student on-task behavior. Teachers who have clearly developed ideas of (a) the relationship between teaching and discipline; (b) the factors motivating student behavior; (c) their own personal expectations for student behavior; and (d) a systematic plan to manage misbehavior have classrooms characterized by a high percentage of on-task student behavior.

—James Levin and James F. Nolan, *Principles of Classroom Management*

Many teachers do not understand the powerful impact that faulty and ineffective instruction has on student attitudes, behavior, discipline, community building, and motivation. They do not realize that teachers can *cause* discipline problems through flaws in their planning, organization, and delivery of instruction. Inappropriate and ineffective instruction can lead to student boredom, confusion, discouragement, lack of direction, disengagement with the material, lack of motivation, lack of attentiveness, lack of respect for the teacher and the other students, and lack of accountability for their own learning. Each of these problems can lead to major disruptions in the classroom. This fact cannot be overstated!

We can have great relationships with our students and can build a positive learning community only as we effectively plan and conduct instruction. These tasks are among the most crucial in teaching. In fact, instruction is our "reason to be." If we motivate our students in every other area but do not motivate them to learn, we have not succeeded as teachers. Classroom activity isn't just about having fun or even about building relationships. It's about learning.

How can we use our planning and instruction to motivate every student in our classroom to want to learn and do well? How can we teach in such a way as to minimize discipline problems and maximize student learning? We need to become familiar with effective strategies and use them in ways that suit our personalities and areas of giftedness as well as our students' ages, interests, abilities, and personalities.

Planning Instruction

Instructional planning is the process by which teachers select and organize a learning experience that will maximize achievement and satisfaction—for both the students and the teacher (Cruickshank, Bainer Jenkins, and Metcalf 2003, 139). The decisions we make during our planning will have a profound effect on our students' classroom attitudes and behavior and on the outcomes of the learning process (Shavelson 1987).

Types of Time

Amount of instruction time is an area that is often overlooked in instructional planning. It is amazing how much time in school is taken up with noninstructional activities. When we see just how little school time students actually spend in learning, we will try to make every minute count in our classrooms!

Let's take a closer look at how time in schools is spent. "Research on teaching has established that the key to successful classroom management (and to successful instruction as well) is the teacher's ability to maximize the time that students spend actively engaged in worthwhile academic activities (attending to lessons, working on assignments) and to minimize the time that they spend waiting for activities to get started, making transitions between activities, sitting with nothing to do, or engaging in misconduct" (Brophy 1988, 3). Research shows that "the wise use of time will maximize opportunities for learning and minimize opportunities for disruption" (Weinstein and Mignano 2003, 154) and that, generally, "time on task is consistently related to increased learning" (Cruickshank, Bainer Jenkins, and Metcalf 2003, 353).

It is important that we understand the different types of school time:

Mandated time. Mandated time is "the formal time scheduled for school or academic activities." Determined by the length of the school year, the length of the day, and the length of the class periods, it is the *maximum* time available for instructional activities (Cruickshank, Bainer Jenkins, and Metcalf 2003, 353). However, not all mandated time is used for instruction. There are recess breaks, lunch breaks, assemblies, breaks between classes, and other noninstructional activities. Thus only a portion of mandated time is actually allocated to instruction. Also, in some schools, the amount of mandated time is less than it is in others. For example, when I first started teaching in 1970, the mandated time was 200 days of six hours for a total of 1,200 hours per year. In the last place I taught, the mandated time was 190 days of five hours for a total of 950 hours per year. We must keep the amount of mandated time in mind when planning and organizing our instruction.

Allocated time. Allocated time is the amount of mandated time scheduled for academic activities (Cruickshank, Bainer Jenkins, and Metcalf 2003, 354). Rosenshine (1980) found that only about 75 percent of mandated time is allocated to academic tasks. The rest is consumed by nonacademic activities. Thus only 7.5 of every 10 teaching days are allocated for instructional activities. If our mandated time is 190 days, then our allocated time would be only 142.5 days (75 percent of 190) for scheduled academic instruction. So before we even start, we've already lost almost 50 days.

Academic instruction time. Academic instruction time is the amount of allocated time during which we are actually conducting instruction (Cruickshank, Bainer Jenkins, and Metcalf 2003, 354). Some researchers have found that less than 60 percent of allocated time in elementary schools and less than 45 percent of allocated time in high schools is actually spent in academic instruction. Unbelievable! Even though we may not be able to control the amount of mandated and allocated time, we can and should do something about our academic instruction time. Elementary teachers may allocate 50 minutes 5 days a week (250 minutes a week) to teach math to their students. However, during each class period, things other than instruction will be happening, including handing out papers, giving directions, socializing, preparing materials, or intervening in discipline problems. According to Walter Doyle (1986), only about 150 minutes of the 250 minutes will be spent in academic activities. That's appalling! Only 86 days in elementary schools and 64 days in secondary schools are spent on academic instruction time.

Academic learning time. Academic learning time is the amount of academic instruction time during which students are actively engaged in learning (Cruickshank, Bainer Jenkins, and Metcalf 2003, 354–55). During this time, students are not daydreaming, doodling, or misbehaving but are actively and successfully involving themselves in learning activities. The fact that teachers are teaching does not mean that all students are engaged in learning 100 percent of the time. Gary Borich (1992, 13) refers to this time as the engagement rate—"the percentage of time devoted to learning when the student is actually on-task, engaged with the instructional materials, and benefiting from the activities being presented." Some say that effective teachers maintain an academic learning time of about 80 to 95 percent of academic instruction time. However, others say that in most classrooms academic learning time is only about 30 percent of academic instruction time. Surely not!

Academic learning time needs to be productive time. This means that students must be doing work that is meaningful and appropriate, not just carrying out assigned tasks. For example, students shouldn't be spending 15 minutes of a 30-minute mathematics period coloring their worksheets. Such students might be on task, but they are not learning mathematics. Teachers need to define the *purpose* of the activities they plan in the classroom. Practicing things incorrectly is also wasting academic learning time. Teachers know that certain instructional activities engage students more effectively than others do. Do you see what a problem it is for those students who are motivated to learn when they see how much time is "wasted"? Do you see the challenges we face in guarding instructional teaching time so that students have genuine, uninterrupted learning time? An overhead timer can enable us to hold ourselves and our students accountable. It will help us not waste time and not allow one activity to stretch into the time allotted for the next one.

So we need to be guarding against the loss of academic learning time. But instead, we often exacerbate discipline problems by not starting classes on time and not getting students involved in meaningful, productive work. Too much time is wasted in taking attendance, collecting lunch money, handing out assignments, handing in assignments, and making announcements. We need to use the available time for instruction rather than other tasks. I am also very concerned about the amount of academic instructional time that is given to review. As a student in such classes, I would wonder why I should pay attention the first time my teacher taught something when I knew she was going to review it later. It seems to me that we ask for trouble, especially from well motivated or highly academic students, when we spend too much time on review.

Types of Plans

Long-range plans. Before the start of the school year, it is necessary and helpful for us to develop long-range plans that include a general outline of the course content and the weeks or months when we will teach each topic. Long-range plans are very general overviews of the curriculum that can be written on a single page for each subject area. This kind of planning done before the beginning of the school year enables us to make sure that we have time to cover the necessary content. Good planners will allow time to cover the curriculum adequately and will not run out of time at the end of the year. New teachers should, if possible, work with experienced teachers at the same grade level to develop their long-range plans. Teamwork is important here. Although teachers may have very different teaching styles and priorities, they can be stretched by working together, and they may find that they can incorporate useful suggestions from others into their own plans.

Unit plans and lesson plans. Before the first day of school, it is wise to prepare our unit plans for the first month of school as well as our day-to-day lesson plans for the *first full week*. Because of the large amount of administrative paperwork at the beginning of the school year, especially during the first week, we should plan ahead so that we have scheduled enough time for all the necessary paperwork. At the end of the previous year—but before June—it is a good idea to order specific resources from the district's resource center for the upcoming school year. Because there is a high demand for these resources and because we should start teaching on the first school day, we need to make sure that all necessary resources are available and in working condition. These include a TV/DVD player, a CD player, an overhead projector, a screen, several overhead pens, the necessary textbooks, and enough student supplies. Planning for instruction before school opens gives us an opportunity to make arrangements for audiovisual equipment, materials for the classroom, and field trips on the dates we want them. Placing orders before school starts will ensure that we will beat the rush of other teachers needing the same equipment, materials, and field-trip locations.

Plans for audiovisual aids. Many incredible technologies are available to aid in teaching and learning subject matter. Becoming familiar with them and then using them in our classrooms will make us more effective teachers. But doing so takes planning.

Sequencing of lesson plans. How fast will we pace our lessons? How will we motivate our students? How will we formulate clear and unambiguous questions? How will we present examples that move from the simple to the complex? How much will we review? How will we provide for individual differences? How will we formulate worthwhile assignments? How will we keep time allocations in check to maximize instruction? (For instance, we won't let a scheduled math lesson of 50 minutes cut into the next language arts lesson by

30 minutes because of a mismanagement of on-task behavior.) In planning instruction, we should closely monitor student learning so that we do not waste time on course material that students have already mastered (Zabel and Zabel 1996). As the school year progresses and we get to know our students well, our planning will more fully reflect their individual needs, ability levels, learning styles, and interests.

Activity plans. We can increase students' engagement in learning by creating and maintaining a highly interactive instructional pattern. It is wise to plan activities for students who have finished their work and to offer a variety of assignments with different levels of difficulty. Obviously we can't plan a separate activity for every student on every assignment. However, students will be more motivated if they realize that the teacher is making allowances for their unique ways of learning.

Conducting Instruction

Much conventional wisdom assumes that students must be motivated by something other than lesson *content*, and this assumption has some merit. External rewards such as grades, praise, recognition, treats, and privileges are popularly recognized as prime motivators of student learning. Don't forget, however, that students can and should be motivated by the lesson content itself.

Many teachers know the content of the subject area they teach. They know *what* they teach, but they may not have learned *how* to teach it effectively. They don't know how to motivate students and engage them in the learning process. *How* we teach is often as important as *what* we teach, so we need to know *both*!

Strategies for Conducting Instruction

Teachers can increase the quantity and quality of academic learning time by employing some practical strategies. Competent teachers can minimize the effect of distractions as well as prevent behavior problems that result from poor instruction. "Student learning and on-task behavior are maximized when teaching strategies are based on what educators know about student development, how people learn, and what constitutes effective teaching. Understanding and using the research on effective teaching enhances the teacher's instructional competence and helps to prevent classroom management problems" (Levin and Nolan 2004, 102).

Start and end each lesson on time. Have all materials, equipment, and activities planned and ready to go so that you can start at the beginning of the class period. Have a specific place to keep certain types of materials so you won't waste time looking for them.

Distribute materials ahead of time. Have them on students' desks when they come into the class. When this is not possible, use the very end of the previous learning activity to prepare for the next one.

Enforce rules and procedures. Enforce rules and procedures that help students to be on time and prepared to learn.

Have directions written out. Having directions written out allows students who are ready to start the next activity to do so. In that way, you free students from having to wait until other students are ready. Effective teachers figure out other creative ways of giving directions so that they don't have to speak to the class all at once. Pictorial presentations help younger students to understand directions. Require students to listen the first time by making it a policy not to repeat instructions that were clearly given.

Pick up momentum/pacing. Start lessons on time, keep them moving ahead, bring them to a satisfactory close, and make smooth transitions from one lesson to another. Momentum "refers to the flow of activities and to the pace of teaching and learning maintained in the classroom" (Cruickshank, Bainer Jenkins, and Metcalf 2003, 356). Jacob S. Kounin (1970, 108) found that "the dimension of movement management, including both smoothness and momentum, is a significant dimension of classroom management. Within this dimension it is more important to maintain momentum by avoiding actions that slow down forward movement than it is to maintain smoothness by avoiding sudden starts and stops." Generally, moving rapidly through material will maintain students' attention. But effective teachers don't go so fast that most of the students can't keep up. Momentum is one aspect of teaching in which some teachers could do better. There are teachers who meander around course content rather than setting a clear direction and guiding students through the material. Regardless of the instructional method effective teachers use at a particular time, they keep up the momentum. They don't underestimate the impact that momentum/pacing has on classroom management and classroom learning. They are also aware that activities must be changed more frequently in the lower grades.

Make smooth instructional transitions. Much class time is wasted through ineffective instructional transitions. "Transitions are points in instructional interactions when [the] contexts change" (Doyle 1986, 406) in some way, such as moving from one activity to another. Making such transitions is one of the most difficult areas for new teachers. Ineffective transitions provide students with an opportunity to get off task, to misbehave, and to lose momentum. Effective teachers reduce the potential for disruption by (a) preparing students for upcoming transitions; (b) establishing clear, efficient transition routines; (c) having a clear beginning and ending for each activity; and (d) monitoring transitions (Weinstein and Mignano 2003, 160).

Use questions effectively. Effective teachers involve students in answering thought-provoking questions. Many first-year teachers ask questions that can only be answered yes or no or that require only one-word responses. The inability of teachers to use effective questioning techniques often encourages students to be uninvolved in the lesson. Most students don't have to pay close attention and think deeply to answer yes or no. Effective teachers use a variety of questions that require lower- and higher-level thinking, go deep and broad, and relate to both content and process. They build upon students' responses by acknowledging each response, reinforcing the response, providing feedback or clarification, probing more deeply, redirecting the question to other students, or rephrasing the question. Good teachers use questions to help students understand and stay focused.

Make use of wait time. Wait time is the amount of time teachers wait for a student's response after asking a question. The term also refers to the pause after the student's response and before the teacher's further comment. Many teachers are not comfortable with silence, so they fill up much of the time with teacher talk. Most researchers have concluded that five to seven seconds of wait time is adequate for receiving a response. Until you are used to the silence, five to seven seconds seems like an eternity. Remember, however, that the deeper the level of thinking required to answer the question, the longer the wait time should be. Learn to be comfortable with wait time. Watch the faces of your students. Do they understand the question? Are they thinking about the answer?

Use group alerting. The term *group alerting* refers to a teacher's efforts to gain student attention and inform students of what they are supposed to do (Kounin 1970, 117). Many teachers do not know this technique. Many teachers first call on a student to answer a question and then ask the question. This practice says to the other students that they don't have to think of an answer. One way to keep students alert is by first asking the question, pausing, and then calling on a student to answer it. In this way, all the students will be thinking about how they might answer. The more your students are involved in learning, the less likely they are to cause problems in the classroom.

Use instructional clarity. "Instructional clarity refers to the teacher's ability to provide instruction that helps *students come to a clear understanding of the material*. Thus, clarity is something students achieve, not something the teacher does" (Cruickshank, Bainer Jenkins, Metcalf 2003, 365; italics in the original). Ways to improve instructional clarity include logically organizing and conducting instruction; informing students of the objectives of the lesson; emphasizing important points; summarizing the major points; using examples and nonexamples; using explanations, elaborations, and analogies; and monitoring student understanding. Effective teachers are clear in their instruction. Often when students don't understand what is being taught, it is because the material isn't being taught clearly. If students don't understand, they may give up and start to distract others. Clear teaching that engages students is at the heart of instruction.

Provide feedback. Feedback "is primarily intended to (1) inform students about the quality and accuracy of their performance and (2) help them learn how to monitor and improve their own learning" (Cruickshank, Bainer Jenkins, and Metcalf 2003, 369). Students need to know what they have done correctly and what they have done incorrectly. They need to know how they are moving toward reaching their goals and what hinders them from reaching those goals. According to Vernon and Louise Jones (2004, 217–219), feedback needs to be immediate, realistic, useful, and positive. When feedback demonstrates that students need further work in certain areas, mini-lessons, reteaching, and practice may be necessary. In such cases, teachers can group together students who are struggling with similar problems.

Be enthusiastic. As teachers, we need to be excited about the topic we are teaching, the activity we are involved in, and the students we are teaching so that we can contagiously excite and motivate our students. A teacher's enthusiasm must be genuine, and the students must perceive it as genuine. Some students sit in classes with teachers who seem uninterested in, bored by, and uninvolved in their subject matter. Such teachers open doors for students to follow their lead. After all, why learn the material if it bores the teacher? When students aren't involved in their own learning, they will often begin to distract others and hinder them from paying attention and learning. For teachers, a lack of proper preparation and a sense of being overwhelmed will often dampen their enthusiasm.

Use phases of learning in instruction. The phases of learning are (a) setting the stage, (b) disclosure, (c) reformulation, and (d) transcendence. Harro Van Brummelen (1998, 115) develops these phases in the following way. *Setting the stage* attempts to make learning personally meaningful to students. Teachers pose problems and relate material to students' lives while students explore and search for relationships. This process builds interest and invites engagement with the material. *Disclosure* builds on the students' experiential knowledge and consists of presenting, explaining, analyzing, and demonstrating material while the students collect information, integrate and conceptualize it, and draw inferences and conclusions from it. *Reformulation* requires students to apply the concepts and theories they have just learned to specific situations as they solve problems and manipulate the material in various ways. Students work on different assignments. Teachers encourage the process by questioning, providing reinforcement and practice, and monitoring student learning. *Transcendence* brings students to the place of making the material their own, of building on it by improvising and inventing, and of moving forward to the point where theoretical reflection becomes reflective action. Learning becomes integrated into students' thoughts, and then the students can act out what they've learned and use it in different settings. The phases of learning are closely tied to the students' learning styles. Recognizing the phases of learning is important, for even when teachers are using a specific textbook or curriculum, they are responsible for implementing these phases of learning. Teachers must bring the material off the page and into life.

Be redundant. Being redundant refers to reviewing general principles, concepts, and procedures. It does not mean just repeating the course content a few times. Rather, it has students "apply the same rules to different tasks, so that they generalize information or skills" (Zabel and Zabel 1996, 133). It's not just a review of the material. Sometimes redundancy is overdone, and it leads to student boredom. Although in some situations, the opposite is true. Material may be too disconnected and disjointed if it is not reviewed properly.

Remember the ripple effect. The ripple effect in this context is the phenomenon by which a teacher's words or actions directed at one student tend to spread out and affect the behavior of other students (Kounin 1970, 2, 140). Teachers in the early grades often use this concept to encourage good behavior. For example, a teacher may say, "Johnny, I like the way you have your books out and you are already working on the questions. Good for you!" Such a comment encourages other students to do what Johnny is doing. It also keeps the focus on students who are doing what the teacher asked rather than on the ones who are distracted or misbehaving. When problems occur, it is wise to nip them in the bud and not let them grow. In any circumstance, a calm, kind, Spirit-filled manner is most effective.

Be "with it." Being "with it" refers here to teachers' knowing "what is going on in all areas of the classroom at all times" (Kounin 1970, 74, 143–144). Teachers who have this trait can reduce the incidence of student misbehavior. Some teachers have a limited focus, on one student, one activity, or one corner of the room, and totally overlook whatever else may be going on. Think of all the things that students can do "when the teacher isn't looking."

When teachers overextend their lives, when they don't get proper sleep, food, and exercise, their students are often the ones who suffer. In such cases, teachers aren't as alert and able to handle the multiplicity of tasks required to teach effectively.

Become skilled at overlapping. The term *overlapping* refers in this context to a teacher's ability to attend simultaneously to two or more events in the classroom (Kounin 1970, 74, 143–144). Effective teachers are able to multitask. Training our students to follow procedures will enable us to be more successful in overlapping.

Eliminate satiation. When students get their fill of a topic, they may be experiencing satiation, which often brings on boredom, frustration, and misbehavior (Kounin 1970, 126–127). High-ability students are especially prone to satiation because they grasp concepts and information more quickly than their peers but must often listen as teachers repeat the material in different ways to help other students learn. Making different learning activities available to students who are ready to move on minimizes the chance that these students will become satiated with a topic and will therefore become uninvolved in learning or cause distractions in the classroom. A caution is in order here. Teachers shouldn't make assumptions about high-ability students. Teachers need to be careful that they don't automatically praise these students when their effort may be mediocre—even though their results are better than average. Teachers might "raise the bar" for these students and give authentic praise only when they have risen to their best effort. This caution doesn't mean that teachers should give high-ability students a score of 2 out of 4 on a criterion-referenced assignment when students meet the standard, but it does mean that they should push these students to go beyond average.

Be consistent. Consistency is one of the least talked about yet most important educational considerations. Since consistency often has a low priority, inconsistency is common among teachers. We as teachers must learn to attain and maintain consistency between our philosophy and our practice and between various educational practices such as instructional methods and discipline. There are important benefits in doing so. First, our students will find it easier to interpret our expectations. Second, when we maintain consistency, it is often because we have tried harder to clarify principles and apply them appropriately, thus improving our educational practice. Third, maintaining consistency has a positive impact on our commitment, so we create better educational programs, assure that our students are successful, and determine for ourselves what principles to apply in our teaching (Edwards 1993, 239–240).

Use intraclass grouping. Often teachers interact with one student while all the other students are waiting. James S. Cangelosi (2004, 66–67) provides an example. A physical education teacher is conducting drills on throwing the "two-hand chest pass" by having the students stand in a single line as he tosses the ball to the first student, who then returns it to the teacher. He then does the same thing with the second student. In this class, students spend more time waiting for their turn than practicing the skill. Another teacher uses a different approach to teaching the "two-hand chest pass." He divides the students into groups of two or three. As each group practices, this teacher circulates around the class to see how the students are doing, offering encouragement and pointing out mistakes in technique.

Anticipate times when students must wait. Similarly, we waste time when we conduct homework checks without giving students something to work on while we do so. Thomas L. Good and Jere E. Brophy (2003, 122) indicate four things that can happen when students must wait with nothing to do (and three of them are bad): "Students may remain interested and attentive; they may become bored or fatigued, losing the ability to concentrate; they may become distracted or start daydreaming; or they may actively misbehave." Plan ahead! What do you want other students to be doing when you are conducting homework checks or working with one student?

Be aware of distracters. Examples of distracters would be absenteeism, tardiness, daydreaming, transition times, a student lacking supplies, a student catching up after an absence, or a student being pulled out of class. Our ability to handle such events will determine the effectiveness of our instructional time, so it is wise to know how to deal with these distracters before the school year begins. How will you accommodate students' completing work at different times? What are students to do when they finish their work? It is important to find effective procedures to manage students who must leave the classroom for remedial work or special classes. Try to have input on the scheduling of students who will be out of the classroom. It is effective to make a chart showing when various students will be out and when the whole class will be together. You need to know this information in order to plan well.

Closing Thoughts on Instructing Effectively

As you become skilled in planning and conducting instruction, you will see the positive effects in your classroom and on your students. Effectiveness in planning and conducting instruction will minimize disruptive behavior and will help your students learn more effectively. Everybody wins!

QUESTIONS: INSTRUCTING EFFECTIVELY

1. Which three of the techniques discussed in this chapter do you think might be hardest for you to implement? Why? What can you do now about improving your ability to use those techniques?

2. Rank in order the five techniques that you think most affect the quality of classroom instruction. These could be techniques mentioned in this chapter, but feel free to add any techniques you think are missing.

3. What problems not mentioned in this chapter affect the quality of instruction? Name at least three.

PART THREE

DISCIPLINE AS OPPORTUNITY FOR DISCIPLESHIP

One of the most demanding aspects of the teacher's role is to discipline and disciple students. In chapter 4, we discussed the importance of the teacher's being a model, an authority figure, a servant, and a mentor. In this section, I hope you will see how these roles must come together in order for the teacher to be an effective discipler of students.

As you read this chapter, it is vitally important that you distinguish between disciplining (working to shape the actions of students) and discipling (influencing students to become disciples of Jesus Christ). Notice which word you are reading as you continue.

The principles of disciplined living, taken from Scripture, are good for all our students, whether or not they are Christians. Yet education is about educating the hearts and minds of children and young people. In this section, I want you to see the bigger picture when you think about disciplining students. The basic truth is this—any time teachers view discipline within the context of the bigger picture, they are potentially moving into the realm of discipling their students. When you see discipline in the context of discipleship, you realize that discipline is far more than putting out immediate fires or just making students behave. Discipling goes beyond behavior to involve the whole student. It goes beyond an outward conformity to rules to a change of heart. Discipling is about making disciples, influencing our students toward being changed from the inside out, motivating them to learn and grow in such a way that they become followers of Jesus Christ. This focus includes seeing our students as who they are in the light of God's truth. It includes helping *them* see who they are—people created by God, specially designed by Him with physical traits, gifts, abilities, talents, dispositions, personalities, and desires, and people placed on this earth in the time and place God ordained so that they would come to know Him (Acts 17). Remember this: Your students, whether or not they are currently Christians, were created to bring God glory by operating fully, willingly, and joyfully in their created uniqueness.

This goal, of course, can't be fully reached without a commitment to Christ and the ongoing work of the Holy Spirit. Yet there is much that Christian teachers can do to move students toward becoming disciples of Jesus Christ. We must take advantage of the many opportunities to sow seeds every day. We must work within the context of families and not just with individual students. We must let the Spirit of God clearly lead us. And we must be willing to talk to our students about having an inner change of heart.

When I was teaching in a Christian school, I was prompted to ask my grade-eight students how often they had been asked (specifically and individually) by an adult about their relationship with Jesus Christ. Most of these thirty students had been attending church and Christian schools all their lives up to that point. Only one boy indicated that he had ever been asked by an adult about his relationship with Christ—and he had been asked by a Sunday school teacher at his church. None of the other young people had ever been asked individually about their relationship with Christ. How sad! This experience reminded me that I shouldn't take for granted that children in a Christian school are being confronted about their need for the Savior. If you are in a Christian school, I hope that before this school year is over, you will take time to speak with each student individually about his or her relationship with Christ.

Further, my challenge to you as a Christian teacher is to do everything for the purpose of discipling the students handpicked by God to be in your classroom at this time. Teach math, interact with parents, decorate your room, discipline—all with the vision of discipling your students to become followers of Jesus Christ. Remember that even at a Christian school you are on a mission field. Discipling requires that we stay focused on what is eternal. To the degree that our ministry stops short of that, it is not truly discipling. As a Christian teacher, you have an incredible privilege and an awesome responsibility to disciple your students toward a saving faith in Jesus Christ and an inner and outer transformation by God's Spirit. I am more convinced than ever that the whole purpose of being a teacher is to disciple our students.

CHAPTER TWELVE

VIEWING STUDENT MISBEHAVIOR

Teaching is difficult under the best educational conditions, and this failure to take into account the needs of students or teachers makes what is already a hard job almost impossible. Any method of teaching that ignores the needs of teachers or students is bound to fail.
—William Glasser, *The Quality School*

Why do students misbehave? Who or what is to blame for students' misbehavior? How we answer these questions depends on our worldview.

Understanding Who Children Are

Many people believe that children are born good but get messed up by their environment. These people would suggest that children misbehave because there is something in their environment (or something lacking in their environment) that causes them to misbehave. According to James Levin and James Nolan (2004), societal changes exert much influence on student behavior. One can certainly argue that what is going on in society influences our students.

Others believe that children are born neutral—neither good nor bad. Still others believe that children are born with a sinful nature and misbehave because it is in their nature to do so. Scripture supports the latter view. The impact of sin is universal (Romans 3:9–12, 23; Ephesians 2:1–5), and the human heart is desperately wicked (Genesis 6:5, Romans 7:18). Scripture indicates that we cannot change our inherited sin nature by ourselves (Jeremiah 13:23, John 8:34, Romans 7:18–25).

What do you believe? Are children born good, or are they born with a sinful nature? Do students misbehave because they are products of their environments? Are students responsible for their misbehavior? Can they be held responsible if there is something outside themselves, in their environment, that influences them to misbehave? What if they have come from a dysfunctional or even abusive home? What if their parents are currently going through a divorce? What if a parent or close loved one is dying? Do people's environments excuse their misbehavior? What allowances, if any, should teachers make for students? What if children haven't been taught what appropriate behavior is— are they still responsible for their behavior? What is the most you as a teacher can do? manage? discipline? mentor? disciple?

The way we answer these questions will determine the direction we take in dealing with our students' misbehavior. If we believe children are born good but are corrupted by their environment, we will focus on creating a learning environment that will bring out good behavior. If we believe children are born good and that left to themselves they will do what is right, we will have a fairly nonstructured classroom and children will be directing their own learning while we facilitate them. If, on the other hand, we believe that children are born with a sinful nature and that left to themselves they will not always be good or do what is right, we will have a fairly structured classroom in which we will take on a more active leadership role in students' learning and discipleship. Among other things, we will be involved in teaching children the difference between right and wrong.

The beliefs that children are born good and that they are born sinful are polar opposites, so the two cannot be held simultaneously. We need to make sure that we are not deceiving ourselves by holding a biblical worldview yet taking worldly approaches in our practice. It is obvious that holding to the biblical view—that children are created by God as His image bearers, are born with a sinful nature because of the fall, and yet are able to become new persons in Christ (see chapter 3)—is not the politically correct thing to do. And yet the biblical view is the truth. On the other hand, just taking *one* part of this view—for instance, that the child is born with a sinful nature—is at best incomplete and in fact wrong. Understanding the whole of who children are is essential to knowing how to discipline and disciple them properly.

Challenging Students

What challenges do students present to us? As mentioned before, if the present trends continue, we are likely to have more than one student in our classroom who is disruptive, unmotivated, angry, hostile, working below grade level, violent, or coming from a dysfunctional family. We may also have students who are discouraged about their opportunities, their abilities, and their present level of skill attainment. We may be dealing with large class sizes, students who are experiencing emotional stress, students who have a wide range of ability levels, and students who have special needs. We may have students who are affected by poverty, crime, abuse, or addiction. More students than ever before are coming to school unprepared to follow rules or to respect adult authority. They lack necessary life skills. And our school may be lacking the resources to help us deal with these problems. What can we do?

We can refuse to be discouraged. God has not called us to disciple perfect children. Perfect children don't need discipling. Instead, God invites us to be patient with the students He's handpicked for our classrooms—all of them. And He reminds us that He isn't finished with them yet. And He isn't finished with us either. He invites us to join Him in what He wants to do in the lives of our students—and in us. We need to work in full submission to Christ and to allow Him to work in us and in our students (Philippians 4:6, Psalm 46:10).

What Causes Misbehavior?

There are at least two theories to explain what causes unproductive student behavior. The first theory is that students misbehave because their *basic needs are not being met* within the environment in which the behavior takes place. This theory would imply that, in order to disciple our students, we need to meet their basic needs. The second theory is that students misbehave because they *lack specific skills* in communicating effectively, resolving conflict, solving problems, and organizing work. If we hold to this theory, then with respect to discipleship, we should teach specific content to help our students develop effective skills in living and working with others.

So do these theories help us deal with student misbehavior? Perhaps if we familiarized ourselves with students' basic needs and sought to create an environment in which those needs were met, our students would be less likely to misbehave. Perhaps if we provided opportunities for students to develop specific skills in problem solving, conflict resolution, interpersonal communication, and study habits, there would be fewer behavior problems in our classrooms. Both are true, but our focus can't be on just stopping misbehavior. This is too limiting a goal. We must want to *disciple* our students—to help them move from where they *are* to where they *could be*.

But what if we already believe that children are created by God as His image bearers, that they are born with a sinful nature, and that they will do what is wrong if left to themselves, but that they are capable of becoming new persons in Christ? Is it still important that we know what students' basic needs are and what skills they may be lacking? Yes, it is.

In this chapter, we will identify some unmet needs that may be causing, or at least influencing, our students' misbehavior. We will also look at this topic through the eyes of Scripture.

What Are Students' Needs?

What are some of the needs that students have? Fourth-year education students at Trinity Western University answered this question in the following way. Students need to (a) know that they are special; (b) know that they are not the center of the universe; (c) know where they fit in the broad scheme of things; (d) have food, shelter, clothing, safety, and support; (e) have goals and direction; (f) have structure; (g) have high, realistic expectations set for them; (h) be touched; (i) be listened to; (j) be free from fear; (k) have role models to emulate; (l) have friends; and (m) have meaning in life.

Josh McDowell (2000), in his video series *The Disconnected Generation: Saving Our Youth from Self-Destruction*, identifies six needs of today's youth. His understanding is supported by other education researchers. His suggestions provide guidelines for meeting students' needs within the context of discipleship. McDowell says that children and young people today need the following:

A sense of authenticity. We must be real with our students. It is unwise to try to be people we are not. Students need to be in authentic relationships and environments that allow them to grow. McDowell suggests that we need to *affirm* our students, because when students don't feel that we identify with them, they are less likely to stay connected to us emotionally, and they are less likely to grow. David Elkind (1981) also found that children need relationships that permit change and growth. Too often we keep thinking of students as they were at the beginning of the year or as they were last year or as if they were at the level of a sibling we formerly taught—and we treat them in accordance with our flawed thinking. When we treat them in that way, we are not allowing them to change. We are holding them to their past.

A sense of security. Students need to interact with their teachers in ways that are safe and socially meaningful. McDowell suggests that we need to *accept* our students. If we want to strengthen our loving bond with our young people, we must accept them for who they are even while we gently invite them to grow. There needs to be physical and emotional security for every student in our classroom. Anger and a lack of self-control on the part of teachers can diminish this sense of security. We must be Spirit-filled in working with our students.

A sense of significance. Stanley Coopersmith (1967, 38) identifies a sense of significance as "the acceptance, attention, and affection of others." Our students need to know that they matter to other people. He also found that they need a sense of their own competence. Students need to do something well to develop their own sense of competence in a socially valuable task. McDowell suggests that we need to *appreciate* our students. The more we encourage our students for who they are and what they do right, the less we will have to rebuke or discipline them for doing something wrong.

A sense of lovability. William Glasser (1986) and Rudolf Dreikurs and Pearl Cassel (1972) identify the related needs to belong, to be socially accepted, and to be valued by others. When these needs are not being met, students will misbehave to gain attention, power, or revenge. If even misbehavior doesn't work, students may just give up, feeling that they'll never be able to "fit in." McDowell says we need to show *affection* to our students. Affection communicates care and helps them feel close and connected to us. A failure to sense any affection from others often shows up later in immoral relationships in which our students are "looking for love in all the wrong places." God-given love enables us to love our students.

A sense of importance. Erik Erikson (1963) identifies the need for children to develop a sense of who they are, which relates to their need to feel important. McDowell says that we need to be *available* to our students. If we want them to feel more important and connected to us, we must give them more of our time. Time spent on preparation outside the classroom will free us to be available to our students during school hours.

A sense of responsibility. Glasser (1986) talks about giving students a sense of power when they know and clearly understand the rules, the procedures, and the material that must be learned, as well as why these things are important to them. What *we* value, our students will value—if we enthusiastically emphasize it. Students need to take responsibility for their learning in order to function productively in the classroom. McDowell says that we need to hold students *accountable.* We need a system of discipline that gives young people every opportunity to learn and to mature.

Is Maslow Right?

One of the key people to advance a theory about children's needs is Abraham Maslow, whose concept of "basic human needs" incorporates many of the needs outlined above. He suggests that there is a hierarchy of basic human needs and that lower-level needs generally take precedence over higher-order needs. According to Maslow, the highest level of need is *self-actualization* (the need of individuals to reach their full potential and to express themselves completely and creatively), followed by *self-respect* (the need to have a positive view of oneself), *belongingness and affection* (the need for acceptance by peers and respect from adults), *safety and security* (physical, psychological, and emotional), and finally the *physiological needs* (food, shelter, clothes, sleep, sound, light, temperature, design, time, intake, mobility, touch, pacing). Levin and Nolan (2004, 40) indicate that having these basic human needs met is a prerequisite "for appropriate classroom behavior." And these needs cannot be met without assistance from other people.

Abraham Maslow is a widely recognized authority on the subject of people's needs. In fact, the field of psychology builds much of its theory and practice on his work. But how does Maslow's hierarchy compare with Scripture? Take some time to stop and think about this question before you read further. What deficiencies, errors, or problems do you see in Maslow's theory? In what ways does Scripture support or refute it? Jay Adams refers to this well-known theory when he writes, "In Maslow's construct of the human being, unless [a person's] needs are met at lower levels, higher-level activity cannot be expected from him" (Adams 1986, 42). This theory means, among other things, that people cannot be held responsible for obedience to the biblical commands to love God and their neighbor if they have been deprived of lower-level satisfactions.

Nowhere does Scripture suggest any such idea. Nowhere does the Bible even hint that Christians must have other people meet their basic needs before they are supposed to obey God's commandments.

Another concern about Maslow's hierarchy is that "Under the guise of meeting needs, sin is excused" (Adams 1986, 57). Maslow's focus is on having others meet one's basic needs. Where does personal responsibility for behavior enter in?

Additionally, today's society has minimized any distinction between "desire" and "need." The Bible delineates our needs at the barest minimum—food and covering (1 Timothy 6:8). Jesus says, "Only one thing is necessary" (Luke 10:42)—and that is to hear Jesus and believe His Word. Matthew 6:33 turns Maslow's hierarchy completely upside down: "Seek first His Kingdom and His righteousness, and all these things will be added to you."

This may be somewhat confusing, so let me try to make it clear. There are two sides to this issue. On the one hand, God calls us to reach out to our students and meet their needs when it is appropriate and in our power to do so. But on the other hand, we must also convey to our students that they are still responsible and accountable to obey the biblical commands to love God and their neighbor even if they have unmet needs. Therefore, there is never an acceptable reason to disobey God's standards.

Who Is Responsible?

So who is responsible for our students' behavior? Are students, teachers, or parents responsible? Or, are all of them responsible?

Students

Students definitely should be held responsible for their own behavior. This truth needs to be strongly conveyed to them. Society makes excuses for just about everything, and now society has made it socially acceptable to cast the blame on someone or something else for less than adequate behavior—for lying, child abuse, poverty, violence, adultery, stealing, deception, fraud, and many other sins. We must convey to our students (and ourselves if we haven't yet believed Scripture) that no matter what we have been through, no matter what type of family we come from, no matter how much we think has been stacked against us, "[God's] divine power has given us everything we need for life and godliness through our knowledge of him who called us by his own glory and goodness. Through these he has given us his very great and precious promises, so that through them you may participate in the divine nature and escape the corruption in the world caused by evil desires" (2 Peter 1:3–4, NIV). We do not have to be products of our environment. We do not need to live with a victim mentality. God has given us all we need to live a godly life! We can move forward and leave the past behind. We can use what someone meant for evil as something that becomes a beauty mark in our lives for God's glory. God is in the business of giving beauty for ashes.

We need to help our students break free from thinking that they can't be held responsible for their behavior because so much has come against them. Instead, we can and should speak life and hope into their lives. They can rise above their circumstances. They can make right choices in the midst of whatever is going on in their lives. We need to speak this truth with compassion and not judgment, with gentleness and understanding. Some of our students are going through some very difficult and hurtful times. We may be going through difficult times too. Yet we need to declare to our students and to ourselves that, even in our darkest situation, God is there, extending to us all that we need to come through this darkness victoriously. We have hope.

Teachers

Teachers also must take responsibility for student behavior. We need to hold before our students the ideal in Christian behavior as illuminated in Scripture. Sadly, many young people today do not have a grasp of Scripture and would not know where to find what Scripture says about Christian behavior. The good behavior prescribed in Scripture is the result of a transformed mind and a changed heart.

Students need to understand that Christian behavior involves two things: putting something off and then putting something on. We need to do both. If we just take something bad off and do not replace it by putting something good on, we will be vulnerable to the attacks of Satan. If we put something good on without taking something bad off, there will be an inner decaying of the bad and an eventual collapse of everything in our lives. Scripture tells us that we need to "put off" our old self, "which is being corrupted by its deceitful desires" (Ephesians 4:22, NIV). This old self is evidenced by sexual immorality, impurity, lust, evil desires, greed, anger, rage, malice, slander, filthy language, lies, idolatry, witchcraft, hatred, discord, jealousy, selfish ambition, dissensions, factions, envy, drunkenness, orgies, bitterness, and brawling (Colossians 3:5–9, Galatians 5:19–21, Ephesians 4:31). But that is not enough. We must also "put on the new self, created to be like God in true righteousness and holiness" (Ephesians 4:24, NIV), "which is being renewed in knowledge in the image of its Creator" (Colossians 3:10, NIV). We are to "put on" or "clothe ourselves with" Jesus Christ (Romans 13:14), with compassion, kindness, humility, gentleness, patience, forgiveness, love, peace, diligence, joy, goodness, faithfulness, self-control, and tenderness (Colossians 3:12–17, Galatians 5:22–23, Ephesians 4:32). We must convey to our students that Christian behavior is not a series of dos and don'ts but a loving, willing, joyful, and obedient response to our heavenly Father, who loved us so much that He gave His Son for us. It is not a series of rules but a relationship. Christian behavior is not bondage. It is not restricting. It is a liberating, joy-filled expression of our love for Christ. We have the privilege of walking alongside our students and helping them see the scriptural truth that will enable them to be all that God wants them to be.

Additionally, our lives need to be examples for our students in speech, life, love, faith, and purity (1 Timothy 4:12). We need to model Christian behavior consistently, willingly, and joyfully, both in and out of school. We need to live what we preach. Our walk talks more than our talk talks! We have the awesome responsibility to model for our students a supernaturally transformed person who has a genuine, vibrant, living, and dynamic relationship with the living God. This is our challenge.

Parents

Parents have been given the responsibility of training children in the way they should go by teaching them God's Word, fearing the Lord, serving Him, and obeying Him (Deuteronomy 6:5–25). Many of our students' parents need help to become better parents. As previously mentioned, many schools are now taking on this responsibility by hosting parenting classes and providing parenting resources that may be accessed through the school resource room. As teachers, we must be open to parents, take the time to care about them, and help them become better parents. This is no more and no less than what God calls us to do. Like all Christians, we have a ministry of compassionate love— to bring reconciliation, to help the poor and broken, and to build relationships for God's glory. We are called to sow seeds that will bloom in eternity, but we do not do it all alone. We sow, another reaps, but it is God who gives the increase. Student behavior is a joint responsibility.

Closing Thoughts on Viewing Student Misbehavior

Dealing with student misbehavior is undoubtedly a challenge. We should not see it as an onerous task but as an opportunity to impact lives for eternity—a God-given opportunity to disciple our students. In this matter of behavior, our focus should not be on the particular misbehavior but on the opportunity to educate the heart.

Meeting students' needs is one part of the solution for student misbehavior. Another part is teaching students appropriate skills—such as taking personal responsibility for their own behavior and attitudes, developing and maintaining positive interpersonal relationships, understanding others, working cooperatively with others, and developing and using problem-solving skills. More detailed strategies for applying these two solutions are given throughout this book.

QUESTIONS: VIEWING STUDENT MISBEHAVIOR

1. If teachers were to know their students' basic needs and then meet these needs, do you think that most classroom misbehavior would disappear? Explain your answer. Do you think this focus on meeting students' needs is a necessary part of motivating students toward acceptable learning and behavior?

2. Briefly describe at least three ways in which you can use unmet student needs as a catalyst for discipleship in your classroom.

3. If teachers were to provide opportunities for students to develop specific skills in interpersonal communication, stress reduction, and dispute management, what effect might these efforts have on the tone of the classroom community and on the interpersonal relationships in the classroom? How might these skills affect your ability to disciple your students? Are there other skills that you think are more important or effective in setting the tone of the classroom and in developing meaningful, supportive classroom relationships? Elaborate.

4. How do student accountability and responsibility fit into this discussion?

5. Comment on the following quotations by Jay Adams in *The Biblical View of Self-Esteem, Self-Love, Self-Image*:

   a. In Maslow's construct of the human being, unless his needs are met at the lower levels, higher-level activity cannot be expected from him.... This means, among other things, that man cannot be held responsible for obedience to the biblical commands to love God and his neighbor if he has been deprived of lower-level satisfactions that are requisite for obedience (1986, 42–43). [If this idea were true, how do we explain the beautiful spirit among many of this world's poor, who are rich in faith toward God?]

   b. To love God and to love other people (the sum of the commandments and, for that matter, the entire Scriptures) is not possible for a person until all his other needs have been met. Reaching out to other persons is a self-actualization activity that depends upon the fulfillment of needs at all lower levels (32).

6. Who are the at-risk and needy students in your classroom?

7. What conclusions are you coming to regarding why students misbehave? How does your worldview/foundation provide a basis for the conclusions you are drawing?

8. What is the difference between discipleship and discipline? What does discipleship look like in your classroom?

9. Why do you think student needs have become a primary concern for educators today? Some would say that making student needs a primary concern is an attempt to explain away the problems our education system is facing. Do you agree? Why or why not?

CHAPTER THIRTEEN

USING RULES AND PROCEDURES IN DISCIPLINE

The corrections of discipline are the way to life.
—Proverbs 6:23b, NIV

In an age when we are told to "do your own thing," "be whatever you want to be," "strive to reach your full potential," and "get your own needs met," having rules and obeying them is not popular. Obedience implies that someone else is "calling the shots" for us, that someone else is in authority, that someone else is telling us what to do. Certainly, putting ourselves in the position of obeying someone else is looked down upon in society today. In fact, most of the dictionary's synonyms for the word *obedient* have negative connotations: "submissive to the restraint or command of authority; docile, tractable, amenable, biddable" (*Merriam-Webster* 2005, 342). However, God has standards, boundaries, and rules, and when God asks us to do (or be) something, He wants us to obey immediately, willingly, completely, joyfully, and wholeheartedly. God does not appear to accept any excuses for disobedience. He encourages us to live holy lives pleasing to the Lord (Colossians 1:10). And He says that He has given us everything we need to do so (2 Peter 1:3). Regardless of the home we come from, the teachers we've had, the friends we have, the situations we find ourselves in, and the weather outside, God has given us everything we need to be able to obey His commands. God's rules have been given to us because He loves us and He knows that obeying them will bring us true freedom. Hopefully, you have already begun to experience the joy that comes from willing obedience to God.

Often boundaries and rules are seen as restricting rather than freeing, and therefore students want to avoid them at all costs. Yet the opposite is the case. Years ago, some researchers studied the behavior of children on school playgrounds. What they found was interesting and informative. When playgrounds were bound by fences around their perimeter, children played on the entire field—fully spread out. They found that children appeared to feel relaxed and safe while playing. However, when playgrounds were not bound by fences, children tended to huddle together and play only in the central area of the playground. This has an interesting implication for teachers. Having boundaries (rules) frees children to operate fully anywhere within those boundaries. Not having boundaries appears to limit children.

In today's society, anything smacking of control, boundaries, and standards is angrily rejected as being detrimental to the development of a person's full potential: "No one should tell another person what to do." "Let everyone do what is right in his or her own eyes." "Who are you to tell me what to do?" "What's right for you may not be right for me." "Keep your values to yourself. I'll do what I think is right for me." This thinking is rooted in relativistic, humanistic principles that reject objective truth. Attitudes such as these make the challenges we face as teachers even more difficult. But they are challenges we can meet! Truth is true whether or not we believe it. For instance, gravity is a law, and it works regardless of what we think about it.

Rejection of rules is not new. Scripture relates countless stories of people who did not value the rules set before them, who crossed the boundaries—and suffered the consequences. Saul lost his throne by going against the instructions God had laid down. David lost more than one son because he didn't obey God's standards. Achan and his whole family were put to death because Achan disobeyed God's rules (Joshua 7). There are indeed serious consequences for going against God's laws, just as there are consequences for going against the laws of nature.

In the 1950s, parents and teachers were told never to say no to their children because to do so would seriously damage them. Today our society is even more permissive. We are told never to tell children that they are wrong because each person has the right to determine what is right and wrong for himself or herself. Proponents of such a view say that there are no absolute boundaries that everyone must adhere to. What deadly consequences result from such philosophies in our classrooms!

Does this kind of thinking surprise you? One of the main goals of teachers in many schools today is to develop their students into autonomous and independent people. But autonomous and independent people are their own bosses. They set their own agendas. They don't need anyone else. This approach to living is certainly not based in Scripture. God has created us to be interdependent people rather than autonomous and independent people. What does that interdependency (or autonomy and independency) look like in our classrooms?

To get the most from this chapter, you will have to come to grips with the following issues: the concepts of authority and classroom leadership, the desirability of structure within the classroom, the work of God in a person's life, the fact that there are consequences for every action, the reality of objective truth, the human tendency to hide behind excuses, the reality of God's absolute standards for behavior, and your view of the child. Wow! Are you ready?

The first part of this chapter will focus on rules. The latter part will focus on procedures.

Rules

"Rules focus on appropriate general behavior in order to avoid discipline problems…. Rules provide the guidelines for those behaviors that are required if teaching and learning are to take place" (Levin and Nolan 1996, 130). Rules, or management decisions, "should be driven primarily by concerns about continuity and quality of instruction rather than by concerns about exerting control over students for its own sake" (Brophy 1988, 2).

Again, many people in today's society have trouble with rules. Some say that rules communicate negative expectations. Others hate the idea of rules because rules mean that someone else is in control. These people suggest that we should take a more positive approach, focus on building a sense of shared community, do away with "rules," and instead establish "behavioral standards." Call them "behavioral standards" or call them "norms," but they are still rules and they are necessary for living in community.

The field of psychology has influenced what goes on in classrooms today. Much has been written on having students develop the rules so that they will "own" them. Proponents of this view believe that if students *own* the rules, they will be more likely to *obey* them. This isn't how life works. God never invited us to create the rules for our lives. He lovingly laid them down for us even before we were born. He never asked for our input. The police never asked my opinion on what speed limits should govern our roadways. When I played basketball (many decades ago), nobody asked me to help set the rules for the game. They were already there, and I had to play the game by the existing rules or I would be disqualified (fouled out!).

Seldom are we able to set the rules and boundaries that guide so much of our lives. This is okay. We must help our students understand *that they are always responsible for their own behavior, whether or not they helped set the rules.* If they get stopped for speeding, even though they didn't set the speed limit, they are still held responsible for disobeying the law. This truth doesn't mean that we have to be heavy-handed and come down hard on students with respect to rules. Doing so would undermine the benefit and purpose of having rules. As we communicate the rules that we have prayerfully developed for our classrooms (within the context of the bigger picture of discipleship), we may often find that students are more than willing to obey them.

When talking about rules, we must talk about the consequences that result when the rules are broken. Should we give students the opportunity to pick their own consequences—giving them a choice between two or three? Where else does that happen in life? Are lawbreakers given the opportunity to choose their consequences? When we speed and get caught, do we get to choose our consequence? It is true that God let David choose which consequence he wanted for disobeying God (2 Samuel 24), but this is definitely not the normal pattern in Scripture. Normally the consequences of lawbreaking are already laid out in the law. It is a very important and fundamental principle of life and we must help our students understand the reality of it—that *when we break a rule, we have automatically given someone else the power to choose the consequence.* This principle doesn't have to be stated harshly. We can speak the truth in love. But we must make it clear that we are giving students an important life truth. If our students embrace this truth, it can set them free to become all that God intends them to be.

Rules are so much more than a poster on our classroom wall containing five or six statements of desired behaviors and attitudes. Rules provide an incredibly rich starting point for discussion of real-life issues. We shouldn't miss this opportunity even with the youngest students. We can talk to them about life, about rules in life, and about boundaries that are there for their good. We have the privilege and responsibility to help them see how positive rules can be.

Principles for Using Rules in the Classroom

Help students learn to view rules as the starting point for being successful.
Motivate your students to focus *beyond* the rules. Rules just define the playing
field. In order to win in sports, in music competitions, or in public speaking
contests, people must participate according to the rules. Give your students
examples such as this: To win the 100-meter sprint, an athlete must cross the
finish line first, run within his or her lane, be free of drugs, and not have a false
start. Knowing these rules, the athlete can then focus on conditioning, practice, speed, and improvement. Students need to be taught to obey the rules
but then to move past the rules and focus on what they can accomplish on the
playing field. Rules provide boundaries, but within those boundaries students
need to be challenged to become all that God intends them to become. Remember the school fence? Students don't keep looking at or checking out the
fence. They know it's there, but they play within the fence's boundaries without giving much thought to the fence itself. That's as it should be with rules.
Students need to know where the fence is, and then they need to live within it
to the best of their ability.

Students need to be shown the value of rules in their personal lives. We as
teachers need to show our students that the rules are meant for their good.
If possible, give examples from your own life that show the benefit of having
rules. I hope you have some examples!

Remind students that every choice they make has a consequence. The biblical laws of the harvest state that (a) you will reap *what you sow* (if you sow
corn, you reap corn), (b) you will reap *more* than you sow (you sow a seed and
reap a crop), and (c) you will reap in a *different season* than you sow (there is
springtime and harvest). Another biblical truth is that sin *takes you farther*
than you ever intended to go; it *keeps you longer* than you ever intended stay;
and it *costs you more* than you ever wanted to pay. Fully comprehend and incorporate these truths in your own life, and then share them with your students.
These truths help to put "rules" into the context of discipleship.

**Communicate the rules clearly to your students, providing a meaningful
rationale for each one.** Put yourself in their shoes. How can you state rules so
that students will want to obey them? Your rationale can be put in the context

of building community, developing motivation, or encouraging discipleship. Providing this context for your rules will give your students the big picture and help them see how the rules are for their good.

Always model your respect for the rules by following them. Your students should never see you breaking rules. Yes, that means they should never see you speeding—not because they didn't catch you, but because you don't speed! Your attitude about the rules in your life will definitely influence how you deal with the rules in your classroom. I pray that you have already genuinely come to the place where you value rules, or boundaries, in your own life and see them as beneficial, not meant to restrict you but to set you free to be all God wants you to be.

Teach students that rules provide guidelines or benchmarks that can help them examine their own behavior. Children sometimes see rules as a teacher's trick to catch them misbehaving so that they can be punished. Instead, students should be taught to see rules as friends that warn them of what not to do so that they won't misbehave and deserve punishment (Jones and Jones 2004, 257).

Rules must be formulated with understanding of the social and cultural context. In our multicultural society, we must be aware that "differences in values, norms, and expectations resulting from cultural differences do have several implications for teachers. First, teachers must understand that schools are culturally situated institutions.... Therefore, school and classroom rules and guidelines must be seen as culturally derived. Second, teachers should strive to learn more about the cultural backgrounds of the students they teach.... Third, teachers should acknowledge and intentionally incorporate students' cultural backgrounds and expectations into their classrooms.... Finally, when students behave inappropriately, teachers should step back and examine the behavior in terms of the student's cultural background" (Levin and Nolan 1996, 144–145). This approach makes some sense, but our biblical foundation must determine how far we go with this kind of thinking. There is an agenda within multicultural education that seems respectful of various cultures and religious beliefs, but in some places it appears that everything except Christianity has come to be viewed as acceptable.

Guidelines for Developing Classroom Rules

Jones and Jones (2004), Levin and Nolan (1996), and Weinstein and Mignano (2003) provide several guidelines regarding rules. Effective classroom rules are (a) reasonable and necessary; (b) meaningful and understandable; (c) supportive of teaching and learning; (d) consistent with school rules; (e) clear enough that students understand what is required of them; (f) brief and simple (as few as possible, five to eight should be enough); (g) written with a positive focus rather than a negative one, and (h) developed in conjunction with teaching strategies that help students meet their personal and academic needs.

Rules are not a one-way street. If students are expected to obey the rules, then the learning environment should respond sensitively to their needs and interests. If students are expected to support rules and procedures that enhance learning, then the learning process should show respect for students and their needs.

When students understand the purpose of rules, they will be more likely to view them as reasonable and fair, thus increasing the likelihood that they will actually obey them. Therefore, it is highly desirable that students be given an opportunity to express their understanding of the rules and their commitment to abide by them. Written contracts signed by students and their parents can be very useful. You might include rules for the classroom in the package of information sent home at the beginning of the school year, along with a request that they be read and signed. Students will be more likely to behave in accordance with rules if they know that the rules are accepted by significant others, such as their parents and peers.

Classroom rules should address general conduct, interpersonal behavior, and treatment of property.

Procedures

"Procedures are routines for behaviors that occur at specified times or during particular activities. They are directed at accomplishing something rather than primarily aimed at managing disruptive behavior.... Procedures are clear-cut systematic steps or directions that reflect behaviors necessary for the smooth operation of the classroom" (Levin and Nolan 1996, 128).

We shouldn't underestimate the value of having effective procedures in place. Having clearly defined procedures will lead to a more orderly learning environment. They will save much time and eliminate many potential problems. Procedures are not posted, but rather they are taught, practiced, and used as needed. Here are some places and situations for which we need to develop procedures (Jones and Jones 2004; Weinstein and Mignano 2003; Evertson, Emmer, and Worsham 2006):

Room Use

Consider desks, tables, storage areas, learning centers, stations, shared materials, teacher desk, sink, pencil sharpener, student desks, other student storage areas, and equipment areas.

School Areas

Consider washrooms, drinking fountains, main office, other offices, library, hallways, playground, sick room, telephones, and lunchroom.

Whole-Class Activities and Seatwork

Consider student participation, signals for getting students' attention, interaction among students, makeup work, out-of-seat policies, and activities after work is finished, as well as marking assignments, distributing books and supplies, turning in work, handing back assignments, and obtaining help.

Small-Group Activities

Consider student movement into and out of groups, expected behavior of students in groups, and expected behavior of students out of groups, as well as how to bring materials to these groups.

Miscellaneous

Consider beginning and end of the school day, student conduct during delays and interruptions, fire drills, housekeeping and student helpers, collection of money, attendance, headings for papers, movement about the room, places to sit, entrance to and exit from the classroom, and line up procedures.

Student Accountability

Consider work requirements, communication about assignments, monitoring of student work, checking of assignments in class, grading procedures, and academic feedback.

Teaching Rules and Procedures

It is wise to take time at the beginning of the year to explain the rules and procedures to be followed in the classroom. During this time, you can discuss with the students the value of the rules and procedures and can give specific examples of each rule. You can also teach procedures through the use of examples and demonstrations. Because students seldom learn all the rules and procedures the first time, be sure to provide practice and feedback. Time spent in this way at the beginning of the year is time well invested. Additionally, throughout the year, you will need to monitor, review, and enforce classroom rules and procedures.

Be creative in how you teach rules and procedures. For example, you could use posters, game shows, puppets, and other activities to help students learn them. Then have your students practice, practice, practice!

Movement within the classroom, especially for younger children, requires specific procedures. For instance, you could have students line up according to which students are ready to go first. You should also praise the group that is ready to line up first. Rhymes, songs, and poems that clearly express expectations help young children to remember specific procedures.

Consequences for Not Obeying Rules and Following Procedures

The general rule of thumb is that it is not the *severity* of the consequences that motivates students to want to obey, but the *certainty* of them. Three types of consequences are described below (Levin and Nolan 1996):

Natural Consequences

Natural consequences are outcomes of behavior that occur without teacher intervention. For example, a teacher is unable to record a student's grade if an assignment is handed in without a name; a student gets a low grade on a test because of failure to study; a student gets the wrong results because of incorrect laboratory procedures. Natural consequences are directly related to student behavior. They remove teachers from negative involvement with students and clearly communicate a cause-and-effect relationship between behavior and consequence.

To the degree that natural consequences are safe and conducive to students' learning, use them. However, you should realize that many times natural consequences are unsafe or they inhibit student learning. Using natural consequences must be somewhat limited in the classroom because of the inherent ethical, moral, and legal restraints that prohibit teachers from allowing certain outcomes to happen. For example, one of the natural consequences of students' disobeying rules in the gymnasium or the science laboratory is that the students can be physically hurt. Teachers have to intervene to keep them safe. Similarly, the natural consequence of students' not bringing work to school or not completing assignments is that the students quite likely will not learn. In these cases, teachers are wiser to use logical consequences.

Logical Consequences

Logical consequences are related specifically to behavior, but they require the intervention of teachers. For example, students have to pay for the damage they have caused to their textbooks, or students have less time for recess because they did not line up correctly. Logical consequences are used more often than natural consequences. Because these consequences are directly and rationally related to student behavior, they are powerful influencers of future behavior. Students are more likely to respond favorably to logical consequences because they understand that they flow logically out of their behavior. This type of consequence puts the responsibility for appropriate behavior on the students. Often teachers give them a choice: for example, to stop the disruptive behavior or to suffer the logical consequence. Not much negative press has been given to the use of logical consequences in classrooms.

Contrived Consequences

Contrived consequences are "more commonly known as punishment. The strict definition of punishment is any adverse consequence of a targeted behavior that suppresses the behavior.... punishment takes on two forms, removal of privileges and painful experiences, both of which may or may not suppress misbehavior" (Levin and Nolan 1996, 133). (It should be noted that removal of privileges may be a logical consequence as well as a contrived consequence.) Contrived consequences receive almost nothing but negative press because many see punishment as having a negative effect on students. Although this type of consequence can be distressing to both the teacher and the student, it can begin a meaningful and appropriate process that produces positive results.

Moving Beyond Consequences

Students should learn early in the year that behavior and consequences are linked, even regarding contrived consequences. This understanding of the connection is especially important in today's society. Many young people have not yet realized that there are consequences for their behavior. We need to remind them that every choice they make has a consequence, either good or bad.

After using any consequence, but especially a contrived consequence, it is very important that once the bad behavior is stopped, we take the time to teach our students what the desired behavior looks like. We shouldn't quit after simply stopping the bad behavior. We must be forward looking, helping students see how they could do better next time. For practical matters, we can have them practice the desired behavior—such as walking (not running) in the hall and focusing their attention on the teacher during instruction.

Most misbehavior needs some level of teacher intervention. Make sure that your intervention doesn't cause more disruption than the students' misbehavior. Remaining calm and intervening immediately will have a positive ripple effect on the other students.

When it becomes necessary to intervene, be sure to do so in a manner that does not embarrass the students. Students' embarrassment will often increase disobedience and invite negative attitudes. Usually it is better to intervene in private rather than in front of others.

Closing Thoughts on Using Rules and Procedures in Discipline

Rules and procedures are necessary in our personal lives and in our classrooms and schools. In fact, rules and procedures are necessary wherever people interact. Rules and procedures identify what good behavior looks like. They are necessary for the efficient and effective running of classrooms because they increase the likelihood that what goes on in the classroom will be conducive to learning. Rules can motivate students to stay focused on their learning. Rules enable teachers to teach and students to learn in a safe and supportive environment. Rules and procedures increase instructional learning time. Rules can be used to build community, motivate our students to grow, and provide the basic building blocks for discipleship.

QUESTIONS: USING RULES AND PROCEDURES IN DISCIPLINE

1. How does your view of authority determine whether and how you will develop rules in your classroom?

2. Basing your answer on your view of the child, how desirable do you think it is to have structure in a classroom? How do you define structure? Support your response.

3. What five or six rules will you have in your classroom? Provide your rationale for each one.

4. Are there absolute standards for behavior? Define what you mean by the word *absolute*, and give examples of such standards that you will have in your classroom. Support your response.

5. How do you make sense of the relationships among the following concepts: God's work in a person's life, logical consequences, contrived consequences, and your role as the teacher in giving consequences?

6. What role should punishment have in students' lives? Support your response from your worldview/foundation.

7. How will you hold students accountable for following the rules? How will you help students follow the rules out of an intrinsic motivation to do so rather than out of a fear of punishment?

8. In what specific ways, if any, have you been influenced by society's thinking about the subject of this chapter?

CHAPTER FOURTEEN

APPLYING BIBLICAL DISCIPLINE

Whoever loves instruction and correction loves knowledge,
but he who hates reproof is like a brute beast, stupid and indiscriminating.
—Proverbs 12:1, Amplified Bible

Understanding Discipline

When people think of discipline, they often think of control, punishment, and authority. Some teachers view discipline as one of their most negative, time-consuming, and emotionally draining tasks. Disciplining students is something some teachers wish they never had to do. But note the following: "For some educators, discipline means the power of the teacher to control the behavior of their students.... For other educators, discipline means an opportunity to teach students a set of values about how people can live together in a democratic society.... Discipline is perceived as the process of helping students internalize these values and develop self-control over their drives and feelings" (Long and Morse 1996, 238). Thus, not all teachers see discipline in a negative way.

In Scripture, we are told many things about discipline: We should not despise God's discipline or reject it (Proverbs 3:11). We should be happy when God reproves us (Job 5:17). Wise people love discipline (Proverbs 12:1). Discipline is for our good, and it shows God's love for us; it may not be joyful at the time it is happening, but it will bring peace and righteousness to those who are trained by it (Hebrews 12:6). Children are to be disciplined while there is still hope (Proverbs 19:18).

Discipline and Authority

Discipline and authority are God's ideas—not ours. Therefore, we must take seriously the authority entrusted to us as teachers. As noted before, biblical authority encompasses dominion and service. We must see both of these aspects as desirable. Many teachers shirk the *dominion* aspect of authority, while others look upon *service* with disdain. When we walk in biblical authority as leaders in our classrooms, our students are more likely to learn from us and to accept God's authority over them. We have the opportunity to model God's authority and build it into our students' lives.

In Scripture, the concepts of authority and discipline are linked. Both are exercised within the context of discipleship. One dictionary defines *discipline* as "training that corrects, molds, or perfects; control gained by obedience and training; orderly conduct; a system of rules governing conduct" (*Merriam-Webster* 2005, 139). Scripture refers to discipline as a calling to soundness of mind—to wisdom. Discipline helps our students see life from God's perspective. It can develop self-control, character, orderliness, and efficiency. It encourages obedience and acceptance of authority and control. It offers a system of rules for conduct.

The words *discipline* and *disciple* come from the same Latin root word *discipulus*, meaning "learner." According to the dictionary, discipled people are people who follow someone, learn that master's teaching, and share it with others. In Scripture, we see that Jesus discipled the disciples, and it was evident in their behavior that they followed Him. Jesus spent much time with His disciples. He poured His life into them. He helped them understand deep truths and called them to a high standard of behavior, as seen in the commandments He gave them in the Sermon on the Mount. He rebuked them harshly at times yet at other times encouraged them. He served them in humility. He spoke what each person needed to hear, out of deep love and concern. These are all things that godly teachers should do when they are discipling students. In the process of discipling, we build relationships and understanding. We call our students to the highest standard of character. We encourage them and give them hope. We speak truth to them in love. We care enough about our students to confront them and challenge them to grow toward Christlikeness. This type of discipline is discipleship.

Here are some eighth-grade students' responses to the question, What is discipline? "Discipline is what gets in the way of me doing the same thing again." "Discipline is correcting you to help you be ready for your oncoming adult life." "Discipline is, in a way, making life easier for the person."

Here is one that is a little longer but very insightful:

> "Discipline is getting across to the person that he has done something wrong
> and you want to correct it. In a sense, you are showing you care about that
> person by stopping him from doing that. Usually, if you're in trouble, you
> don't realize that the person is telling you that. When you discipline, you
> should do it in love, not in anger. You should first make it known to him

what he has done, and then make sure that he acknowledges that. Then, discipline in such a way that it's a way of communicating. It is usually for our good so when we are older we won't go out and steal and turn out to be criminals. It is hard to take, and sometimes you may feel like rebelling when you are punished. The person should feel sorry that he did what he did if he is punished in the right way. When you discipline, it should not be in front of others because it is usually humiliating...."

And one more: "Discipline is, in my mind, restrictions that sometimes keep us from what we like to do. It also, keeps us from harm."

I thought these comments were very insightful and interesting coming from eighth-grade students. Try this activity in your school. Ask eighth graders for their definitions of discipline. See what they say. Get them to write their definitions down so you have them for later. Of course, there may be some major differences in how today's students understand discipline.

Discipline is a training ministry based on a godly relationship in which there is a balance between freedom and control, firmness and love, prevention and correction, will and spirit, and words and actions. Discipline is much more than just having well-run classrooms. More importantly, discipline points children toward living their lives in a dynamic relationship with Jesus Christ and being conformed to His will. Discipline is "an opportunity to redirect students: to strive against sin, to overcome weakness, to build inner peace and righteousness, and to partake in the holiness of God. Through discipline students must realize the grace of God (Hebrews 12)" (Van Brummelen 1998, 68). In Scripture, discipline is always done within the context of a relationship. The same should be true of our classroom discipline.

Discipline and Discipleship

In the context of discipleship, discipline deals with attitudes and motives as well as behavior. Somewhere years ago, I heard that discipline doesn't elevate the conduct of students above the root (cause) of their conduct because conduct is only the "fruit of the root." In disciplining for discipleship, we must deal with root causes. Doing so with a gentle spirit that flows from a godly character will make an impact on our students for Christ.

Discipling incorporates many aspects of discipline, but discipling is broader and goes much deeper. Discipline becomes discipling when it moves beyond just dealing with the current behavior and takes the whole child into consideration. Discipline becomes discipling when it involves instruction, when it paints the big picture of who students can become, and when it helps them see how they can improve in the future. Discipline becomes discipling when it supports God's vision for each child and when it is not limited to our own perspective of our students. Discipline becomes discipling when it helps our students on their way to becoming all that God created them to be. This type of discipline does not speak judgment, discouragement, and hopelessness into the lives of students. It acknowledges that sin has consequences even while speaking faith into their lives and giving them hope for a better future.

Discipline becomes discipling when we give students everything they need (everything that is appropriate and within our power to give) to help them make the best choices in the future. This kind of discipline focuses on future growth and not just on the suppression of the bad behavior at hand. Discipline that is discipling takes into account the whole student—body, soul, and spirit. It focuses on the uniqueness of each child and chooses to work within each one's uniqueness. It includes crying out to God for His vision to be fulfilled in each student. It moves beyond the natural realm. Effective discipling brings about inner transformation not just outward conformity.

Discipling gives us the focus for our leadership in the classroom and our reason for motivating our students to learn, grow, and succeed. It is what enables us to have hope for each of our students. Discipling can give us purpose for everything we do in our classroom. It provides the foundation for building community—not just for the sake of a happy, safe, and productive learning environment but for the purpose of discipling students to become willing disciples of Jesus Christ.

Although discipling encompasses the teacher's role of mentoring, discipling goes beyond mentoring. Discipling invites students into a mentoring relationship with us, within the context of God's standards for living. That is, as we disciple children, we are seeking to make them disciples of Jesus rather than disciples of ourselves. Discipling is shaped by, influenced by, and focused on what is eternal.

The Goal of Discipline

The goal of discipline within the context of discipleship is for students' lives to be the outgrowth of godly thinking and godly feeling—a deep inner conviction rather than just an outward conformity to rules. Since discipleship deals with attitudes and motives as well as behavior, there should be less and less external control (rewards and punishments) and more and more internal control (willing obedience) under the direction of the Holy Spirit. We have the responsibility to teach children that true obedience comes from the heart out of a love for God and a desire to obey His commandments. Therefore, we *expect* obedience from our students. We don't ask them for their permission to make them obey us. Many teachers say to their students, "Sit down, okay?" What if it isn't okay with them? We must be clear, calm, and assertive.

All discipline must be for the growth and improvement of students. Discipline can provide hope for students when it is done in a personally affirming manner. It starts as an outer stimulus that urges students to do better and become better. But the goal of discipline is to develop an inner drive that causes students to pursue God and His righteousness. That kind of discipline will last, and not just for their year in our classrooms, but for eternity.

Principles of Discipline

The following "principles of discipline" are taken from Ollie Gibbs and Jerry Haddock's *Classroom Discipline: A Management Guide for Christian School Teachers* (1991, 3–18). These authors understand that discipline must be done within the concept of discipleship. What they offer is no "bag of tricks" for handling challenging students. The type of discipline they describe requires the long, hard process of building relationships with students; walking with them consistently, prayerfully, and lovingly, sometimes through very difficult times; and leading them toward a life lived in joyful submission to Christ.

Discipline Is Related to Disciple

"The purpose of discipline is to disciple students in the Lord's way" (Gibbs and Haddock 1991, 4). Just as Jesus invested three years in discipling His disciples, so we need to invest our teaching years in discipling our students. This process takes time, effort, and commitment to relationships. Students need a lot of sincere praise to be able to receive correction. Encouragement is huge in children's lives. We need to send messages of warmth, smile a lot, laugh with our students, and enjoy them while we are training them. This approach is not just a gimmick to get students to behave. This type of discipling focuses not on punishment but on having ongoing, edifying input into our students' lives.

Discipline Is a Mark of Sonship

Godly teachers discipline within a context of love and concern. We discipline students because we care about them in a way that is similar to the way parents care about their children. Parents (and teachers) who care will take the time to discipline their children (or students) in a godly manner. Indeed, discipline *is* a mark of sonship (Hebrews 12:5–11). Thus disciplining our students is not a one-time thing. On the contrary, it builds growth and maturity over time.

Discipline Provides a Framework for Godliness

Discipline should give students a strong foundation in God's Word so that they grow in their faith and learn to live according to God's principles. Discipline helps them make personal decisions for life that reflect biblical values.

Discipline Involves Submission to Authority

In today's society, submission to authority is often viewed as a sign of weakness. We need to help our students understand that submission to authority is vital to the proper development of their relationship with God and with other people. In addition to expecting our students to submit to us, we as teachers need to model submission to our own authorities—school administrators, political leaders, and most of all, God.

Discipline Includes Learning by Observing

We need to practice what we preach and model appropriate attitudes and behavior. Our students often learn more by watching what we do than by hearing what we say. If we are to have a godly impact on them, we must stay connected to Christ and model godly living (John 15).

Respect Is Foundational to Effective Discipline

Our students need to have respect for God, for themselves, and for others. Discipline teaches and demonstrates consideration for others. Our students need to understand that respect is reciprocal (people are often treated in the way they treat others), universal (everybody wants to be respected), and feasible (our students can always find grounds for respecting others).

Peers Play an Important Role in Discipline

Gibbs and Haddock (1991, 16) say, "Maturity is a process that involves association." In discipling, wise teachers realize the effect peers have on students' attitudes, behavior, and achievement, and they make use of peer pressure for the benefit and growth of their students.

When looking at these seven principles, we can see that discipline is far deeper than just pulling tricks out of a hat to make students behave. We must be looking for more from our students than mere outward conformity. Even in Christian schools there are students who have learned how to conform outwardly without having a heart change. We must be discerning, and we must be prayerful. True disciplers care enough to look for a heart change deep within those they disciple. Discipleship requires making a heartfelt commitment to our students, before God, that we will do all we can to move them toward becoming disciples of Jesus Christ.

Misconceptions About Discipline and Authority

Before we discuss biblical discipline in depth, there are some misconceptions about discipline and authority that need to be identified and addressed. Our world has, perhaps, influenced the way we think about authority and discipline. Consider the following views that reflect much current thinking: (a) Doing things on our own and in our own way is a sign of maturity. Independence (versus interdependence) is highly valued. (b) Accepting discipline, correction, admonition, chastisement, or instruction is foolish and is a sign of weakness. (c) Acknowledging that we need guidance and discipline makes us inferior to the person who is offering us advice or disciplining us. (d) Providing guidance and discipline makes us better than the one who is receiving our guidance and discipline. (e) People have all the answers within themselves, so we don't really need advice (discipline) from others. (f) Once we have been disciplined, we will automatically learn from the experience, and we will not need to be disciplined in the future. (g) Discipline equals punishment.

As we look at biblical discipline, evaluate where your thinking about discipline has been influenced by current thinking and where it needs to be renewed to bring it into line with God's view of discipline as identified in Scripture.

Biblical Discipline

Presented here is a fivefold examination of biblical discipline based on my understanding of Scripture: instruction, warning, consequences, correction, and ongoing follow-up. At least two writers have also influenced my thinking: Bill Gothard (1984a, 1984b) and Jack Fennema (1977).

Instruction

The first step in biblical discipline is instruction. Without it, we would not have an effective means of disciplining or discipling our students. This instruction refers to the type of teaching that brings life (Proverbs 4:13). It systematically and intentionally teaches students how to walk on the right path, how to discern right from wrong. It teaches students where they are and where they need to go—using Scripture as a guide. Instruction is not just presenting rules to be memorized but teaching truth that can be applied to life.

The goal of instruction is to transform students' natural inclinations, to convert the soul, to build character, and to make wisdom attractive. Instruction is showing students divine standards for living and God's reasons for those standards. "True instruction enables the child to see life situations from God's point of view [wisdom]. It also provides him with sufficient information to successfully perform specific tasks. The degree to which he is able to do this will determine his ability to develop mature attitudes, meaningful goals, and successful relationships" (Gothard 1984a, 1).

Jack Fennema (1977, 58–78) points out that instruction is done primarily through two means: words (instruction that is taught) and actions (instruction that is caught). Instruction that is taught should be presented in a manner that is planned, organized, structured, authentic, and authoritative. On the other hand, instruction is caught mainly through classroom atmosphere and personal interaction. Yet, according to Fennema, caught instruction is the most likely to help students (a) develop a sense of joy by acting upon who they are in Christ, (b) share in communal love by learning to work together, (c) respect others by learning to work separately, and (d) develop a sense of security by learning to work within structure.

On the basis of Psalm 19, Gothard (1984a, 10) says that instruction should include the following:

Law of the Lord. The laws of the Lord are the basic principles of Scripture that pertain to life and godliness. These laws are "perfect" (complete) and able to convert the soul (mind, will, emotions) by replacing the natural inclinations of students and transforming their minds.

Testimony. Instruction should include illustrations of the ways that people have applied the principles of Scripture in the past. Illustrations of what didn't work are also effective. (I once saw a photo of the Titanic with an inspirational caption that read "Failure: The purpose of your life may be to show others what not to do.") We can draw examples from our own experience as well as other people's lives.

Statutes. Instruction should include specific standards. We must state these clearly. Scripture says that statutes bring joy by giving practical direction in difficult situations.

Commandments. We need to show our students what is right and what is wrong. God's revealed way is "pure" (clear and precise), and it "enlightens the eyes" (provides fresh insight for living). We must instruct our students in more than just facts. We must help them see the concepts and principles that the facts are based on.

Fear. We need to keep before our students the importance of the fear of the Lord, since it is the beginning of wisdom.

Judgments. Instruction includes letting students know that there are always consequences for every action. These reproofs are to be "desired more than gold" because they warn God's servants to avoid bad consequences and seek good consequences ("great reward"). God reproves those He loves. God's reproofs lead to great reward if we allow ourselves to be changed by them.

The necessity for effective discipline, according to Gothard, is amplified by the fact that the child's natural inclinations are directly contrary to God's principles of life. In contrast to what many believe, the Bible teaches that children are not born good. Everyone is born with a sin nature, and therefore we can't focus only on our students' outward behavior. In disciplining, we must communicate to the total person: the body, the soul (mind, will, emotions), and the spirit. Teachers must communicate in different ways with each aspect of their students, and they would be wise to learn these ways. Although Gothard (1984a, 4–6) writes mostly to parents, his directions, which are summarized below, can also be useful for teachers.

Communication to the spirit of the child. Communicating to the spirit of our students is the key to developing deepening relationships with them, and therefore it is the most vital form of communication. A child's initial instruction is with the spirit. Even before a child learns the meaning of words, he "reads" the spirit of his parents. Facial expressions (especially the eyes) reflect the spirit. In the same way, we can communicate all the essential qualities of God—love, joy, peace, longsuffering, gentleness, goodness, faith, meekness, and temperance (Galatians 5:22–23). It is our calling to work at connecting our spirit with the spirit of each student. Unless we do, we cannot effectively disciple our students. (On a personal note, I'm learning the importance of communicating with the spirit through the challenge of loving someone with Alzheimer's disease, my mom. I am finding that I can still connect with her— my spirit with her spirit—through the eyes. It's amazing! Even though her body is breaking down and her mind no longer understands reality, she still is able to communicate well with her spirit. Through her I'm learning much about who we really are as people!)

Communication to the mind of the child. It is wise to know the mental frame of reference of our students because this knowledge helps us speak meaningfully into their worlds. Words and expressions have different meanings to different people, and, to some, certain words have no meaning at all. Children often learn through pictures. Therefore, we need to help children build larger and clearer pictures of words and then help them relate these pictures to spiritual truth. We need pictures to define words such as righteousness, faith, prayer, meekness, and humility. (This practice is similar to that of keeping a good Bible dictionary handy to look up words that we are not sure about when we are studying Scripture.)

We also have the opportunity to create curiosity about truth through the use of stories, parables, and questions. Our instruction must be designed to achieve specific, clearly defined goals. We must organize and communicate information effectively to help our students see, internalize, and achieve God's purpose for their lives.

Communication to the physical needs of the child. We need to identify the basic physical needs of the children in our classrooms (see chapter 12). Many children are coming to school malnourished, insufficiently clothed, physically exhausted, or abused in any number of ways. Many schools are trying to address these needs. We must seek solutions when it is appropriate to do so.

Gothard (1984a, 7) is correct when he says that there must be inward preparation in the hearts and minds of [teachers] if they hope to communicate effectively with the whole child. It is not all about how students receive discipline; it is also about how teachers administer it. Gothard says that teachers need to answer the following questions: What do I hope to accomplish in this conversation (Proverbs 10:21)? What past ideas or experiences will affect the listeners' responses (Proverbs 18:15)? What words will be the most effective (Proverbs 16:23)? Are students aware of their needs (Proverbs 15:2)? How can I motivate them rather than cause them to react to my words (Proverbs 15:28)? What facial expressions and body language will support and increase the effect of my words (Proverbs 16:1)? How do the facial expressions of students reflect how they are responding (Proverbs 18:4)?

Warning

The second step in biblical discipline is warning. Its main purpose is to clarify and reemphasize instruction. Warning follows instruction and happens when students choose not to apply the instruction to their lives. Warning is meant to accomplish at least four things. First, we must determine whether our instruction was clear. Did students understand the instruction, the standards we taught, the expectations we set forth? Asking ourselves such questions gives us the opportunity to make sure we don't jump to any wrong conclusions. Sometimes students misbehave because they honestly did not understand what was expected of them. Second, we must take the time to find out the cause of the misbehavior. Was the student being defiant? Was the student being childish? Was something else going on? We may choose to handle each of these causes of misbehavior differently. Third, we need to ask ourselves whether we might have contributed to the student's behavior in any way. Is the student reacting against us? Are there unresolved issues between us and the student? Fourth, we must find ways to communicate what was wrong and how it can be corrected. How can we appeal to their consciences in such a way that students will understand and accept that they have done wrong and that there are consequences? How can we help students determine what is inappropriate and unacceptable about their behavior? Remember, biblical discipline goes much further than just stopping bad behavior.

This warning step provides us with the opportunity to show genuine concern for students who are going the wrong way. This step is not about threatening students. Warning should appeal mainly to the consciences of our students. Does our warning prompt their consciences to convict them that they have done wrong? Are our students concerned more about the consequences of misbehaving than about the misbehavior itself? By appealing to their consciences, we bring warning in line with what the Spirit of God wants to do in their lives. Warning provides the opportunity for children to measure their behavior by God's standards rather than by what everyone else is doing. The apostle Paul appealed directly to the consciences of those with whom he worked, and he gained lasting results (2 Corinthians 4:2, 5:11).

Warning also has another component to it. It alerts students to dangers, snares, and coming evils; it puts them on guard about certain acts; and it gives notice to them to stay away from something.

If it becomes obvious that our students did understand the instruction and still disobeyed it, we must move to the next step—consequences.

Consequences

The third step of biblical discipline is applying consequences for misbehavior. At times the consequences will be minimal, and at other times they will be more severe. As we take this step with our students, we want to encourage them to confess and ask forgiveness from whomever they have offended. Students should understand that confession involves the following seven steps: (a) addressing everyone involved; (b) avoiding "ifs," "buts," and "maybes"; (c) admitting what they did specifically; (d) apologizing; (e) asking for forgiveness; (f) accepting consequences; and (g) altering their behavior. I am more convinced than ever that genuine confession, in which we follow the seven steps above, is rooted in eternity. Somehow we are living by the value system of eternity when we genuinely confess, specifically ask for forgiveness, and actually turn away from what we did wrong.

Students should also be taught that forgiveness means (a) we will not bring the matter up again; (b) we will not talk to others about it; (c) we will not dwell on it ourselves; and (d) we will relinquish all desire to get even or retaliate. Read these again, now, for your own life. Is there someone you aren't forgiving (according to the above definition)? This is a key issue in life. Every one of us will have many opportunities to choose to forgive someone. I've heard it said that when we do not forgive someone, it is like taking poison and hoping the other person will be hurt. From experience, I can tell you that forgiveness sets you free. When someone has hurt you or done you wrong, certain "friends" will want to hang around; they are pride, fear, self-pity, bitterness, and resentment. Don't let them stay. The sooner you forgive, the sooner you will be rid of these friends and the sooner you will be set free.

We should never make students apologize until the apology is genuine. If they are unwilling to do so at this time, we still have opportunity to walk alongside them in the next two steps, correction and follow-up.

The previous chapter dealt with specific types of consequences. When it comes to giving consequences for misbehavior, we want the whole process of giving consequences, including the consequence itself, to build students up not tear them down. Remember that what we are doing is in the context of discipleship. We want the process to help students realize that certain behaviors are not acceptable, but at the same time we want to convey that we genuinely care—not just about changing their behavior but about understanding what is going on inside them. We can't just pick consequences haphazardly. Consequences have the power to bring deep and lasting changes in students' lives, so we should prayerfully consider what consequences are appropriate for specific students. When giving consequences, we need to be consistent, clear, and fair.

Correction

"A wise and successful [teacher] will use instruction, warning, [consequences,] and correction to first reinforce the conscience of [the] child and then appeal to it" (Gothard 1984b, 2–3).

Correction is the fourth step in biblical discipline that occurs after instruction, warning, and consequences. Correction refocuses students on desirable and appropriate future behavior and attitudes. It gives suggestions, godly advice, and biblical direction. It speaks affirmation about who students are and who they can become. Too often discipline stops at step three, and then students don't know what desirable behavior looks like. They only know what undesirable behavior is. When we include correction, we take the time to dialogue with students about how they can handle things differently in the future. We can seek their input. Often they have some ideas. We can use this step as a further teaching moment, when we show students that we care enough about them to go beyond just stopping bad behavior and that we really want them to know how to behave in the future. We want to convey to our students that we are sharing the responsibility for their future conduct. This step provides the opportunity for students to develop with us plans for their future behavior and to covenant with us about how they will live out the plans they have made (Fennema 1977). Correction shows students how to stay on the path. It helps them to see what they can do differently next time.

Ongoing Follow-Up

Follow-up is the fifth step in biblical discipline. This step is not necessarily done in a formal manner. It entails walking alongside our students on an ongoing basis. It takes into account the uniqueness of each student. It requires intentional encouragement and regular mentoring. It necessitates letting students know that we have seen their improved behavior, that we can tell they really are trying. Follow-up includes continuing to take opportunities to speak into the lives of our students in ways that influence their character and fuel their desire to know, love, and serve God.

This fivefold process is all about discipline within the context of discipleship. Biblical discipline cannot be separated from discipleship. We discipline biblically by (a) clearly setting forth biblical standards of behavior (*instruction*); (b) caring enough to confront our students by lovingly *warning* them when they disobey; (c) applying *consequences* that will give them hope that they can change; (d) graciously and gently helping students see how they could do things differently in the future (*correction*); and (e) walking alongside them in such a way that we can continue to make an impact on their lives (*follow-up*).

Responses to Discipline

What should we look for from our students as appropriate and ideal responses to discipline? Students who have responded well to discipline (Hebrews 12) have hearts that have been changed by the working of the Holy Spirit and lives that reflect those changed hearts. Students such as these have come to value discipline (and being discipled) because they see that it leads to peace and righteousness. Students who have responded well to discipline have become effectual doers of the Word of God—not forgetful hearers (James 1:25). These students are on their way to becoming responsible and "response-able" disciples of Jesus Christ!

Closing Thoughts on Applying Biblical Discipline

"[God] disciplines us for our certain good, that we may become sharers in His own holiness. For the time being no discipline brings joy, but seems grievous and painful; but afterwards it yields a peaceable fruit of righteousness to those who have been trained by it (a harvest of fruit which consists in righteousness—in conformity to God's will in purpose, thought, and action, resulting in right living and right standing with God)" (Hebrews 12:10–11, Amplified Bible).

QUESTIONS: APPLYING BIBLICAL DISCIPLINE

1. What do you think is the difference between "discipline for discipleship" and "discipline for control"?

2. Using this chapter, Scripture, your worldview/foundation, and anything else you find helpful, list ten components that you believe are necessary elements for the model of discipline you are developing.

3. Give a title to the model of discipline you are beginning to develop, and briefly explain why you chose it.

4. Reread the "Misconceptions About Discipline and Authority" section of this chapter. Which of these nonbiblical views have influenced you? Evaluate which areas of your thinking about discipline need to be renewed to bring them into line with God's view of discipline as identified in Scripture.

5. How can teachers best communicate to the spirit, mind, and body of a child?

6. Read again the material in this chapter on confession and forgiveness. Before you apply these concepts in your classroom, what do you need to confess? To whom? What and whom do you need to forgive? What is preventing you from doing so? What are you going to do about it?

CHAPTER FIFTEEN

RESPONDING TO VIOLATIONS AND CONFLICT

People take time! Dealing with discipline takes time. Children are not fax machines or credit cards. When they misbehave, they tell us that they need help in learning a better way. They are telling us that there are basic needs not being met that are motivating the behavior.
—Allen N. Mendler, *What Do I Do When ...?*

So far in this book we have dealt mainly with prevention strategies that will minimize misbehavior and maximize learning and student growth toward becoming disciples of Jesus Christ. We have discussed at length strategies such as building meaningful and appropriate relationships, arranging the classroom effectively for learning, teaching rules and procedures, managing student work, getting off to a good start, enhancing student motivation, and building a biblical pattern of discipline. These are all vital preventive measures. Teachers who implement effective preventative strategies radically reduce the possibility of problems developing and increase the likelihood of creating an atmosphere in which students want to learn.

However, to stop there would be naive and wrong. In today's society, we have many children and young people who are hurt, confused, broken, angry, abused, and lost. They are reaching out for attention, love, acceptance, and even control. It is highly probable that teachers will have some of these students in their classrooms. Many children have been deeply hurt by those meant to protect them and, as a result, have come to believe that adults are not to be trusted. Many young people have no concept of the value and desirability of having boundaries and authority in their lives. For these young people, and for *all* students in today's classrooms, teachers have the privilege and awesome responsibility before God to make their classrooms sanctuaries—havens of rest; places where all students belong; places where all students feel safe, welcome, loved, and accepted; places where teachers build meaningful relationships with students and have the opportunity to mentor and disciple them.

The topic of this chapter troubles me somewhat. The potential for seeing students who violate rules and cause conflict as *problems* or as *misbehaving children* deeply concerns me. That is *not* my intention in writing this chapter. Students should never be seen as problems. Some students can be very challenging, but God has created every student in His image and for His purpose. Teachers need to pray for wisdom and discernment to see their students as God sees them.

In case you haven't picked up this truth yet, God has *divinely appointed* each student to be in our classrooms. It is not by chance that a certain child is in your class. God has you there for each child—and He has each child there for you. Remember this when you are facing the challenges that will come!

My purpose in this chapter is to provide you with some meaningful and appropriate ways to get involved in the lives of these students so as to make an eternal difference for God's glory. These strategies can do more than stop problems; they can enable you to guide your students "in the way they should go." You'll want to use these strategies to enable you to minister to your students more effectively and to help them develop into true, growing disciples of Jesus Christ. Remember that no method of motivation and discipline will be equally effective with all students. That is why building relationships with students is so important. Different strategies will affect different students differently.

Seeing Conflict as Opportunity

Before we go any further, a "mind shift" about how to view conflict may be necessary. Too often conflict is seen as bad and unhealthy. That view of conflict is sad—and wrong: "Conflict is a normal part of life in a fallen world. Conflict is a thread that runs throughout Scripture, beginning with Lucifer's rebellion, continuing through the Old Testament as *God uses conflict to form His people*, and then into the New Testament, where Acts 15 details serious conflicts in the early church. Jesus Himself was no stranger to conflict. He *initiated* conflict when He cleansed the temple (Matthew 21). He *resolved* conflict concerning the adulterous woman (John 8). He *avoided* conflict when He disappeared while being confronted in Nazareth (Luke 4)" (Rosa 1998, 27; emphasis mine).

In the classroom, teachers have many opportunities to use all three approaches: to initiate, resolve, and avoid conflict. Godly teachers pray for wisdom to know what they should do in specific circumstances. As long as teachers see conflict as bad or unhealthy, they will have difficulty taking positive action to resolve it. They will just want the conflict to end, so they will do whatever it takes to stop it. However, conflict can provide teachers with the *best* opportunity to interact with students on a very deep level. From my experience, I can tell you that conflict in the classroom opens doors to talk personally with students about what is going on in their lives. Such discussions seldom take place when teachers are talking only about assignment expectations.

Conflict can be initiated when students cheat, disobey classroom rules, defy the teacher's authority, make negative outbursts, or do not complete their homework, or when they are moody, late, absent, or generally uncooperative. Through such conflicts, I have had the opportunity and responsibility of walking alongside students who were being shifted from foster home to foster home and being physically, sexually, and emotionally abused in each place. Conflict has given me the opportunity to discover and walk alongside a student who had lost her virginity and who was afraid she was pregnant. Conflict exposed the fact that a student felt he was no good and that he would never amount to anything. Conflict exposed that a student who had tremendous rage inside him had been adopted and then abused by his adoptive family. Conflict brought to light the fact that some students were dealing with a friend's suicide. One student's repeated failure to do homework led me to find out that this student's father had left the home and was living with another woman even though he had always told his children that such behavior was wrong. Because of the moodiness and negative outbursts of some students, I realized that they felt as if nobody liked them or that they couldn't meet my expectations and just wanted to give up. Because of a cheating incident, I found out that a person close to one of my students had been convicted of fraud. I've walked alongside students who sneaked out of the house at night to be with friends whom the parents didn't approve of. Because of a seemingly unrelated conflict, a student revealed that a family member was abusing drugs, was making drugs available to her, and was encouraging her to try them.

I know of a public school teacher who had a student who was acting out in class. This teacher learned that the child's mother had just been put in prison. The dad was already there, and this young child was living with some unrelated men. Both parents gave permission to the teacher to have the child live with her until they were out of prison. The teacher led that child to the Lord.

These are some of the reasons discipline can become so much more than just getting students to hand in their homework, come in on time, and not fight with others. Often violations of the rules expose something much deeper that the student is going through. Teachers need to do their best to get to the bottom of things so that they truly can walk alongside these students and help them face whatever they are going through. These are opportunities for discipleship.

These experiences show that conflict—even seemingly unrelated conflict—can give teachers incredible opportunities to speak into their students' lives. Students often open up if they are invited to do so. Teacher-disciplers don't view conflict as just something they must shut down as quickly as possible. Rather, they ask God how He wants to use these conflicts in ways that will make a positive difference in their students' lives. By doing so, teacher-disciplers can begin to allow the full pattern of biblical discipline (see chapter 14) to be worked out. God can also use these conflicts to show teachers what part of their own character needs to be transformed.

Often life change or life redirection begins when the conflict that occurs is handled in a way that gives hope to the young people involved. Conflict provides teachers with opportunities to walk alongside students in ways that focus on personal growth and personal life issues. Effective disciplers don't miss these opportunities.

Seeing Problems as Problems

Another false belief is that conflict in the classroom is a *people problem.* "Actually conflict arises because there is *a problem that needs to be solved.* When we hold the false belief that conflict is 'me against you,' it becomes increasingly difficult to resolve the problem through communication.... Recognizing conflict as an opportunity to solve a problem frees us to use communication as a problem-solving tool" (Rosa 1998, 27).

Conflict does not have to pit teachers against their students. As noted above, conflict is about finding solutions to problems together. Teachers and students should be working together, not against each other. In seeking solutions to problems, teachers can build bridges to students. Working together to solve a problem helps the teachers and the students see each other in a different light. Conflict provides the opportunity to graciously and gently (yet firmly) invite students to grow. These divine appointments take time and selflessness.

When Bad Conflicts Happen to Good Teachers

Experience in the area of conflict is an effective teacher, but only if the experience is rooted in appropriate beliefs, theories, principles, and training. We need to build our practice of discipline on absolutes and filter it through our foundation—the Word of God.

Perhaps there was a time when "good" teachers had fewer discipline problems than other teachers. However, even in well-managed classrooms the brokenness, hurt, apathy, and emptiness of many young people today are making conflicts more widespread than ever before. Most of our classrooms are likely to include hurting, lonely, angry, abandoned, and abused children and young people. These students may be a challenge for even the best of teachers—but *they don't have to become discipline problems.*

Working through discipline challenges as opposed to simply having good control takes more than just knowing one or two "tricks of the trade." Discipline is far too complex and interpersonal for teachers to depend on gimmicks and tricks. Remember that no method of discipline is equally effective with all students. Therefore, discipline has to be done in the context of a caring, mentoring, discipling relationship with students.

Further, once we have dealt with a discipline challenge, we must let it go! With God's help, we truly can forgive and forget. We shouldn't continue to feel bad about having a conflict with a student when what we did was for the student's good. We must care enough to confront our students—to say the hard things that they *need* to hear. But we must also love them enough to go beyond the confrontation and help them see how they can do things differently in the future and how they can become transformed people.

Our major challenge with respect to discipline is that we must be careful not to (a) expect too much, (b) act too soon, or (c) quit too early, something I heard years ago at a teachers conference. We must also know the difference between godly and ungodly practices of classroom discipline. Ungodly classroom discipline includes such things as belittling, berating, and embarrassing students; displaying a vindictive spirit; blowing up; striking back; speaking negatively about students to others; and disciplining students in front of others. Godly discipline, on the other hand, includes committing ourselves to helping, serving, and loving our students; committing ourselves to working personally with every student; praying consistently for our students, asking God to give us a deeper understanding of each one; letting our students know that we care; working with our students' parents; and always displaying hope for our students' future.

Types of Misbehavior

What types of misbehavior might we see in our classrooms? C. M. Charles (1999, 2–3) identifies five types of misbehavior. The first three are becoming more common in today's classrooms:

1. *Aggression*: physical and verbal attacks by students on the teacher or the other students

2. *Immorality*: acts such as stealing, cheating, and lying

3. *Defiance of authority*: refusal, sometimes in a hostile way, to do as the teacher requests

4. *Class disruptions*: talking loudly, calling out, clowning around, tossing objects, walking about the room, and the like

5. *Goofing off*: fooling around, dawdling, daydreaming, and not doing assigned tasks

Although there are many types of misbehavior, perhaps they can all fit under a general definition: "A discipline problem exists whenever a behavior interferes with the teaching act, interferes with the rights of others to learn, is psychologically or physically unsafe, or destroys property" (Levin and Nolan 2004, 19), and whenever it is unhealthy, is unwise, contradicts the Word of God, or hinders students from becoming all God wants them to be.

Corrective Strategies

Effective teachers spend more time preventing misbehavior than correcting it! This book has already outlined a number of proactive teaching skills and strategies that can prevent misbehavior:

- Building solid teacher-student relationships (chapter 4): One helpful strategy is to talk to each student personally every day.

- Building community among students (chapter 5): One helpful strategy is to take time at the beginning of the year to play getting-to-know-you games.

- Building effective parent-teacher relationships (chapter 6): One helpful strategy is to send an introductory newsletter home introducing ourselves, our expectations, and our vision for the year. In the newsletter, we can also invite input from parents.

- Getting off to a good start (chapter 8): One helpful strategy is to learn the names of our students before the end of the second day (preferably the first day).

- Arranging our classroom in ways that will enhance learning and not disrupt it (chapter 9): One helpful strategy is to arrange seating so that we can see all students at all times.

- Effectively managing student work (chapter 10): Helpful strategies include letting students know that we know how they are doing, and showing interest in their work.

- Making sure instruction keeps students on task (chapter 11): Helpful strategies include changing the pace of our instruction, improving transitions from one subject to another, and using our entire teaching time for instruction.

- Using rules and procedures to motivate students to take charge of their own learning and behavior (chapter 13): One helpful strategy is to show students right at the beginning of the year what the boundaries are.

- Redirecting the behavior of off-task students by showing them what they could and should be doing (chapter 14): One helpful strategy is to affirm another student who is demonstrating appropriate behavior.

Determine Response Ahead of Time

Before misbehavior occurs, we need to determine what our response will be. One option is to choose to ignore the behavior if it is not disruptive to others. If we ignore the behavior, it may eventually stop—especially if the student is misbehaving to get attention. There are obvious limitations to this method of planning ahead. Sometimes ignoring misbehavior may cause the student to escalate it in the hope of getting our attention.

Sometimes other students are encouraging the disruptive behavior. When this happens, we can't ignore it. We also need to teach our students how to respond when another student is misbehaving.

Use Minimal Consequences

We should keep the consequences as minimal as possible, as long as they are effective. If we use the strongest intervention first, we won't have anything left to deal with students' escalating misbehavior.

When I was taking my teacher training, I decided to put restrictions on myself regarding what interventions I would and would not use in my classroom. I determined that I would *use my eyes* as much as possible (this was fun because it meant that I had to be aware of what the students were doing). I determined that I would *never raise my voice at students* (I have only raised my voice at students twice in my thirty-two years of teaching—and both times what I said loudly was the student's name). I determined that I would *never send students to the principal's office or out into the hall.* (I kept the first one; I have never sent a student to the principal's office. I may have sent a few students out into the hall to give them time to pull themselves together and to feel ready to come back into the classroom and participate.)

In handling misbehavior, it is best to start with nonintrusive, nonverbal responses because they give students the opportunity to exercise self-control.

They also minimize disruption to the teaching/learning process, reduce the likelihood that students will become more unruly, and maximize future options for intervention.

It should be noted that there may be times in today's society when it is legitimate to send (or take) students to the principal's office. A violent child who is intentionally causing physical harm to others must be removed from the classroom. Choosing this option doesn't mean that we have lost control or that we aren't willing to invest the time needed to get to the root of the problem. It means that we have a zero-tolerance policy on violence. We can't allow children to harm others, and for their own good, as well as the good of others, they need to be removed from the classroom.

In the early years of my teaching career, I learned the following at a teacher convention. I have never forgotten it, and I have practiced it in my classroom. Our best tool in dealing with misbehavior is our *eyes*. Students usually look at us just before they do something wrong. It's actually quite interesting to watch human nature at work. But when we make eye contact with them, we let them know that they need to be doing something more productive. One great thing about this method is that it doesn't interrupt our teaching. If making eye contact doesn't work, we may want to try using our *eyes and proximity*. We can keep on teaching as we move closer to the disruptive student. If this method still doesn't work, we might then consider using our *eyes, proximity, and minimum voice* (just saying the student's name). We want to train our students to follow these cues. Next, we can use our *eyes, proximity, and silence*. We will seldom need to take time away from teaching when we use these strategies. Finally, we can use *eyes, proximity, and consequences*. While students are transitioning into the next activity or the next class, we should take time to speak one-on-one with the misbehaving student.

Use a Sense of Humor

We must have a sense of humor. Students can be very funny when they are misbehaving. We need to know when it is appropriate to enjoy a laugh with them and when it is necessary to speak firmly to them about their behavior. Many times the two go hand in hand. After my years in the classroom, I could tell many stories about how humor has been effective in diffusing tension and redirecting students' behavior to more productive pursuits.

Respect Your Colleagues

It is unfair to make students skip another teacher's class as punishment for something they did in our classes. I am surprised that many students are kept back from physical education, art, music, and drama as a punishment for misbehaving in another teacher's class. We don't have the right to use this method. In effect, we are telling our students that the other teacher's class is not important and it's okay to miss it—not the message we want to send, even if the other teacher agrees to let the students stay back. Also, we are showing disrespect for a colleague. There are other, more effective ways to discipline students. Additionally, if the class we keep our students from is one of their favorites, we are taking away something they enjoy. "Exactly!" you say. But we should never use school subjects to punish students. They need to have the opportunity to excel in the subject areas they enjoy.

Be Creative

What limitations are you going to put on yourself with respect to how you will work with students who misbehave? Think of five—at least—and write them down. Then choose to follow through on what you have written. Don't just try to follow through. There is a vast difference between *choosing* to do something and *trying* to do it. Choosing brings success. Trying often does not. Further, choosing to give up unproductive forms of discipline forces you to be more creative in finding productive ways to discipline.

Use Time-Outs

Teachers often provide time-outs for students who are showing signs of frustration, fatigue, or anger. This strategy should be used sparingly, but there are times when students need to get away from what is going on so they have time to think. When tension or emotions are interfering with learning, a time-out is called for. This strategy is effective even with older students. I've used it with middle school students (mainly girls) who needed time to debrief friendship issues. I've given them a certain amount of time to work things out and then come back and get to work. If we get to know our students well, we can tell when they genuinely need the time to work things out and when they are just trying to get out of schoolwork. (Yes, they will try!) We also might want to help them develop conflict resolution skills.

The Purpose of Interventions

Our interventions should be concerned with building students up and encouraging growth in their lives. To achieve these goals, we must stay flexible and look forward—not backward. We also need to communicate our optimism to students that things will work out. Remember that interventions are just one step in biblical discipline (the third step, consequences). Interventions, therefore, need to fit within the five-step process of biblical discipline: instruction, warning, consequences/intervention, correction, and ongoing follow-up.

Skills for Conflict Resolution

Earlier, I said that students often misbehave because their needs are not being met. At that time, I also indicated that students often misbehave because they don't have the social skills that would enable them to prevent conflict or to deal with it when it happens. Students (and teachers) must be taught the skills needed for conflict resolution. There are at least six skills that we all need to learn before conflict occurs and to use when conflict happens.

Listen Actively

The first skill to use in resolving conflict is to listen actively (Rosa 1998, 27). Active listening focuses on what is being said. While someone else is speaking, we should be actively involved in what the person is saying, not focusing on how we'll respond. Thus we may need several seconds after the other person stops speaking to think about our response. Some experts say that we should use empathetic and nonevaluative listening, taking the time to paraphrase what the person has said. In any case, before responding, we need to make sure we have heard and understood what the person has said. It is good to take the perspective of the other person and try to really hear what he or she is saying.

Stay Focused

The second skill to use in resolving conflict is to stay focused (Rosa 1998, 28). We do so by dealing only with the present problem and its solution. How often have you been in situations in which you were trying to resolve a problem and the other person kept bringing up things from the past? When dealing with misbehavior, we should be careful to give a focused response that is appropriate for both the situation and the people involved.

Share Primary Feelings

The third skill for conflict resolution is to share our primary feelings. For example, anger is a secondary feeling; it is almost always preceded by feelings of hurt, frustration, or fear. We must identify our primary feelings. Sharing secondary rather than primary feelings usually moves us further away from being able to deal with the problem. It's often more difficult to deal with our primary feelings (Rosa 1998, 28). Doing so makes us more vulnerable, yet it brings us back to the central problem we are trying to solve.

We move closer to resolving conflict when we take responsibility for our statements by using the personal pronouns *I* and *me*. Some experts say we should never say *you*. I disagree. There are times when "you" statements are needed, but they should be made gently, in kindness, in love, and with a gracious spirit. Godly teachers need to speak lovingly but also honestly and directly to students. We can and should explain how we feel and why.

Model Nonthreatening Techniques

The fourth skill for conflict resolution is modeling nonthreatening techniques. Our words, the tone of our voices, and our body language all communicate something during conflict (Rosa 1998, 29). We should be sure that what they communicate is a desire to resolve the problem. How we share is as important as what we share. If we need to (and often we do), we should take time to reflect on the problem before meeting with the student. This practice enables us to organize our thoughts and strategies as well as giving the student time for reflective thinking. I attended a Leadership Summit conference (2006) where Peg Neuhauser, author of *Tribal Warfare in Organizations* (1988), talked about the anatomy of a conversation. She said that it consists of the transaction (what is being said) and the relationship (how it is being said). She noted that there are four possible impacts of every conversation: build, maintain, repair, or damage relationships. Wow! There is no neutral effect.

Use Effective Communication Skills

The fifth skill to use in resolving conflict is effective communication. We must talk directly *to* students rather than *about* them. We should talk respectfully and courteously to the individuals concerned rather than to the whole class. According to Neuhauser (2006), we must use language as a tool and not a weapon.

Know Modes of Conflict Resolution

The sixth skill in resolving conflict is to know and use the modes of conflict resolution. These include, but are not limited to (a) sharing (both can do it); (b) taking turns (your way this time, mine the next); (c) compromising (give up some and get some); (d) getting outside help (ask a classmate or teacher to get involved); (e) postponing (let's resolve this later when we cool down); (f) avoiding (let's agree to disagree and still respect each other); and (g) using humor (is this really important?) (Classroom Law Project n.d.).

Glasser's Problem-Solving Model for Conflict Resolution

Many teachers use William Glasser's model (1965), modified by Jones and Jones (2004, 337–338), in their classrooms because it provides a usable framework for dealing with classroom conflict:

Step 1: Establish a warm, personal relationship with the student.

Step 2: Deal with the present behavior. (What happened? What did you do?) Talk and listen to each other.

Step 3: Make a value judgment. (Is it helping you? others? Is it against a rule?)

Step 4: Work out a plan. (What can you do differently? What do you need me or others to do?) Brainstorm solutions. Make the process one of finding solutions rather than gaining a personal victory.

Step 5: Make a commitment. (Are you going to do this?)

Step 6: Follow up. (I'll check later and see how the plan has worked.)

Step 7: Make no put-downs, but do not accept excuses.

Rewards and Punishments

Rewards are something desirable that students receive in return for accomplishment, effort, or other appropriate behavior. What role do rewards have in classrooms? Do children need incentives to encourage them to work hard, complete assignments, and follow classroom rules and procedures?

Some examples of rewards are grades; symbols (happy faces, check marks); recognition (certificates, "star of the week" awards, activities such as free-reading time or appointments such as room monitor); and material incentives (a pencil, a book).

We should use rewards with caution and after much thought. It has been shown that the use of extrinsic rewards can reduce students' intrinsic motivation to engage in the rewarded activity. Do external rewards communicate the implicit message that "this is an unpleasant or boring task, so a reward is needed to maintain engagement"? When using extrinsic rewards with students, teachers can counteract the potentially negative effects by pointing out the usefulness of the skill to be learned, by choosing materials and activities that have high potential for sustaining interest, and by modeling and demonstrating personal interest and enthusiasm for the task.

Punishments, penalties, or consequences may be needed to deter certain kinds of behavior. A punishment is something undesirable that students receive or have to do because their attitude, behavior, or speech was inappropriate. Students should know that their actions will have consequences. Some educators say that students should be informed of what the penalties are and when they will be used. Others say that students need to know only that there will be consequences. As noted previously, it is the *certainty* of consequences not their *severity* that motivates most students to stay within the boundaries of acceptable behavior.

Some examples of punishments or penalties are reduced grades for late assignments, loss of privileges, detentions, in-school suspensions, confiscation of property, and negative marks in a check or demerit system. In using punishment, we should still focus on keeping the classroom atmosphere positive and supportive. Punishments or penalties should serve mainly as deterrents. We should use them sparingly and only with correction and follow-up.

Age-appropriate rewards and punishments or penalties should be planned to suit the behaviors they are intended to encourage or deter. Rewards that are too easily earned or are too difficult to achieve lose their motivational effect. Penalties that are harsh or too frequently used place us in opposition to our students and minimize our ability to disciple them.

Closing Thoughts on Responding to Violations and Conflict

For effective teaching to take place, we must be competent in managing student misbehavior in order to maximize the time spent on learning and to use misbehavior to disciple our students. When consequences are warranted, they should be appropriate, controlled (not disruptive), calmly administered, personal (teacher to student), and limited (so as not to affect other classes or students), as they remind the students of their classroom rules.

QUESTIONS: RESPONDING TO VIOLATIONS AND CONFLICT

1. How does conflict provide the opportunity to disciple your students? Remember that discipling goes further than disciplining.

2. In what ways might using the strategies described in this chapter either enhance or interfere with building relationships with your students and among your students?

3. Which types of consequences do you think fit best with your foundational beliefs? Why? What consequences will you never give in your classroom? Why?

4. What is your philosophy of rewards and punishments? Is it wise to issue rewards for good behavior and accomplishments? Why or why not?

5. Why do you think educational theorists use the word *penalties* for the word *punishments*? Are they missing or avoiding some aspect of punishment by changing the word?

6. What biblical principles or truths are you applying when you use rewards, penalties, and punishments?

PART FOUR

PERSONAL GROWTH IN COMMUNITY:
GROWING THROUGH CHALLENGES

As leaders in our classroom communities, God invites us to grow into Christlikeness. Teaching isn't just about leading *students* toward growth and maturity. Teaching, as I'm sure you've already recognized, provides ongoing opportunities for *us* to grow as well! In fact, teaching is about living, moment-by-moment, with an ever-increasing measure of godliness. We need to understand that God wants to use the ministry of teaching to fashion us into Christlikeness.

Therefore, we need to understand that God is with us in everything we go through as teachers. It doesn't matter how many other people are involved or how complex the situation is—God is working in the situation for us! He wants to use every circumstance and every relationship to transform our lives.

As you read these final two chapters, open yourself up willingly to God's specific direction. God's challenge is before you. Each one who is reading this is probably going through a challenging situation or relationship right now. As you press on through inevitable challenges, don't just seek to survive. Begin to see those challenges as opportunities for God to work at a deeper level in your life. Allow God to refine you so that others will be able to see Christ in you. Learn to grow through adversity.

CHAPTER SIXTEEN

GROWING AND LEADING THROUGH ADVERSITY

Ministry

The foundation of ministry is *character*.

The nature of ministry is *service*.

The motive for ministry is *love*.

The measure of ministry is *sacrifice*.

The authority of ministry is *submisison*.

The purpose of ministry is the *glory of God*.

The tools of ministry are the *Word of God and prayer*.

The privilege of ministry is *growth* [deeper, closer, larger].

The power of ministry is the *Holy Spirit*.

The model for ministry is *Jesus Christ*.

—Warren Wiersbe, *Making Sense Out of the Ministry*

In our career as teachers, we will face many challenges and obstacles, and some of them will seem insurmountable. These may come in the form of difficult life situations—medical issues, the death of a family member or a close friend, a change in marital or financial status, or even some unpleasant consequences of our own sin or the sin of others. (Yes, even godly people still sin.) These could also come in the form of professional challenges—an unreasonable school administration, seemingly impossible colleagues, difficult students (and their parents), or a demanding workload. Often we will face life challenges at the same time we are dealing with professional challenges.

What does God want us to do when we are facing adversity? Does He want us just to *survive*—to hold on for dear life and ride, white-knuckled, through the storm? No! God desires that we do more than just survive adversity. He has not called us to a joyless, unhappy, discouraged life. He has called us to a life that is more than barely existing. The life God has called us to is an abundant life (John 10:10). So how does adversity fit with God's desire for us to have an abundant life?

Called to Grow

In difficult times, it is good to remember that every obstacle, every challenge, every adversity we face is subject to God's power. Nothing is outside His power to change. Since everything is possible for God, He could easily change our difficult situation or remove us from it—but He doesn't always choose to do so. If we experience adversity, it must be that God is allowing it for His eternal purposes and out of His unconditional love for us. God allows adversity in our lives because it is in adversity that He invites us into a deeper intimacy with Him and a growing ability to live as He wants us to live. Through adversity, God calls us to grow in grace, to become more like His Son, Jesus Christ.

God desires that adversity will lead us not to discouragement, defeat, and depression but to the glorious, holy, and abundant life that Christ died to give us. But whether it does so is up to us. Our response to adversity will determine how much we will grow. In adversity, we can choose to believe God or to believe the facts of the situation in which we find ourselves. Growing through adversity is a choice we make, and that choice begins in our thoughts. When we think that God has forgotten us, that others are to blame for our situation, that nothing good can come out of such pain, or that God is not a loving God because He has allowed this to happen to us, we are listening to the lies of the enemy—and doing that will surely lead us to defeat. Alternatively, we can choose to live the victorious life that God has planned for us. This chapter will outline the choices we must make.

Fulfill Your Responsibility as a Teacher

The truth is that God calls us to continue to lead our students even while we go through adversity and deep pain. No matter how deep our pain, we are called to continue to walk before our students in a way that models the presence of God in our lives. From experience, I can tell you that it hurts. I ache when I think of the adversity that many teachers have gone through and will continue to go through. But I can also tell you that God is sufficient to meet your every need and to give you the strength to carry on—and even to walk through the pain with peace and a deep-rooted joy.

You see, our lives, with all their ups and downs, go on even while we teach. We can't stop everything in our classrooms in order to deal with the adversity in our lives. The need to keep going is perhaps the single most difficult aspect of teaching. It is very difficult to remain fully present, self-controlled, and filled with the right spirit during times of great trial. It is very difficult to focus on setting the right tone in our classrooms when our greatest desire is to be elsewhere, sitting at the feet of Jesus and receiving His direction and peace. Yet, despite weariness, emotional pain, fear, and dissension, we are called to continue to teach with Christlike character. God has promised that He will provide all we need to bring us through each day victoriously. We have been called to live above life's circumstances. No matter what is going on, either inside or outside the classroom, God wants us to model for our students how to go through adversity in a God-honoring way. God wants us to lead our students. The need to fulfill our other responsibilities while we are dealing with adversity provides a wonderful opportunity to grow much deeper into Christlikeness.

Trust in God's Provision

Sometimes it seems that the challenges and responsibilities we face are more than we can carry. In these situations, we should be encouraged and should not lose hope, because God is with us. He will carry us when we can't go on. He can give us the strength, the courage, the wisdom, and the grace to do the things we can't do ourselves. We only need to let Him transform us as we respond to His leading in the challenges we face.

As God's children, we do not have to be prisoners of our circumstances. With God's help, we can control our responses to adversity. God has given us everything we need for life and godliness (2 Peter 1:3–8). God calls us, no matter what our circumstances, to add to our faith moral excellence; to moral excellence, knowledge; to knowledge, self-control; to self-control, perseverance; to perseverance, godliness; to godliness, brotherly kindness; and to brotherly kindness, Christian love. He tells us that if these qualities are increasing in our lives, we will be neither useless nor unfruitful.

Remember That God Is with You and for You

God has promised to be with us in *every* circumstance. He is in every situation and every relationship, whether or not we have yet acknowledged His presence. God has not left us by ourselves. He sees exactly what we are going through. He knows our pain, fear, hurt, and anger. He knows what has been done to us through no fault of our own, and He knows what pain we have caused ourselves. In all of this, He is there to help us in ways that will build us up and not tear us down. He is there to work out His plan for us to become more like Christ, to give us a future and a hope (Jeremiah 29:11).

God is always working, and His timing is perfect. God is at work in the challenges, obstacles, and adversity we face even when we are unaware that He is working or unaware of how He is working. Let's allow that truth to encourage us. Adversity gives us an opportunity to trust that God is working deliberately, lovingly, and carefully to carry out His purposes in our lives.

Isaiah 64:4 says that God acts on behalf of those who wait for Him. Believing this truth will enable us to give the situation and all we are going through to Him and not lean on our own understanding. Often God will require some action on our part (obedience, submission, humility, confession and repentance of sin) for Him to work His will. Victory through adversity doesn't just drop down from heaven. We need to work with God on what He wants us to do to bring it about.

As you already know, God sometimes calms the storm, but at other times He calms us while we go through the storm. Put another way, God sometimes takes us out of a difficult situation, and sometimes He gives us all we need to walk through the situation in victory. Even though we experience pain and heartache, we also have peace and contentment in the knowledge that God is in control. What we need to know is that whatever He chooses to do in a given situation He does because He loves us and wants to give us a wonderful future. God always has the bigger picture in view.

Let God's Word Guide You

God will give us very specific, personal direction for whatever challenges, obstacles, and difficulties we face, but we must stay in His Word to know His direction. God tells us to constantly "be renewed" in the spirit of our minds—to have a fresh mental and spiritual attitude (Ephesians 4:23). Being renewed requires us to be intentional about getting into God's Word every day. We must take the time to see what God is saying to us. He speaks loudest when our hearts are most quiet. Therefore, we need to turn off all the noise. Isaiah 30:15 says that our strength is "in quietness and trust." God promises that if we acknowledge Him in all our ways, He will direct our path and make our way straight (Proverbs 3:6). So many people go to other people to get direction. But God wants to build such a close relationship with us that we will go to Him first (and many times only to Him). Then, when necessary, we may seek out others for confirmation of His direction to us. But the counsel of others is never a wise substitute for the counsel of God. Scripture shows that serious consequences have come to those who sought the counsel of humans instead of the wisdom of the Lord. Ask God to increase your hunger for His Word.

Be Willing to Die to Self

Fruitful, God-glorifying ministry comes when we die to ourselves and to our own ambitions, hopes, and dreams. John 12:24–26 says, "Unless a grain of wheat falls into the earth and dies, it remains alone; but if it dies, it bears much fruit. He who loves his life loses it, and he who hates his life in this world will keep it to life eternal." God has been teaching me the truth of the *seed* in Scripture. First Corinthians 15:36–38 reminds us that seeds must die so that life and fruitfulness can come but that we do not sow the fruit itself; we sow only "a bare grain." And then we have to wait to see what fruit God will grow from it. We have no idea the unique harvest that God will bring about out of our death to self. The death of self in God's children will bring a harvest in many areas. The challenges that come give us the opportunity to die to self so that life and fruitfulness may be harvested. Doesn't that give you hope? God knows the crop He wants to bring to life as we die to self.

Scripture says that we are continually being given over to death so that "the life of Christ" may be manifested in our mortal bodies—"We have this treasure in earthen vessels, so that the surpassing greatness of the power will be of God and not from ourselves." The apostle Paul says that death to self comes through trials and tests and challenges: "We are afflicted in every way, but not crushed; perplexed, but not despairing; persecuted, but not forsaken; struck down, but not destroyed; always carrying about in the body the dying of Jesus" (2 Corinthians 4:7–11). Scripture further says that tribulations bring perseverance, proven character, and hope (Romans 5:3–5).

Having specific children in our classrooms, dealing with certain parents, finding out that people are gossiping about us, facing attacks and criticism, experiencing unfair treatment, dealing with our aging parents, dealing with our own sickness, struggling with interpersonal relationships—all of these, and countless others, can provide opportunities to die to self.

Take Your Thoughts Captive

Adversity will come. But focusing on the wrong things as we walk through adversity will cause us additional pain, heartache, and emotional duress, and ultimately it will destroy us. I could write a book just on this—the importance of our thoughts as we face difficult life situations and professional challenges. Our thought life is truly the battle front. I speak from experience and on the basis of the truth in God's Word. Focusing on how big the obstacle is, how unrelenting the adversity is, how impossible the relationships seem, how no one understands, and how others are involved will only discourage and defeat us. I know of people who are still thinking wrong thoughts years after a situation has taken place. How destructive! How painful! How deadly! We are set free only by believing the truth of God, by allowing ourselves to be transformed by the renewing of our minds (Romans 12:2).

We need to understand that, no matter how terrible, adversity cannot rob us of joy or peace. Having joy and peace is a choice; and having them comes from choosing to believe the truth of God in our circumstances. What we think about, not what we experience, will determine whether we have joy and peace. We can choose our thoughts. If our thoughts are not in line with God's Word, we must change them. We will become what we think. Remember that God is in the circumstance with us; His purposes and plans for us are good. He created us for a purpose, and He wants to use the situation to move us closer to that purpose. If we fill our minds with these truths, we can be full of joy and peace as we walk through adversity. The light is *in* the tunnel (not just at the end of it) when we go through it with God!

Unfortunately, our thoughts can become an open door for the enemy. Truth is one piece of the armor of God that we are to put on daily (Ephesians 6: 13–14). Focusing on the problem (rather than on what God wants to do in our lives through it) will enable the enemy to keep attacking us, but the enemy's attack is not what God intends for us. Are you still replaying over and over in your thoughts what happened yesterday? a week ago? last year? years ago? You know whether your thoughts are in line with God's truth. Replaying the facts of the situation, casting blame on ourselves or others, discussing the situation with others every chance we get, speaking derogatorily about those who were involved, and trying to figure out over and over again how we might have done something differently will discourage and ultimately defeat us. (Knowing what we could have done differently and choosing to do that next time is a positive thing—the problem is our *replaying* of what we could or should have done differently.) We need to take captive every thought and destroy every speculation that is not in line with God's Word (2 Corinthians

10:5). The enemy often makes us believe that his thoughts are our thoughts. We need to recognize these thoughts for what they are—one of Satan's most effective tactics for hindering our walk with God.

God's Word says that if we want to be transformed, we need to think differently. Transformation comes about by the renewing of our minds (Romans 12:2). God promises that the truth will set us free (John 8:32), but only if we allow it to. Therefore, we need to let our minds dwell on whatever is true, honorable, right, pure, lovely, of good repute, excellent, and worthy of praise (Philippians 4:8). We need to focus on God's truth—that God is in the situation for our benefit, that He wants us to accept responsibility for our part in it (no matter how small), that He asks us to give up our need to defend ourselves, that He calls us to forgive those who have done us wrong, and that His plan through it all is for our good. Focusing on God's truth will set us free to move forward in ministry and in growth toward Christlikeness. That is why it is so important that we view every challenge, every adversity, every obstacle, and every relationship through the truth of God. What we think about during challenging times will ultimately determine how long we will be influenced by the situation and who we will become because of it.

Acknowledge the Sovereignty of God

God can remove every obstacle that hinders His plan for our lives as we ask and allow Him to. No one else can determine the destiny God has for us, even though at the time we may think that others can affect it. Only we can. Joseph, in Scripture, is a perfect example. What his brothers did to him (selling him into slavery in Egypt) was grossly unfair. Surely, God couldn't have been in it. These brothers wanted evil to happen to Joseph. They were operating out of jealousy and hatred. But God used what the brothers meant for evil to bring about good in Joseph's life and in the lives of many other people. It doesn't matter *why* people do what they do to us. It doesn't even matter *what* others do to us. God will deal with those people. What matters is that God can turn it all into good.

As we face challenges and adversity, we should remember that our students, our colleagues, and our school administration are not obstacles to overcome. They are divine appointments that God wants to use in our lives to bring about growth in character. How do we respond when people mistreat us? Do we put them down? Do we try to defend ourselves? Do we withdraw from those who have hurt us? Or do we lovingly try to speak into the situation?

As we go through adversity, we should recognize that adverse situations do not *create* our character—they just *reveal* it. "Someone once asked, 'What do you get when you squeeze a lemon?' The answer is not just 'lemon juice,' but 'you get what is inside'" (Bonner 2000, 53). Therefore, we should use these situations to let God show us what He wants to do in our lives. Even though it is painful to acknowledge that our character needs work, it is an incredibly blessed place to be—a place where we admit that we have made mistakes and that we need help. When God exposes things in our lives that need to be changed, He does so because He wants to help us change them. The fire of purification is hot because it has the warmth of His presence. Let Him work in you. Stop focusing on others. Let God have His way in making you into the person He created you to be.

Forgive Others and Yourself

We already know that if something doesn't work in teaching, we should do something else. We need to use this truth in our own lives as well. If who we are isn't effective, then we must let God change us. We must not keep saying, "That's just the way I am."

When we face adversity, we must move beyond anger and unforgiveness. Rotten roots always produce rotten fruit. We should never give the emotional "friends" called fear, pride, self-pity, resentment, and bitterness permission to walk with us through adversity. We must recognize these, not as friends, but as enemies who will discourage us, keep us longer in the situation, and ultimately destroy us. We must address the feelings we have because feelings don't die when we bury them alive. They fester and hinder good fruit from being produced in our lives.

One way of doing battle in the Old Testament was to "stop up" the wells of the enemy and throw stones on their good soil. We need to recognize that our enemy wants to stop up the well of our minds and clutter the field of our hearts with stones of worry, anxiety, fear, discontent, selfishness, compromise, thoughts of the past, and reminders of our own sin. The enemy will do everything he can to keep us from being fruitful. It is important that we recognize these stones for what they are and prevent them from entering our minds and taking up residence in our hearts.

Control Your Words

Let's take it a step further. We must not only control our thoughts, but we must also control our words. Too often when we are facing adversity, we speak death rather than life into the circumstances. We speak, among other things, about the impossibility of the situation ever working out for our good, the unfairness of it, and the roles of other people in it. Scripture says that life and death are in the power of the tongue. What we say *does* affect our lives. We often shape our lives by words that hurt rather than by words that build up. Our words can either agree with God's view of the situation (and speak life) or agree with the enemy's view of the situation (and bring death). What we say will come out of what we think. If we believe that God is in the situation, we won't speak about how impossible it is, because we will know that "with God all things are possible" (Matthew 19:26).

Recognize Who You Are in Christ

Knowing who we are in Christ is another foundational truth that will enable us to grow through adversity. Knowing that we have been created by God—in His image, for His purpose—and that we have been given worth by Him will enable us to overcome any lies the enemy slings at us. When we come to the realization that we are special because Christ loves us and died for us, we will be set free from any addiction we have to other people's approval, any need we have to evaluate ourselves in relation to others, any perfectionist tendencies we have, any need to perform in order to achieve worth, any tendency to be a workaholic, any temptation to let our job/ministry/position rather than God define us. God alone gives us worth! No one else can add to or subtract from the worth He has given us, but the enemy doesn't want us to know that. What others say and do to us can hurt us deeply at times, but it cannot change the fact that God created us in His image, for His purpose, and with inestimable worth. Let's not let others define us.

Knowing who God has created and gifted us to be will enable us to seek ministry and employment in those specific areas suited to our giftedness and will prevent us from getting into adverse situations because we have made wrong choices. There are two common mistakes that people make. First, many people keep moving up the professional ladder until they have gone beyond their area of giftedness. They often do this because they want more money or more prestige, but their hard-won position often brings conflict and challenges that defeat them. Knowing who we are can help us to feel satisfied with ministering in our current position, even if it brings us little recognition and few monetary rewards. It can prevent us from getting into situations that God never intended for us. Second, although many people are content to be in the positions they are in, they keep adding more and more responsibilities to themselves until they are headed toward burnout. This is adversity just waiting to happen. When we get overloaded, we should ask ourselves why. What have we taken on that prevents us from doing things well and from having the priorities God intends us to have?

Adversity can come if we let our job define us. We should never define ourselves by our job, nor should we let others define us that way. We are so much more than a job or a career and more than one characteristic that others may use to define us. Would losing your job tomorrow destroy you? It is possible that God could call you into an entirely different ministry or even into no job at all. Would you be okay if one of these things happened, or are you hanging on to your job too tightly?

Also, we should never evaluate our worth by the amount of our salary or by the perks we receive. We may lose those as well. Let's learn to recognize that we are so much more than whatever benefits we may receive. We must let God tell us who we are and what His purposes are for our lives.

Move Beyond Self-Inflicted Adversity

The following section is for those of you who have inflicted problems on yourselves. I haven't written this section to judge you. I've been in this situation myself more times than I care to admit. It's a hard and painful place to be. But the important thing to remember is that God still loves you and wants to use whatever situation you are in to bring confession, repentance, and growth. Below I share six truths that I have learned and that I am continuing to learn while going through situations created by my own sin, carelessness, and mistakes.

1. Let God show you what part of the situation is your responsibility. Choose to take your eyes off the responsibility of others. This will enable God to work more deeply within you. He will do what He will do in the other people's lives. That's not your concern. As you seek to determine your responsibility, recognize that you will always be able to find people who take your side. That doesn't mean that you are right. It doesn't matter whether others say that you are right or whether they understand why you did what you did. Let God tell you what your responsibility is. Keep your conscience sensitive to Him.

2. Once you know your responsibility, take responsibility for your part. Don't make any excuses. Give up any need to make yourself look good or to minimize what you did. Admit your part specifically and fully, without any qualifying statements, to those God tells you to confess to. Doing so sets you free from being chained to other people, especially if you think they might be in the wrong as well. I have learned that this type of confession and repentance has the fingerprint of God all over it. I've truly been blown away as I've come to realize that this kind of godly sorrow over sin, followed by confession and repentance, somehow taps into the value system of eternity. When you repent in this way, somehow in return God gives you unconditional love for those who were in the situation with you, even if they hurt you or did something wrong. It has made me bow in awe and reverence that God can use my repentance and confession to change my heart toward others. The two don't seem to be related at all, but somehow, in God's grand scheme of things, they are.

3. Choose to act on the basis of truth and not feelings. Choose to get up after you have failed. Let God bring you to the place of genuine repentance. Refuse to replay destructive thoughts. Refuse to speculate about what others are thinking and saying. Let it go. These are choices. Don't just *try* to get up after you've failed. *Choose* to get up!

4. Recognize that God wants to use your failures to do a powerful work in your life. He will do this as you spend time every day in His Word and in

prayer. It is His Word that will show you where you went wrong and what you can do right in the future. It is His Word that will direct you, comfort you, and let you know that He has paid the price for your sin. Erwin W. Lutzer (1988) titled one of his books *Failure: The Backdoor to Success.* Praise the Lord that failure is not final!

5. Learn as soon as possible that relationships are more important than productivity and more important than doing your job well. Much of the adversity you face or will face on the job is centered in relationships. Remember that relationships take time and action. Not all your colleagues or students will be models of godliness all the time (neither are you), but you should actively reach out to them and encourage them anyway. This is part of your calling. Build people up. Speak the truth in love. Strive to live at peace with all people—even those you think require more grace.

6. Find an accountability partner. Having an accountability partner is crucial in walking through adversity. Give your accountability partner permission to ask you anything. Choose to be absolutely honest with the person. Your accountability partner should be someone you trust to give you godly counsel and to say the difficult things you need to hear. You must agree to prayerfully consider and then act upon every direction that God shows you through your partner.

Closing thoughts on Growing and Leading Through Adversity

I hope that this chapter has helped you see adversity from God's perspective. He will use it in your life to teach you, if you will let Him. I hope you will use it to grow into Christlikeness for God's glory.

QUESTIONS: GROWING AND LEADING THROUGH ADVERSITY

1. What challenge or adversity are you currently facing? What makes it a challenge? Why do you consider it adversity?

2. What thoughts about the situation are you continually thinking? Be specific.

3. In what way, if any, are you responsible for the challenge or adversity you are currently facing? What will you do about it? What does God want you to do about it?

4. Which thoughts (from question 2) indicate that you are agreeing with the enemy's perspective on the situation? Which thoughts indicate that you are thinking God's thoughts? (One way to tell is that if the thought makes you feel discouraged, frustrated, and powerless, it is from the enemy. On the other hand, God's truth brings hope, sets you free, and gives you the power to carry on with peace.)

5. What evidence do you see that God is working in your adverse situation? Is He removing the adversity from you, or is He helping you walk through the adversity in victory?

6. What three truths have you learned from this chapter that you are choosing to implement in your life immediately? To whom will you hold yourself accountable?

CHAPTER SEVENTEEN

MOVING FORWARD FROM HERE

The ideas we now popularly espouse are reshaping our culture, redefining our destiny, and are at the heart of the rampant evil that we now witness. They are ideas, therefore, that must be seriously questioned or we will find ourselves in some remorse-filled future, wondering how it all happened.

—Ravi Zacharias, *Deliver Us from Evil*

We live in a pagan culture, in many ways a post-Christian and unchurched culture. Our students may never have read the Bible. They may not know the doctrines and the stories of the Bible. They may not realize that God has provided us with guidelines for living life and for getting to know Him. They may not know how deeply God loves them. Many young people are non-Christians and are biblically illiterate even though they attend church regularly and go to Christian schools.

Understanding Our Society

An analogy may help you understand the view of truth that we have adopted in our culture. Three umpires are talking after a baseball game. One says, "There's balls and there's strikes, and I call 'em the way they are." (This is the Enlightenment view of truth, which assumes that there is a real world out there.) Another responds, "There's balls and there's strikes, and I call 'em the way I see 'em." (This is the subjective view of truth, which says that there may be objective truth but that we can know only our own view of it.) The third umpire says, "There's balls and there's strikes, and they ain't *nothin'* until I call 'em." (This is the postmodern view, which denies that there is such a thing as truth and objective reality.) (Anderson 1990, 75) It is the third umpire who represents our culture. Society would like to have us believe that there is no absolute truth and that we can believe whatever feels right to us.

In *Understanding the Times* (Noebel et al. 2006), a worldview curriculum, Frank Beckwith and Greg Koukl say that we are living in a time when society has abandoned the notion of absolute truth and opted instead for *relativism*, which makes truth merely an opinion, or a preference. What *is* good has been replaced with what *feels* good. According to these authors, today's society says that there is no universal moral law for all people, at all places, at all times; the final decision of what is ethically right or wrong is relative—a matter of cultural preference or personal choice. Each person can decide for him- or herself what is right and wrong. But this idea is foolishness. Society has confused *preference*, based on our personal likes and dislikes, with *moral claims*, based on God's absolute standards of right and wrong.

Beckwith and Koukl further describe the culture in which we live as one that reflects *cultural relativism*. That is, society says that because cultures have different moral values, no culture can claim that one is right or wrong. That's absurd! How does it follow that because cultures differ, nobody is correct? People disagree, but that disagreement does not mean that there is no right or wrong.

Yet we also live in a society that reflects *cultural conventionalism*, the belief that society determines what one ought to do. If society says it's moral, then it is moral. Thus, moral statements are no more than power statements made by the ruling majority. So if society says prostitution, abortion, and same-sex marriages are right (even if they go against God's standards), these things are right. This is a very serious error, one that confuses the social code with God's moral code (Noebel et al. 2006).

Our society also reflects *individual ethical relativism*, so right and wrong become a matter of private judgment. We can do whatever we think is right. How can anyone be wrong then? Society says, "Who are you to judge? If there is no truth, then why should I listen to others?" (Noebel et al. 2006).

Paradoxically, even though our society says that there is no such thing as right and wrong, it still insists that Christianity is wrong. Our society is intolerant of all but its own brand of tolerance. We live in a society that, under the guise of political correctness, shuts down legitimate discussion, silences unpopular opinions, and harasses Christians for not accepting the view of the majority. We live in a society that calls us close-minded if we have come to a different conclusion than others have. *Close-minded* means we have reached a conclusion before we have looked at all the facts. *Open-minded*, on the other hand, means that we keep our minds open and look at all the facts in our search for truth—but that only makes sense if there is truth! What if we have had open minds, looked at the facts, and then discovered the truth? Wouldn't it be folly to keep searching for truth after we've found it?

Ravi Zacharias (1997, 68) sums up, noting three "processes" that have made our society what it is. We live in a society that has become secularized: "religious ideas, institutions, and interpretations have lost their social significance." Our society has become pluralized: "a number of worldviews [are] available and no one view is dominant." And our society has become privatized: "[it] compels individuals to restrict all their spiritual and religious beliefs and keep them to themselves."

Further, we live in a society in which people interact with other people by going online, sitting in "wireless" coffee shops to work on their computers, surrounded by other people who are working on theirs. That's socializing now. Even though these people are with other people, they aren't connecting meaningfully with them.

Influencing Society

If the above describes the situation we are in, how in the world do we influence our society in ways that will make a difference now and for eternity?

Accepting the Call

In the midst of a lost and pagan culture, Jesus encourages His followers: "You are the salt of the earth; but if the salt has become tasteless, how can it be made salty *again*? It is no longer good for anything, except to be thrown out and trampled under foot by men. You are the light of the world. A city set on a hill cannot be hidden; nor does anyone light a lamp and put it under a basket, but on the lampstand, and it gives light to all who are in the house. Let your light shine before men in such a way that they may see your good works, and glorify your Father who is in heaven" (Matthew 5:13–16, italics are in original).

What does this mean with respect to teaching? It means that there *is* hope. God has placed us here at this time in history to influence our world for Him. Our teaching is not just "arranging the deck chairs on the *Titanic*," but it can actually make a difference. We have been given the wonderful opportunity to rise to the challenge and join the army of Christian teachers throughout this world whom God has called to make an impact in their classrooms for Him.

Being Salt and Light in Our Classrooms

Jack Fennema (1977, 8–9) suggests three tasks that will enable us to be salt and light to our students and their families. First, we can fill the role of *prophet*—knowing God's revelation and sharing it with our students, helping them learn right from wrong; helping them understand that there *is* truth. Second, we can fill the role of *priest*—bringing people closer to God by modeling (and speaking when appropriate) that we are children of God, by living our lives before our students in such a way that they will see our good works and glorify God. And third, we can fill the role of *king*—being the authority figure in our classrooms, reflecting God's perfect rule, and doing what is best for our students and not what is easiest.

Being salt and light means that we communicate God's truth and Christ's love to those around us. It means that we teach academic content to the best of our ability. It means that we build a community that invites students to get involved and grow. It means that we educate our students for the world they live in so that they understand the culture and they are able to reach out in meaningful ways to others. It means that we address the real questions young people have—questions about transcendence, meaning, identity, and community. And it means that we teach students to stand for what is right even if it means standing alone.

When I think of the role of salt on food, I'm reminded about a trick we used to play when I was a student living in a dorm. We would unscrew the top of the saltshaker but leave it on top so that it looked as if it was still attached. Then, when other students picked up the saltshaker to shake some salt onto their food, the top would come off, and their food would be covered with salt. The food, of course, would be ruined. Some Christians tend to operate in the same way. They drop *all* the salt they have into a person's life. They don't take the time to sprinkle it only where it is needed. We must be careful that we don't dump a shaker full of salt onto the lives of other people. Instead, we should take time to see whether salt is needed at a given time and in a given place. One kind of food on a plate may need salt, but it doesn't follow that everything on the plate needs it. Be careful!

With respect to light, we must not hide our light. People are longing to know that the relationship we have with God is worth staking their lives upon. They long to know that what we have is real. Too many Christians believe they have to be just silent witnesses for the Lord. That is no longer effective—if it ever was! We must not only *live* the faith; we also must *speak* the faith and give reasons for the hope that is within us (1 Peter 3:15). We are called to keep the light shining.

God calls us to introduce worldview questions into the study of culture. He calls us to identify and respond to the source of differences among cultures and among the various participants in our pluralistic society. We must go beyond just passing along the existing culture. Let's provoke our students to think, inviting them to evaluate things and not just accept them without question.

God calls us to *truth*. Many students may have no other way to begin to understand the Christian faith unless we are bold enough to speak the truth to them. We must help our students see how the spiritual affects the physical, and we must help them understand that there is absolute truth and not just the conflicting notions of truth they hear in the media and from many people around them.

God also calls us to *compassion*. Our students need to have us touch their hearts and genuinely care about their lives. We may be the only people speaking compassion into our students' lives on a given day.

We are called to give *hope* to our students. This call goes far beyond helping them be successful in academic endeavors. If we have truth but we are harsh, unkind, and controlling, we will lose our effectiveness with our students.

We are called to teach our students *to think carefully in general and about spiritual and ethical matters in particular*. We have many opportunities to provide our students with the intellectual and moral training they need in order to stand up for truth and biblical morality. We can equip them to give reasons for the hope that is within them. We can encourage students to deal with the questions and issues that are relevant for today. As we teach, we can use Scripture to shed light on all that we are teaching. We can teach our students to consider and contemplate not just act and react (Moreland 2000, 3).

We can't let ourselves be overwhelmed by the enormity of the impossible. Instead, let's start pouring our time and energy into the possible—the people and places that God has called us to. It is an exciting time to be teachers. We have an incredible privilege and responsibility. With our help, our students can learn to understand their culture and can be equipped to defend the Christian faith in the midst of it. As we intentionally become familiar with the Word of God, our students also can become more and more biblically literate as they see how Scripture speaks to their everyday lives. We can have the awesome privilege of seeing our students' lives changed and transformed forever!

Getting Sidetracked from Pursuing the Call

We need to be on guard against the many things that can distract us from following God's call:

Time. The "fast food" lifestyle has, in many ways, influenced our communion with God. Just as fast food is not usually high in nutritional value, so interacting with God only on the run is not spiritually nutritious. In the busyness of our lives, it is easy to let our relationship with Christ decline to the level of fast food. We will always find time to do what we value. If we don't take the time to be with God through His Word, it's because we value other things more highly.

Job or ministry responsibilities. Often, we tend to take on more than we should so that we can do things we are gifted in. But it is unwise to pick up more than we can do well. We need to determine our workload. We need to speak up and say what we are willing to do and what we aren't willing to do. God never intended that we work eighteen or more hours per day. There are always enough hours in the days that we commit to Him, because He will make clear what needs to be done, or does not need to be done, on each of those days. If we find ourselves rushing into our day without taking meaningful, uninterrupted time with the Lord, our relationship with Him will be hindered, and we will have no guarantee that we will be doing what He wants us to be doing.

Relationships. Some relationships we are in are not moving us toward Christ-likeness. How much do the people closest to us love God? How evident is their love for God in their lives? We may need to give up some friendships to pursue God more intentionally. In Scripture, we are urged to choose our friends wisely. It is beneficial to form an inner circle of friends who hold each other accountable.

Choices. The choices we make with respect to how we spend our time and money will influence our walk with God, either positively or negatively. We must intentionally make choices that will move us into a deeper relationship with God through Christ.

Noise and clutter. Many of us find that noise and clutter tend to fill our lives so full that God cannot get through, and we don't even realize how much we need Him. Many people in our society are spiritually anorexic and they don't even know it. They think they are fine, but they don't realize that they are not getting the spiritual nutrients needed to keep them alive spiritually.

Moving Forward from Here

God desires intimacy with us. He urges us to be still and know that He is God (Psalm 46:10). He wants to commune with us. We must recognize that *serving* God (through teaching or any other ministry) is not the same as *knowing* Him. God calls us to get to know Him. He invites us to ask Him what specific things must change in our lives so that we can walk with Him throughout our day. We need to put off all that belongs to the old unregenerate self and put on Christlike character. We need to realize that drawing near to God may begin as a discipline but will surely move toward becoming a delight. We have God's promise that as we draw near to Him, He will draw near to us. He invites us to wait on Him and promises that as we do, we will not become weary or faint; instead, we will soar like eagles above the situation we are in and will be able to see God's truth in it all (Isaiah 40:31).

Closing Thoughts on Moving Forward from Here

As we press on to know the Lord, may we know a joy in ministry that flows out of the overflow of our relationship to God, through Jesus Christ and the work of the Holy Spirit. As we allow God to change us, we will influence others for Jesus throughout our lives and our teaching careers.

May God bless you as you take up the challenge that God has laid before you.

QUESTIONS: MOVING FORWARD FROM HERE

1. What part of being salt and light in your classroom do you struggle with the most? Why?

2. Where is God calling you to? What is His specific call on your life? Is He calling you to teach? Where—overseas, in North America? In what type of school—in a private, public, elementary, middle, or high school? To what type of learner—students with special needs, gifted students, regular students? Be as specific as you can. What has God already made clear to you with respect to His calling on your life?

3. How will you graciously, honestly, and clearly demonstrate your relationship to God in this postmodern culture?

REFERENCES

Adams, Jay E. 1986. *The biblical view of self-esteem, self-love, self-image*. Eugene, OR: Harvest House Publishers.

Anderson, Walter T. 1990. *Reality isn't what it used to be: Theatrical politics, ready-to-wear religion, global myths, primitive chic, and other wonders of the postmodern world*. San Francisco: HarperSanFrancisco.

Anonymous. n. d. Unity.

Augustine. 1952. *The city of God,* trans. Marcus Dods. Vol. 18 of *Great books of the western world*, ed. Robert Maynard Hutchins. Chicago, IL: William Benton Publishers.

Badley, Kenneth Rae. 1996. *Worldviews: The challenge of choice*. Concord, ON: Irwin Publishing.

Barna, George. 1997. The vision thing. In *Leaders on leadership: Wisdom, advice and encouragement on the art of leading God's people*, ed. George Barna, 47–60. Ventura, CA: Regal Books.

BC Confederation of Parent Advisory Councils, BC Principals' and Vice-Principals' Association, and BC Teachers' Federation. 1996. *Building partnerships in schools: A handbook*. Victoria, BC: Crown Publications.

Blendinger, Christian. 1976. Might, authority, throne. In Vol. 2 of *The New International Dictionary of New Testament Theology*, ed. Colin Brown, 601, 607. Grand Rapids, MI: Zondervan.

Bonner, Mickey. 2000. *Brokenness, the forgotten factor of prayer*. Houston, TX: Transformed Publications.

Borich, Gary D. 1992. *Effective teaching methods*. New York: Merrill.

Bronson, Po. 2005. Quoted in Opportunities for creating and strengthening peer programs. *The peer news*, (May 19). www.peer.ca/thepeernews12.html.

Brophy, Jere. 1988. Educating teachers about managing classrooms and students. *Teaching and Teacher Education: An International Journal of Research and Studies* 4, no. 1:1–18.

Burbules, Nicholas, C. 1986. A theory of power in education. *Educational Theory* 36, no. 2:95–114.

Cangelosi, James S. 2004. *Classroom management strategies: Gaining and maintaining students' cooperation*. 5th ed. Hoboken, NJ: John Wiley & Sons.

Charles, C. M. 1999. *Building classroom discipline*. 6th ed. New York: Longman.

Classroom Law Project. n.d. Eight modes of conflict resolution. Portland, OR: Classroom Law Project.

Coopersmith, Stanley. 1967. *The antecedents of self-esteem*. San Francisco: W. H. Freeman and Company.

Cruickshank, Donald R., Deborah Bainer Jenkins, and Kim K. Metcalf. 2003. *The act of teaching*. 3rd ed. New York: McGraw-Hill.

Dodge, Kenneth A. 1993. The future of research on the treatment of conduct disorder. *Development and Psychopathology* 5:311–319.

Doyle, Walter. 1986. Classroom organization and management. In *Handbook of research on teaching: A project of the American Educational Research Association*, ed. Merlin C. Wittrock, 392–431. 3rd ed. New York: McMillan Publishing.

Dreikurs, Rudolf, and Pearl Cassel. 1972. *Discipline without tears*. 2nd ed. New York: Hawthorn/Dutton.

Edwards, Clifford H. 1993. *Classroom discipline and management*. New York: Macmillan Publishing.

Eliot, Thomas Stearns. 1940. East Coker. Quoted in David Spurr, *Conflicts in consciousness: T.S. Eliot's poetry and criticism* (Urbana, IL: University of Illinois Press, 1984), 89.

Elkind, David. 1981. *The hurried child: Growing up too fast too soon*. Reading, MA: Addison-Wesley Publishing.

Emmer, Edmund T., Carolyn M. Evertson, and Murray E. Worsham. 2006. *Classroom management for middle and high school teachers*. 7th ed. Boston: Allyn and Bacon.

Epanchin, Betty Cooper, Brenda Townsend, and Kim Stoddard. 1994. *Constructive classroom management: Strategies for creative positive learning environments*. Pacific Grove, CA: Brooks/Cole Publishing.

Erikson, Erik H. 1963. *Childhood and society*. New York: W. W. Norton & Company.

Evertson, Carolyn M., Edmund T. Emmer, and Murray E. Worsham. 2006. *Classroom management for elementary teachers.* 7th ed. Boston: Allyn and Bacon.

Fennema, Jack. 1977. *Nurturing children in the Lord: A study guide for teachers on developing a biblical approach to discipline.* Phillipsburg, NJ: Presbyterian and Reformed Publishing.

Fennimore, Beatrice Schneller. 1995. *Student-centered classroom management.* Albany, NY: Delmar Publishers.

Focus on the Family. 2006. *The truth project: An in-depth Christian worldview experience.* DVD Series. Colorado Springs, CO: Focus on the Family.

Froyen, Len A., and Annette M. Iverson. 1999. *Schoolwide and classroom management: The reflective educator-leader.* 3rd ed. Upper Saddle River, NJ: Prentice Hall.

Gibbs, Ollie E., and Jerry L. Haddock. 1991. *Classroom discipline: A management guide for Christian school teachers.* Colorado Springs, CO: Association of Christian Schools International.

Glasser, William. 1965. *Reality therapy.* New York: Harper and Row.

———. 1986. *Control theory in the classroom.* New York: Harper and Row.

———. 1990. *The quality school.* New York: Harper and Row.

Good, Thomas L., and Jere E. Brophy. 2003. *Looking in classrooms.* 9th ed. Boston: Allyn and Bacon.

Gothard, William. 1984a. *Principles of discipline: Principles of instruction.* USA: Institute in Basic Youth Conflicts.

———. 1984b. *Principles of discipline: Basic aspects of warning.* USA: Institute in Basic Youth Conflicts.

Greenleaf, Robert K. 1998. *The power of servant-leadership: Essays by Robert K. Greenleaf.* Ed. Larry C. Spears. San Francisco: Berrett-Koehler Publishers.

Hayford, Jack. 1997. The character of a leader. In *Leaders on leadership: Wisdom, advice and encouragement on the art of leading God's people,* ed. George Barna, 61–80. Ventura, CA: Regal Books.

Hill, Leslie Pinckney. 1968. The teacher. In *Sourcebook of poetry,* comp. Al Bryant, 548. Grand Rapids, MI: Zondervan Publishing House.

Hollinger, J. Daniel. 1987. Social skills for behaviorally disordered children as preparation for mainstreaming: Theory, practice, and new directions. *Remedial and Special Education* 8, no. 4:17–27.

Holt, John A. 2007. Ministry is ... Riverside Christian Alliance Church home page. Riverside, CA. http://www.riversidecma.org (accessed February 28, 2007).

Hoover, Arlie J. 1976. *Dear Agnos: A defense of Christianity.* Grand Rapids, MI: Baker Book House. Quoted in Zacharias 2006, 5.

Johnson, David W., and Roger T. Johnson. 1995. *Reducing school violence through conflict resolution.* Alexandria, VA: Association for Supervision and Curriculum Development.

Johnson, David W., Roger T. Johnson, and Edythe Johnson Holubec. 1990. *Cooperation in the classroom.* Edina, MN: Interaction Book Company.

Jones, Vernon F., and Louise Jones. 2004. *Comprehensive classroom management: Creating communities of support and solving problems.* 7th ed. Boston: Allyn and Bacon.

Kauffman, James M., Mark P. Mostert, Stanley C. Trent, and Daniel P. Hallahan. 2002. *Managing classroom behavior: A reflective case-based approach.* Boston: Allyn and Bacon.

Kounin, Jacob S. 1970. *Discipline and group management in classrooms.* Huntington, NY: Robert E. Krieger Publishing.

Kuhl, Julius. 1982. The expectancy-value approach within the theory of social motivation: Elaborations, extensions, critique. In *Expectations and actions: Expectancy-value models in psychology,* ed. Norman T. Feather. Hillsdale, NJ: Lawrence Erlbaum Associates.

Lemlech, Johanna Kasin. 1988. *Classroom management: Methods and techniques for elementary and secondary teachers.* White Plains, NY: Longman.

Levin, James, and James F. Nolan. 1996. *Principles of classroom management: A professional decision-making model.* 2nd ed. Needham Heights, MA: Allyn and Bacon.

———. 2004. *Principles of classroom management: A professional decision-making model.* 4th ed. Boston: Allyn and Bacon.

Long, Nicholas J., and William C. Morse. 1996. *Conflict in the classroom: The education of at-risk and troubled students.* 5th ed. Austin, TX: PRO-ED.

Lutzer, Erwin W. 1988. *Failure: The backdoor to success.* Chicago, IL: Moody Publishers.

Maxwell, John C. 2000. *The 21 most powerful minutes in a leader's day.* Nashville, TN: Thomas Nelson.

McDowell, Josh. 2000. *The disconnected generation: Saving our youth from self-destruction.* Video Series. Nashville, TN: Thomas Nelson.

Mendler, Allen N. 1992. *What do I do when ...? How to achieve discipline with dignity in the classroom.* Bloomington, IN: National Educational Service.

Merriam-Webster Dictionary. 2005. 11th ed. Springfield, MA: Merriam-Webster.

Meyer, Joyce. 2005. *Approval addiction: Overcoming the need to please everyone.* New York: Warner Faith.

Moles, Oliver C. 1993. Collaboration between schools and disadvantaged parents: Obstacles and openings. In *Families and schools in a pluralistic society,* ed. Nancy Feyl Chavkin, 21–52. Albany, NY: State University of New York Press.

Moreland, J. P. 2000. The loss of a thoughtful approach to spiritual formation. Paper presented at Leadership Academy 2000 of the Association of Christian Schools International, Colorado Springs, CO.

Nazigian, Arthur. 1983. *The effective teacher.* Colorado Springs, CO: Association of Christian Schools International.

Neuhauser, Peg. 2006. Tribal warfare. Lecture presented at The Leadership Summit 2006 of the Willow Creek Association, Barrington, IL.

Noebel, David, Kevin Bywater, Jeff Myers, Connie Willems, Jeff Baldwin Jr., Micah Wierenga, Todd Cothran, et al. 2006. Responding to relativism. In *Understanding the Times,* 4th ed., 161–173. USA: Summit Ministries.

Ortberg, John. 2002. *The life you've always wanted: Spiritual disciplines for ordinary people.* Grand Rapids, MI: Zondervan.

Patterson, Gerald, R., John B. Reid, and Thomas J. Dishion. 1992. *A social interaction approach.* Vol. 4 of *Antisocial Boys.* Eugene, OR: Castalia Publishing.

Pazmiño, Robert W. 1994. *By what authority do we teach? Sources for empowering Christian educators.* Grand Rapids, MI: Baker Books.

Rinne, Carl H. 1997. *Excellent classroom management.* Belmont, CA: Wadsworth Publishing.

Rosa, Sharon. 1998. Communicating during conflict. *Christian School Education* 2, no. 4:27–29.

Rosenshine, Barak V. 1980. How time is spent in elementary classrooms. In *Time to learn*, eds. Carolyn Denham and Ann Lieberman, 107–123. Washington, DC: U.S. Department of Education.

Sanborn, Mark. 2006. *You don't need a title to be a leader*. Colorado Springs, CO: WaterBrook Press.

Schell, Leo M., and Paul Burden. 1992. *Countdown to the first day of school: A 60-day get-ready checklist for; Beginning elementary teachers, teacher transfers, student teachers, teacher mentors, induction-program administrators, teacher educators*. NEA Checklist Series. Education Resources Information Center (ERIC): ED 350 115.

Schmuck, Richard A., and Patricia A. Schmuck. 2001. *Group processes in the classroom*. 8th ed. New York: McGraw-Hill.

Shavelson, R. J. 1987. Planning. In *The international encyclopedia of teaching and teacher education*, ed. Michael J. Dunkin. New York: Pergamon Press.

Smith, John K. 1977. The decline of teacher power in the classroom. *Peabody Journal of Education* 54 (April): 201–206.

Steele, Fred I. 1973. *Physical settings and organization development*. Reading, MA: Addison-Wesley Publishing.

Tharp, Roland G. 1989. Psychocultural variables and constants: Effects on teaching and learning in schools. *American Psychologist* 44, no. 2:349–359.

Van Brummelen, Harro. 1988. *Walking with God in the classroom*. Seattle, WA: Alta Vista College Press.

———. 1994. *Steppingstones to curriculum: A biblical path*. Seattle, WA: Alta Vista College Press.

———. 1998. *Walking with God in the classroom: Christian approaches to learning and teaching*. 2nd ed. Seattle, WA: Alta Vista College Press.

Walker, Hill M., Geoff Colvin, and Elizabeth Ramsey. 1995. *Antisocial behavior in school: Strategies and best practices*. Pacific Grove, CA: Brooks/Cole Publishing.

Walsh, Brian J., and J. Richard Middleton. 1984. *The transforming vision: Shaping a Christian world view*. Downers Grove, IL: InterVarsity Press.

Weinstein, Carol Simon, and Andrew J. Mignano Jr. 2003. *Elementary classroom management: Lessons from research and practice*. 3rd ed. New York: McGraw-Hill.

Wiersbe, Warren W. 1983. *Making sense out of the ministry*. Chicago, IL: Moody Bible Institute.

Wlodkowski, Raymond J., and Margery B. Ginsberg. 1995. A framework for culturally responsive teaching. *Educational Leadership* 53, no. 1:17–21.

Zabel, Robert H., and Mary Kay Zabel. 1996. *Classroom management in context: Orchestrating positive learning environments*. Boston: Houghton Mifflin.

Zacharias, Ravi. 1996. *Deliver us from evil: Restoring the soul in a disintegrating culture*. Dallas, TX: Word Publishing.

———. 1997. *Deliver us from evil: Restoring the soul in a disintegrating culture*. Video Series Leader's Guide. Dallas, TX: Word Publishing.

———. 2006. The components of a worldview. *Persuader* 3, no.1:4–5.

p. 5

Relationship
vital in

kingdom living